Marketing Nonprofit Programs and Services

Douglas B. Herron

Marketing Nonprofit Programs and Services

Proven and Practical Strategies to Get
More Customers, Members, and Donors

Jossey-Bass Publishers • San Francisco

Jossey-Bass books and products are available through most bookstores. To contact Jossey-Bass directly, call (888) 378-2537, fax to (800) 605-2665, or visit our website at www.josseybass.com.

Substantial discounts on bulk quantities of Jossey-Bass books are available to corporations, professional associations, and other organizations. For details and discount information, contact the special sales department at Jossey-Bass.

 Manufactured in the United States of America on Lyons Falls Turin Book. This paper is acid-free and 100 percent totally chlorine-free.

Library of Congress Cataloging-in-Publication Data

Herron, Douglas B., date.
   Marketing nonprofit programs and services: proven and practical strategies to get more customers, members, and donors / Douglas B. Herron.
      p.   cm. — (The Jossey-Bass nonprofit sector series)
   Includes bibliographical references and index.
   ISBN 0-7879-0326-4 (acid-free paper)
   1. Nonprofit organizations—Marketing.   I. Title.   II. Series.
HF5415.H395   1997
658.8—dc20   96-25356

HB Printing   10 9 8 7 6 5 4 3   FIRST EDITION

The Jossey-Bass Nonprofit Sector Series

Contents

Preface

Too many of my friends have suffered sleepless nights and stressful days as they struggled to balance their budgets by trimming good staff. Other friends got credit for great performance when they were merely lucky enough to be sitting on a gold mine. The glory was fun while it lasted, but when they moved off the gold mine to other nonprofit organizations (NPOs), they were sorely pressed for quick solutions in more challenging positions. Without a good concept of marketing, they were ill prepared for the chill of the challenge.

How to keep your job is easy to figure out: please the bosses and balance the budget. You can even go backwards in service and dollar volume as long as you end the period with more revenue than expenses.

In today's increasingly competitive world, balancing the budget is not easy. Traditional United Way agencies, for example, have seen their allocations cut; funding has not kept up with the agencies' needs. Competition has even emerged from for-profit centers as well as other nonprofits. If that isn't challenging enough, there are now watchdog groups, state attorneys general, and federal agencies asking for more NPO performance accountability. Improving marketing practices is an excellent way to strengthen your organization's position in this very dynamic world.

Many of the books on marketing have been written by educators drawing on their readings and part-time consulting experiences. This book is different because I am drawing on my more than twenty-nine years of on-the-line nonprofit management experience in Ohio, Maine, Minnesota, California, and Pennsylvania, as well as my experience consulting and conducting marketing workshops with NPO managers throughout the United States and Canada. My purpose is to help you as managers do a better job immediately. You will gain new insights by discovering what others have done and by reviewing basic marketing concepts. I believe simple, proven concepts will serve most of us well. I am less interested in explaining complex theories and methods—NPO managers and I seldom use them.

The roots of this book reach back to when I was serving as executive director of a YMCA. Challenged to balance the budget, develop staff, encourage volunteers, and expand program volume, I realized that working longer hours was not enough to meet higher goals. I had to conceptualize my situation differently.

Fortunately, I won a Bush Foundation Fellowship enabling me to take marketing and management courses offered to experienced business executives at Harvard Business School, Massachusetts Institute of Technology, and Columbia Graduate School of Business. The new learning worked so well that I was soon giving marketing workshops for NPOs all across the United States.

Having closed out my YMCA career, I am now using the same marketing material in my own national fundraising business. The concepts enable my team to help others raise millions of dollars annually.

Marketing Nonprofit Programs and Services is written for people like the thousands of NPO staff members I have worked with. Most of them do not like to read marketing or management books. Typically they prefer to get new information or insights from colleagues or experts at workshops. They pick up management or marketing material in search of solutions to their problems, so this book includes plenty of examples of successful marketing applications.

This book is for management staff on the line, those whose jobs depend on meeting production goals and balancing the budget. They want to know what has worked for others and what is likely to help them succeed. They have little interest in much marketing theory or nonutilitarian information. Thus you are spared any review of service marketing developments since 1950 or multiple definitions of marketing. What you now have in front of you is a very practical guide for anyone in nonprofit management. The concepts are simply presented but are just as relevant to managers of large nonprofits as to small, single-employee organizations. The size of an organization's budget or marketing director's salary does not correspond to marketing expertise. Some people with large salaries and large organizations to manage do not have enough time to focus their attention on customer service, or to redo the marketing arithmetic to get a better return on investment. Although they have the power and the responsibility to improve marketing practices, they may not have the luxury of contemplative time between meetings and phone calls. But reading this book should help even the most experienced manager get and keep customers and consumers of their organization's services.

Reputedly, when legendary union organizer Sam Gompers was asked what he really wanted after already achieving higher wages, shorter work days, more benefits, and better work conditions, Gompers replied, "More." The nonprofit world is very diverse; although more clients, more patients, or more service recipients are not always good for some groups, for others more members and donors may be a very worthy goal. This book addresses the needs of this latter group and does little for those interested in social marketing or cause-related marketing. That has not been my field of experience, and successful marketing experience is what much of the book is about.

This book is an experience-based treasure chest of strategies and methods for weighing options. You can read it as an overview of marketing strategy and planning or as a reference on promotion and service. The book helps you identify the most important benefits sought by your customers, then tells you how to discover more about what customers really want—after all, the purpose of marketing is to attract and satisfy. Next, you are told how to communicate your special message in a message-cluttered world, which should be particularly helpful to the staff of organizations that rely on a mixed base of fees and contributions for support, such as Ys, museums, zoos, theaters, youth groups, and churches. Site directors, executive directors, marketing directors, and chief executives will gain competitive advantages.

Overview of the Contents

In Part One, you will see how marketing is useful to NPOs and how to adapt marketing from the for-profit world. Chapter One shows that we have been marketing all along in our management duties, even if many of us haven't looked at our day-to-day work as specifically marketing related. Chapter Two reminds us to attach a related important benefit to each feature we promote. We overlook this step much too often.

Part Two is loaded with market research tips particularly useful to anyone on a tight budget. Because marketing demands that you be obsessed with learning more about the customer, four separate chapters are devoted to practical market research. Chapter Three tells when to conduct market research and the steps to follow. Chapter Four explains the benefits of target marketing and provides two detailed examples. Much of the information gathered by marketing research, such as leisure reading and favorite TV programs, may not seem relevant initially because we can't afford to advertise through those media, and admittedly we can get lost in the minutia; but by discovering new patterns we can improve our position in the changing marketplace. Chapter Five furnishes strategies and specific steps to help improve your market share. In Chapter Six, you will learn how to personally conduct an audit of an NPO's market practices. The audit reveals comparative advantages and areas that are vulnerable to the competition. A new chief executive or marketing director would want to conduct the audit during his or her first week on the job.

Part Three focuses on how to get more of what you want—customers, consumers, and volunteers. Chapter Seven discusses promotion—the task most NPO marketers are hired to do. Plenty of examples are included in addition to suggestions on how to evaluate the effectiveness of your promotion efforts. Chapter Eight offers good advice on advertising. Chapter Nine follows with the comparative advantages of various advertising and promotion media. Chapter Ten shares useful packaging concepts—brand image, price, place, service, time, volume, and frequency. The last two chapters are more action oriented. Most NPOs want more volunteers: Chapter Eleven reveals how to get them and keep them satisfied through marketing. Chapter Twelve presents a fifteen-step outline that I call the "classic marketing scheme." It helps you quickly review the essential steps of marketing and, again, focus for finer performance.

Acknowledgments

Two friends have been wonderfully helpful in the preparation of this book. I am indebted to C. Fortune Beutell of Rye, New York, my high school friend and early manuscript editor; and to Terry Young, my coworker since 1984.

I am appreciative of the efforts of the entire Jossey-Bass editorial and production team, particularly those of reviewer Elspeth MacHattie.

My son, John, has also played an essential role in the creation of this book. From his home office in San Francisco, John spent many hours on the phone patiently helping me comprehend computer hardware and software. I never wanted to learn about the technology (that was the persistent problem); I just wanted to get my ideas down on paper quickly. There is a parallel to be drawn here. My desire to skip the computer manuals and plunge ahead to the keyboard is similar to that of the time-pressed NPO managers who want a quick solution to their everyday problems; they have little interest in marketing theory. A few minutes with this book, like my few minutes with John, will help.

King of Prussia, Pennsylvania   Douglas B. Herron
August 1996

The Author

Douglas B. Herron is president of Campaign Associates, Inc., a fundraising and marketing firm for nonprofit organizations. With headquarters in King of Prussia, Pennsylvania, Campaign Associates has twenty associates working with clients throughout the United States and Canada. Formerly the capital fundraising division of the YMCA of the USA, Campaign Associates was spun off in 1990 into a private corporation that has since worked with libraries, vocational rehabilitation organizations, a shelter for victims of domestic violence, a state humanities council, and others, in addition to many YMCAs.

In 1984 Herron was recruited to serve as a national field consultant for the YMCA of the USA. He consulted with three hundred independent YMCAs from Washington, D.C., to Maine. His expertise in marketing and fundraising was drawn upon both by the smallest YMCAs, with budgets of $100,000, and by the largest, with annual revenues in excess of $50 million.

Herron has led marketing and fundraising workshops in four countries for the YMCA, YWCA, Boy Scouts, Girl Scouts, Boys Clubs, Girls Clubs, Camp Fire, Jewish Community Centers, Hispanic agencies, United Way agencies, museums, schools, youth camps, Lutheran Camp Directors, Humanics, and the National Society of Fund-Raising Executives. He has taught courses at the University of San Francisco Graduate School, Stanford University, College of the Pacific, and Villanova University.

Prior to joining the national YMCA, he served for five years as vice president for financial development of the San Francisco

YMCA. In his last three years in the one-person development office, capital gifts were averaging $2 million annually, government contracts averaged $2 million, foundation grants were over $500,000 each year, and sustaining memberships were $700,000.

Herron's professional YMCA career started with World Service in Istanbul, Turkey, in 1962. From Turkey he went to the Maine State YMCA for five years as executive director of a rural, non-facility YMCA district in Aroostook County. Herron worked with the YMCAs in St. Paul and Minneapolis from 1968 to 1978, during which time he helped raise capital and build two full-size, attractive YMCA facilities.

From 1990 to 1992 he served as president of the Friends of American Board Schools in Turkey (an international foundation), and later served as president of the council. Herron has also served on the boards of the National Society of Fund-Raising Executives, Camp Fire, and a private school.

In 1975 Herron won a Bush Foundation Fellowship enabling him to study at Harvard Business School, Columbia Graduate School of Business, and M.I.T.'s Sloan School of Management. He adapted the business marketing knowledge into a book, *Marketing Management for Social Service Agencies* (1977).

Herron received his B.S. degree (1961) in social group work from George Williams College, Chicago, and his M.S. degree (1967) in community and international services from Springfield College in Springfield, Massachusetts.

Marketing Nonprofit Programs and Services

Part One

Marketing and Nonprofit Organizations

Chapter One

The Role and Benefits of Marketing in Nonprofit Organizations

Marketing is what nonprofit organization (NPO) managers do all the time. We are constantly searching for ways to increase our membership and supporters. Although for-profit business marketing is now a highly developed process with its own descriptive terms, few NPO managers think and communicate in the business marketer's parlance.

We perform marketing tasks routinely. For example, a family moves to a new community in search of improved living conditions. The thirty-two-year-old father works at a job downtown, and the thirty-one-year-old mother has a part-time sales job near their home. They own their own home, and their income is $60,000 a year (market profile).

The wife becomes concerned that her busy husband is not spending enough time with his personal fitness. He is getting fat. So she calls the local YMCA (brand) to inquire about its programs (products). She calls the YMCA because she thinks it has a good reputation for fitness programs (public image built through public relations). She was told (word-of-mouth advertising) that it is better than similar programs (brand differentiation). The physical director (salesperson) tells her about the combination strength and cardiovascular fitness classes, one of the fastest-growing programs of the YMCA in the 1980s and still a viable program (product life cycle). Before she tells her husband (potential consumer) about the YMCA fitness classes, the wife (potential customer) wants to find out what the fees (prices) are, whether discounts are given (pricing policy), and where the services are offered (channels of distribution). She also says she will call the community recreation department (competition) to see what it has to offer (product menu). The YMCA person assures her that his agency has 50 percent of all the fitness classes in the area (sales claim of market penetration).

A letter from the YMCA invites all members of the family to visit a demonstration fitness class (sample). The letter states that now is the right time to join (asking for the order) because a special fitness class for overweight executives (target market) is starting next week. Also enclosed is a brochure (advertisement) describing the agency's other programs (product mix) of clubs, camps, and sports.

It is to the YMCA's advantage to get more program members (sales) because it must generate more income than expense each year (surplus center) to help pay for necessary general office and national expenses (cost centers, overhead). Some of the valuable services of the general office include accounting, supervision, legal documentation, fundraising (resource acquisition), and public relations.

The family decides it wants the services (benefits) and that the fees are fair, so it continues the marketing transaction by submitting payment and completing a registration form (order). The husband may choose to talk (bargain) with the agency staff over the amount of the fee he should pay. The marketing transaction is truly complete when both sides feel satisfied about the service and the payment (exchange).

Now examine your own customer-client interactions. Look at the process of attracting and registering people who use your organization's services. By attaching business marketing terms to segments of the transaction, you can gain valuable insights on how to improve the process. Not just the marketing director or the executive director but staff at all levels should be able to benefit by pulling the processes apart and reassembling them to increase overall effectiveness. Reengineering our routine steps can lead to greater productivity and less stress.

Why Nonprofits Should Market

Because marketing is what we do all the time anyway, we ought to do it better, for the good of our organization, our supporters, our customers, and even ourselves—better marketing will reduce our stress.

I have witnessed too many NPO managers showing signs of personal stress: physical tension, crankiness, family quarrels, reduced time with friends, ulcers, weight gain, compulsive smoking, and a variety of other symptoms. Perhaps it is no different than the stress felt by anyone in the working world, but stress is undoubtedly a particularly serious problem for leaders in the nonprofit health enhancement, family enrichment, and recreation fields.

Marketing doesn't make miracles, but it can help us gain marvelous insights, focus our resources sharply, get better results, and perhaps reduce our stresses.

I turned to marketing management as one good way to solve some of the problems I faced when managing YMCAs. The old ways just weren't good enough: the work piled up fast, the phone rang, call-back slips covered the desk, everyone wanted to meet with me except the people I wanted to meet with, memos went unanswered, and the paperwork pile turned into desktop compost. Aside from my paperwork, the need for face-to-face communication and greater problem analysis was sometimes overwhelming. I worked long hours but couldn't satisfy the organizational animal's insatiable appetite. The more it got, the more it wanted.

Under stress, we work harder—in ways we've worked before. We add an hour to the meeting, write another request, call more people, and do more tasks ourselves because it is easier than explaining to someone else what we need. Under stress, we tend to work harder, not smarter. Better marketing can help us work smarter and focus on what counts.

There is a perpetual list of social problems and target groups that need attention. In the institution of the American family, for example, we see many signs of trouble—teen runaways, school dropouts, substance abuse, suicide among young adults, child abuse, and households financially stressed because of unemployment or underemployment. Many people need better health care for themselves, for their children, or for their parents. Many people avoid museums and seldom see a live performance of dance, drama, or music. The arts and humanities can enrich lives. The health care and educational institutions can save lives. The need for services normally exceeds the supply.

Despite human needs and organizational stresses, few NPO managers really think they need to learn much more about marketing. On the other hand, they are receptive to anything that will make their jobs easier. Learning new marketing insights will enable us to fulfill our purposes, reduce current job stresses, and soon enjoy life even more than before.

Of course, improved marketing is not always an effective way to solve problems. As Novelli (1980, p.4) stated, "It is not a problem-solving panacea." There is no magic in marketing management that will ensure success. You can improve your odds, though.

A legitimate goal is simply to improve our success rate and get a greater return on our investment, making the effort even more worthwhile. A consistently fine level of performance will be one of the rewards.

Up until rather recently, NPO managers could survive even if they were reluctant to adopt sophisticated marketing techniques. They did not have much reason to become more proficient in marketing because things were fine. For example, at a YMCA program workshop about twenty-five years ago, former YMCA director V. M. Robertson cited seven nonprofit program development models, and every one of them reflected the nonmarketing orientation that many NPO managers held until recently.

1. *Traditional model.* Continue to do things because we have always done them. They exist now, so we will keep them.

2. *Brick and mortar model.* We have a facility, so we seek to fill it with activity. With this model, it is the facility that dictates the program. We have a pool, so we must offer swim classes.

Our hospital must keep its beds full. We have three hundred acres and some buildings in the country, so we run a camp.

3. *Money-making model.* Our summer concert nets us $5,000 each year. It seemed like a good idea when we started, but now we cannot turn loose from it because we need the revenue to balance the budget.

4. *Telephone or front door model.* Someone walks in and wants a macrame group. Or a father calls and wants a Chinese cooking class. So we add two new activities.

5. *Community expectancy model.* We assume the community expects us to have programs for senior citizens or provide a place for teenagers to gather. We respond to the expressed community interest and thereby let the community do our planning.

6. *Mythical community expectancy model.* This is very similar to the previous model. The difference is that in this model we hypothesize community expectation so as to have a rationale for doing what we want to do anyway.

7. *Personal preference model.* We do the things we are comfortable doing.

What all of Robertson's models have in common is planning with little research and little evidence of organizational mission. The organization using these models does not seem to know what business it is in or what its mission is, knowledge we must have if we are to effectively market our services.

Due largely to an increasingly competitive environment, our program services must be more market sensitive and purposeful today. NPO managers need special marketing help because competition, regulations, and higher customer expectations have made managers' jobs more difficult than they were a few years ago. Historically, NPO managers have been charming, highly motivated, positive people. Many were Jacks of all trades, having to be proficient in many diverse hands-on tasks ranging from working with boards and committees and counseling people with problems, to raising money and designing flyers, to leading songs and umpiring games.

The modern need for greater marketing sophistication was first felt by our nation's business managers. Bank officials, for example, once acted as some nonprofit managers have. If bankers put a branch someplace, they thought the customers would just walk in. "Build it and they will come," the *Field of Dreams* movie message, is naive.

At one time Citibank (now Citicorp) management did not court retail customers because each depositor's account was relatively small. But in the mid 1970s, Citibank invested $200 million to pursue some of the $1.2 trillion in U.S. consumer deposits (Salamon, 1981, p. 25). This was a new focus on and appreciation of the value of small customer accounts.

Learning how to motivate smaller retail customers became the goal of one of our nation's largest banks. Citibank officials started by hiring managers with consumer product marketing experience, from General Mills, General Foods, PepsiCo, and Procter & Gamble. They relied more on market research, product development, and advertising, moves that would be routine in a large consumer products company.

Citibank officials felt that without the marketing experts, they would not have known how to do a good job of testing consumer receptivity to new services. When the bank wanted to know how well customers might react to automatic teller machines, for example, it built a $250,000 model in the basement of the *Daily News* in New York. From behind two-way mirrors, bankers and market researchers watched 2,500 customers use the machine. (The researchers bypassed the cheaper route of surveying bank customers through a questionnaire because the customers had never used such machines, and therefore their opinions would have been invalid.)

The once-staid banking business was changing rapidly by 1995. First there were the biggest mergers in the industry's history, followed by the threat of on-line banking services offered by software giants Microsoft, Intuit, and others. Innovations in personal computer software have rewritten the rules on how and where people can save, borrow, pay bills, secure loans, and invest. Some banks, such as Citicorp, have spent years developing their own home banking products, including software and screen telephones. Other banks have joined forces with Microsoft, Intuit, and other providers. Even Citicorp, which avoided partnerships when developing its teller machine network in the 1970s, finally linked up with Intuit.

New technology is transforming the way large corporations conduct their charitable fundraising, too. Several large companies, such as Federal Express, the Gap, General Motors, and Ameritech have begun using an automated telephone system to collect pledges for NPOs. Employees are encouraged to call a toll-free number and use the telephone key pad to indicate the size and recipients of their pledge. IBM recently introduced computer kiosks at seventy-five of its worksites for the Employee Charitable Contributions Campaign. Freestanding, interactive computers enable employees to simply touch the screen to get information about various charities and the fund drive. USAir is using electronic pledge cards that allow employees to submit their pledges using electronic mail.

These new technologies for fundraising, for the most part, are not yet yielding well for federated fund drives. The reason is that they lack the persuasive power of real human contact. A United Way volunteer can field questions and convey with personal conviction the value of charitable services. A volunteer can also challenge donors and catch clues from the audience on how to proceed. Yet companies embrace the high-tech campaigns because they consume less employee time and they are more convenient for employees on the move.

A new CD-ROM product called Benefice by Traq International in Boston helps potential donors find worthy charities. By clicking the mouse on their personal computer, donors can scan a list of NPOs, pull up several screens of additional information about organizations that interest them, and then make their donation decisions.

New technologies require additional skills and usually involve retraining. Six branches of Citibank achieved record growth after providing a course that helped employees lose their Brooklyn accents. How much training does your organization give to staff and volunteers who interact with your customers? Staff responsiveness affects our customer service, our program quality, and our retention rate. Our attitudes toward customers show in everything we do. For example, BanPonce Corp., a Puerto Rican financial services conglomerate, experienced a tenfold increase in deposits between 1990 and 1996 (to $2 billion) by making BanPonce's working-class customers feel more comfortable with the business. BanPonce used bilingual bank tellers and offered hours convenient for people who work late shifts.

Brand loyalty in banking had been easy to maintain until recently, when so many banks merged. The first transaction is the most difficult, but inertia prevents most customers from switching banks frequently. Packaged-goods companies have an easier time making the first sale, but uninterrupted repeat purchases are more difficult. I suspect that most NPOs, like banks, benefit from customer inertia and the tendency toward first-brand loyalty: once we have them enrolled and using our services, customers are not likely to change (unless our service deteriorates). But how do we know what customers want, and what keeps them satisfied?

What Do Customers Want?

How did we get the attitude that we know what is best for the consumer? Was it from the college courses we had in psychology, sociology, and urban problems?

Why are some of us so confident that we know what is best for everyone else? Sometimes we should challenge our organization's assumption of what people need and want. Start by asking yourself what it may feel like for a person who needs or wants your services for the first time. Dick Webster, my associate at the Northwest YMCA in Minneapolis in the 1970s, was a physical fitness specialist. At that time, fitness protocols said that everyone should have a doctor's exam before beginning an exercise program. Yet Webster wisely recognized the requirement as a barrier to people who wanted to join the YMCA and start getting in shape. These people did not want to see their doctor yet. That added step only made joining harder and less likely. So we stopped making a strong suggestion that all fitness class members see their physicians first.

We knew that fitness tests were good for people. We encouraged people to take ours for free. Yet we also knew that people had their own ways of testing their level of fitness. They knew their health habits needed improvement when they were embarrassed by the V shape caused by letting pants out at the back seam. If they were puffing after climbing stairs, if they didn't like their appearance in a bathing suit, they knew they had a problem. We had a solution.

Henry Ford's statement that buyers could have any color car they wanted as long as it was black is not a far cry from NPOs that say you need Boy Scouts, camp, Goodwill, or the local performing arts group. A contemporary Ford dealer might say, "We know they want black cars, so we must convince them we are the best place to buy a black car." Henry Ford merely described his inventory; the contemporary automaker identifies black as a consumer need or want before offering it. The challenge for NPO managers today is to capitalize on consumer-expressed desires for services, rather than just announce the existence of services.

Girl Scouts USA, for example, should probably focus on what thirty-one-year-old women want, because that is their target market for volunteer troop leaders. Local Girl Scout councils should conduct focus-group studies with thirty-one-year-old women to find out their lifestyles, pressures, and aspirations. They could then offer a volunteer group leadership program that responds better to leaders' feelings of time pressure, guilt, and, in some cases, a desire for greater significance.

Lipton Pet Foods promoted its Tabby cat food in a way that showed a sensitive understanding of the sales environment. Through market research, the company learned more about the special relationship between pets and owners. Instead of merely selling cat food, it played on the special personalities of cats and humans. Lipton developed a cat astrology program and spent $7,600 on a short tour of the Hartford, Boston, and Springfield, Massachusetts, areas. The newsworthy cat astrology program was touted on the radio and TV and in newspaper features. Lipton's goal, of course, was to improve its sales and profits through innovative promotions. NPO managers can learn from studying such marketing moves by for-profit companies. If an NPO's primary motive in marketing is to relieve financial pressures, then in a sense, the NPO shares some of the profit motivations of commerce. We have already seen survival-oriented colleges shift from a sales stance (take what courses we offer) to a consumer marketing orientation (what would you like?). To balance budgets, colleges have changed curricula, relaxed dormitory rules, and sought year-round use of facilities. They have developed new services, including vacation courses, summer festivals, and workshops. They even give college credits for life experiences, in effect discounting the degree requirements.

Needs Versus Wants

An exchange underlies most marketing transactions. You give up something of value in exchange for something of greater value to you. The process of exchange works well when it meets both the needs and the wants of the market. Try to blend both needs and wants into your marketing program. Find out what people's problems are and help to solve them.

There often is a significant difference between needs and wants. Many NPO managers organize to give people what they need, rather than respond to their expressed wants. But services can be designed to meet both NPO goals and consumer wants. Table 1.1 shows some successful combinations of goals, needs, and wants.

In our analysis of the marketing exchange, we find other wants and needs that must be satisfied in addition to those of the NPO

Table 1.1. NPO Goals Can Be Compatible with Both Needs and Wants.

NPO Goal	Parent Wants	Child Wants	Program
Health enhancement	Safety for child	Learn how to swim and to have fun in the water	Swimming lessons
Leadership development	Outstanding child	Fun with other kids	Volunteer leader corps
Reduced racism in the community	Life in a safe and happy neighborhood	Improved tennis skills and fun	Tennis camp
Environmental education	Worry-free vacation from the kids	Exciting summer filled with adventure	Summer camp
Financial stability of the agency	A good feeling and relief from guilt and pressure	More programs and services	Sustaining membership campaign

and the consumer (see Table 1.2). Good marketing is the coordination of all these needs and wants.

The needs and wants of all are seldom, if ever, satisfied. Some NPOs may purposely not want to meet the interests of the majority of the population. Their goal may be to serve the special needs of a segment. Religious institutions, for example, are not going to dilute their doctrine to attract more donations.

Most groups want wider support. While holding steadfast to their particular mission, they seek to lead outsiders toward a greater understanding of their mission. They respond to the market the same ways a for-profit business might: offering trial use, greater convenience, easier access for the first-time user, and so on.

NPOs have their own wants for the world around them. They want to create, change, promulgate, maintain, preserve, and resurrect. Responsiveness to someone's interest keeps them alive.

Table 1.2. Who Wants What?

	Board of Directors	Service Users	Employees	Contributors	Suppliers	General Community	Government
Growth	x			x	x	x	
Reputation	x			x		x	
Significance	x			x		x	
Best return on investment	x			x			
Training			x				
Balanced budget	x			x	x		
Security		x	x				
Recognition	x			x	x		
Good performance		x					
Reliability		x					x
No waste				x			
No extravagance				x			
Pet projects		x	x	x			
Low fees		x					
Safety		x	x				x
Easy enrollment		x					
Program and staff continuity		x	x	x	x		
Easy parking	x	x	x				
Easy program access		x					
Wages and benefits			x				
Pleasant environment		x	x				
Advancement			x				
Challenge	x		x				
Good stewardship	x			x			
Prompt payment			x				
Solve problems				x		x	
Taxes							x
Worker protection			x				x
Reports	x						x
Standards							x

Are You Sales Driven or Marketing Oriented?

Too many NPO managers do not understand marketing. The uninformed among us tend to view marketing simply as sales and advertising. Sales is getting more takers of what we have, and advertising is a method of promoting what we have.

You can tell what stage of marketing development an organization is in by observing the actions of top management. When you apply the following guidelines, it is easy to appraise whether management is in (1) a self-satisfied stance with no intention of doing things differently, (2) a promotion push, or (3) a marketing mode.

1. *Self-satisfied stance.* "We are doing just fine. We know what works. We know what the people want, and we will continue to give it to them. Our programs are good, and there are plenty of people in our area who need what we offer. We know what doesn't work, too."

The tell-tale signs. There is no written marketing plan. Staff give routine answers to client inquiries with little regard for the needs of the questioner. There are few new programs and no push for improved customer service. Staff work very regular hours. Last year's plan is the same as this year's.

2. *Promotional push.* "We need a lot more, so let's go out and work harder. We want many more people in all our programs. . . ."

The tell-tale signs. There is promotion to everyone (universal), using selling techniques and a wide variety of promotional elements (flyers, radio PSAs, paid magazine ads, classroom visits, trade shows). More brochures are produced and distributed. Key leadership maintains a high public profile. Staff work long hours and with bursts of energy. More money is spent on promotions, and there are more special events. The same fixed-percentage increase is applied to all enrollment goals across the board.

3. *Marketing mode.* "Let us offer only services and programs that make a significant contribution in keeping with our special mission."

The tell-tale signs. The organization conducts regular audits of the organization's strengths and weaknesses. The management studies census data and the lifestyles of both customers and consumers. Target markets are identified in writing. A written marketing plan is approved months in advance of the promotion phase. Promotional pieces are developed for each audience. Enrollment charts are visible and used in staff meetings. Customer service gets constant attention through staff training and procedural changes. Consumers regularly evaluate all programs. The organization conducts annual studies of similar services offered by others. The organization regularly reviews both the formal and the informal mission statements in light of changing markets.

The difference between sales and marketing can be summarized this way:

Selling	Marketing
Emphasis on program/service.	Emphasis on public needs/wants.
Internal NPO orientation.	External market orientation.
Emphasizes NPO's wants.	Emphasizes potential user wants.
A program/service develops, then NPO figures out how to attract people to use it.	NPO identifies needs and wants of the public, then figures out how to effectively develop and deliver a service to satisfy them.
Results are measured by participation numbers.	Results are measured by user satisfaction and constituency.

Sales-oriented executives think differently than marketing executives. We must recognize the differences so that short-term successes (sales) do not jeopardize the organization's long-term effectiveness. Most organizations need both current sales and the long-term benefits of marketing, but they shouldn't sacrifice one for the other.

You can accurately appraise the dominant thinking of your leadership. The purpose of this appraisal is to avoid sharp peaks and valleys of participation volume, cash flow, and NPO effectiveness in both the long and the short terms.

Sales-driven executives tend to think in the following terms:

• *Participation volume rather than unit contributions toward the overhead costs.* They push for greater enrollments in all programs to meet enrollment goals and to get good work performance reviews and opportunities for personal advancement. They generally do not pay attention to budget details or to controlling expenses, nor do they know the unit contribution of each program toward the overhead costs.

• *Short time frame rather than the long term.* Focused on today's programs, clientele, and organizational pressures, sales-driven executives don't think much about program strategies over the next three years. They don't plan to be around then.

• *Individual customers and consumers rather than market segments.* They know about the individuals who affect their campaign success right now. They are less interested in building leadership and support for the future.

• *Field-work promotional efforts rather than desk-work planning and committee strategy sessions.* They prefer to sell to individual customers rather than get involved in cooperative community planning with other NPOs or funding sources.

Marketing-oriented executives, in contrast, tend to think in these terms:

• *Surplus planning.* They plan enrollment goals around budget needs, community needs, and customer wants. They try to integrate the three to get a comfortable budget. Some goals may be below last year's attainment because of a shrinking market or some demarketing strategies. Marketing-oriented executives work to gain greater market shares and to solidify the organization's reputation for outstanding delivery of services in a few carefully selected areas.

• *Trends, future threats, and promising opportunities.* Marketing-oriented executives keep experience graphs and charts. They analyze risk. They diligently search for changes in the environment that might affect future successes.

• *Customer types and market segments.* They have instant access to written assumptions about the lifestyle details of their typical customers; they also use related census data. Both the Boy Scouts and Girl Scouts, for example, know the fall season enrollments in every grade in every school in their area. They can tell you their saturation level in each school.

• *Systems for market analysis, planning, and control.* Marketing-oriented executives typically maintain maps with overlays, graphs, and charts. Their fascination with the numbers is evident. However, systems alone don't differentiate a marketing person from a sales person. Some of us are fascinated primarily by the challenge of new equipment and pay little attention to the timing of field promotions or the cost of our equipment and time. Some of us are so program oriented that we fail to do a good marketing job; we figure, develop a really good program, and it should sell itself. Still others of us are very promotion minded. We simply assume the program is good, the staff are fine, and all we need to do is promote it more. People will buy the program just because we have told them it's available.

Selling focuses more on the need of the seller. The preoccupation is with exchanging an inventory of goods or services for cash. Marketing embraces the same exchange goal, but focuses much more on the interests of the buyer. This focus is not more noble so much as it is good business. By satisfying the needs of consumers and paying particular attention to all that makes them happy, marketing gets better results.

The fair exchange concept lies at the core of marketing, particularly for nonprofits. Both sides should feel satisfied when the transaction is completed. Marketing is concerned with how such transactions are stimulated, created, facilitated, and valued (Lovelock and Weinberg, 1989, p. 11). For nonprofit service providers, the transactions may be more subtle than in the commercial field because the subsidized prices people pay often do not reflect the true costs to the NPO. Or, in the case of environmental programs and others, the price and inconvenience to individuals may be rather high in order for the larger community to benefit. Lovelock and Weinberg address this point: "The behavior advocated often seems to offer few benefits for the customer; indeed, it may seem to offer more short-term costs, frustrations, and self-denials than any apparent prospect of personal benefits. In many instances, the individual benefits (where they exist at all) are both small in nature and long-term in achievement. Frequently, these benefits take the form of not having something bad happen to you rather than having something good happen—as in undergoing regular medical checkups" (p. 13).

There are many definitions of marketing. Each marketing professor and key executive has a different one. Two classroom definitions are as follows: (1) marketing is a total system of interacting activities designed to plan, make, price, promote, and distribute want-satisfying programs and services to both present and potential consumers; and (2) marketing is ascertaining, creating, and satisfying the wants of people, and doing it at a profit. Although profit making is not our goal, it behooves those in the nonprofit field at least to balance the budget with enough revenue to meet expenses.

My own definition: marketing is every purposeful thing we do to get and keep customers and consumers of our services. "Everything we do" includes not only the big things, such as pricing, promoting, packaging, research, risk analysis, testing, and monitoring, but also a lot of little things. This is particularly true for NPOs. Most of us do a fairly good job of developing programs to meet identified needs, promoting the package, and accounting for the enrollments and finances. Where we may be weak, however, is in dealing with such nuances as schedules that are sensitive to the needs of the time-harassed consumer, bathroom cleanliness, how long the phone rings before it is answered, consumer interaction with the front desk staff, whether the staff get all the best parking places, functioning vending machines, and quick refunds. Inattention to these little things hurts many of our marketing programs most.

My definition of marketing includes both getting and keeping people. Retaining members, volunteers, and supporters is so critical that the national Boy Scout movement made it a priority in its marketing program. The Boy Scouts reasoned that it makes good sense in terms of finances, time, and programming to keep the good support they already have.

Our actions change once we adopt a strong stance of conserving members, volunteers, and donors. We spend more time discovering what is a good experience for them. We give them more of what they want.

Keeping the support we already have is a prime strategy now. There was a time in the 1950s and 1960s, and even into the 1970s, when we did not need to worry much about retention strategies. We had a booming market demand. If someone had a bad experience, we expressed sympathy but did not worry much about it. There was such demand for many of our services that people were in line for the health club locker, the handball court, the day camp slot, or the club group. Most of our efforts focused merely on announcing the existence of our services and signing up the new members. Most of our traditional markets have now changed. There is more competition for potential members, financial backers, and board members. We need to hold on tighter to the people we already have. Arts organizations that once prospered through grants from the National Endowment for the Arts (NEA) were struggling for existence by the mid 1990s. Congressional leaders cited the NEA funds as a good budget item to cut. Similarly, state Humanities Councils experienced flat federal allocations for the first half of the 1990s. With less federal support, local community arts and humanities organizations felt stress. They needed to retain old sources of support while finding new customers and consumers.

My definition of marketing includes seeking both customers and consumers of our services. Customers are those who pay for the service; consumers are those who use it. They can be the same people but more often are different. An example of a customer and consumer being the same would be a thirty-eight-year-old man who enrolls himself in a YMCA fitness class. He makes the buying decision and pays for the class; thus, he is the customer. Because he uses the class himself, he is also its consumer. Frequently, though, NPOs have situations where the customers and consumers are quite different. Good marketing strategy pays attention to both groups.

For a day camp, the customer may be a thirty-two-year-old mother, the consumer an eight-year-old child. If the camp receives subsidies from private donors and the United Way, then there are several more customers whose interests must be attended to. Although it can get complicated, you need to do a customer analysis only once. You can simplify the process by drawing a profile of your most typical customers and consumers and focusing on their concerns.

I used to think that NPO marketing was just concerned with getting consumers. I added customers to my definition when I discovered that Boys Clubs and some Hispanic agencies serving disadvantaged communities already had plenty of consumers. The Boys Club members paid only $2 a year, so those executives were obsessed with getting more revenue to support the centers. With the notable exception of Detroit in the early 1980s, most Boys Clubs were directing their marketing efforts to obtain more financial supporters rather than more children.

The District of Columbia Humanities Council in 1995 had a program popular with the older residents of housing projects in some of the city's poorest neighborhoods. In the program known as City Lights, scholars shared neighborhood history. People were encouraged to share their own experiences and add to the oral history of Washington, D.C. None of the program consumers paid for the programs, but good event attendance was a critical element to keeping City Lights funded. The customers, in this case, may have been the Humanities Council members who annually approved the allocation of a portion of their National Endowment for the Humanities funds for City Lights.

Challenges in Nonprofit Marketing

Distinguishing between those interested in consuming your services and those buying your services is a critical marketing task. Market research is the way you find out what various publics want. Do not be surprised, however, if the top management of your NPO does not want to commit significant time and money for such research. Top corporate executives have a low opinion of marketing research and marketers' contribution to strategic planning, according to Rabin (1981).

Rabin reported that company executives rated their marketing managers highest with the basics—pricing and sales. Only a small percentage of his small sample were pleased with their marketing staff's research. The biggest disappointments cited were weak accountability and productivity. Present-day professional marketing journals and papers regularly report identical observations. Marketing scholar Mel Moyer wrote, "Formal market investigations in nonprofit enterprises are quite rare" (Herman and others, 1994, p. 254).

Social marketing problems are more formidable than the typical marketing problems facing commercial marketers. There are nine significant differences between NPO marketing and that of commercial enterprises.

1. *The nonprofit market is more difficult to analyze than the for-profit market*. It is harder to get funding for consumer research studies and harder to complete studies in a timely manner. There is also less pertinent secondary information available to NPO managers.

NPO managers are usually reluctant to adopt bold marketing management strategies. The element of risk looms larger than when business is done as usual. Theodore Leavitt (1960) called the reluctance to risk a "fear of the inexact—the fear of playing the odds, and the rejection of imprecise data" (p. 45). Decision making seems to be one of the inherent weaknesses of marketing; even a professional marketing manager may find it difficult to arrive at a decision because of a seeming lack of data. Additional information can often be uncovered, but managers must weigh the cost of getting more information against the benefit they feel it will lend to the final decision. If an attribute of a good manager is an ability to read the environment correctly and make timely decisions, then the cost of collecting more information must always be considered.

Gathering more data may result in even more management tension and frustration. We can handle only so much data at a time. For expedient decision making, we must restrict the information we consider. McKenzie and Tullock (1981) suggested that if you have difficulty understanding the world you live in, you are probably attempting to consider too much information, not too little!

Economist Kenneth Boulding (1970) said it a little differently: "It is a very fundamental principle indeed that knowledge is always gained by the orderly loss of information; that is, by condensing and abstracting and indexing the great buzzing confusion of information that comes from the world around us into a form which we can appreciate and comprehend" (p. 2).

The field of management science has effectively used many shortcuts for better decision making. These include systems analysis, mathematical modeling, probability theory, queuing theory, PERT, the critical path method of project control, story boarding, and other techniques. For the nonprogrammed, nonroutine decisions, a manager must act on the basis of incomplete information. Such marketing activities as advertising, public relations, and determining why people buy something are extremely difficult to quantify and place values on.

Tight-budget NPO managers frequently find the costs of sophisticated and reliable research data prohibitive. Here are several options for them: join with sister agencies in similar communities and fund a cooperative project with each agency bearing only a portion of the total costs; recruit a specialist as a volunteer to do the task; get a consumer product company to adopt the project as part of its community service; hire a specialist or consultant occasionally; or borrow from someone's related research.

2.   *Picking target markets is more difficult for NPOs.* Although NPOs do not have stockholders seeking personal financial gain, they do have boards representing the interests of service users and the broader community. Because of the extensive committee work and consensus-seeking process involved, we often end up with low-risk ventures. Dramatic extremes filter out in the process of getting universal approval. Unfortunately, programs patched together by committees often appeal to few because they aim too broadly. It is particularly difficult to get board and committee volunteers to agree on narrow target markets.

When consulting with the Girl Scouts of Orange County, California, for example, I learned that they did not need more girls as much as they needed volunteer troop leaders. There were many more girls in the county who were interested in the Girl Scouts than there was a proportionate number of volunteer leaders available. Those who became troop leaders quickly found themselves overloaded with groups much too large. The quality of the experience diminished for both the girls and the volunteers. The solution would have been to focus Girl Scout promotional efforts on recruiting more volunteers, not more girls.

I surmised that the Girl Scout target market for leadership, at that time, was a thirty-one-year-old mother. This was a woman who married at twenty-two, had her first child at twenty-three, and now wanted her eight-year-old to enjoy the benefits of Girl Scouting. My contention was that the Girl Scouts could gain greater benefits by focusing their resources on that one target market than on a universal appeal for volunteers. However, the Girl Scouts leaders said they could not target this market. Instead they directed their appeals and research to both men and women ages twenty-one to sixty-one. Target marketing was politically unsavory for them at the time, as it is for most NPO leaders. Yet I suggest in the following chapters that knowing who is most likely to respond to us and understanding those people are paramount even if we cannot concentrate our limited marketing resources on them exclusively.

3. *NPO leaders have more freedom to act simply out of commitment to an idea or value.* Millions of volunteers and staff have a chance for self-actualization and self-fulfillment. Sometimes, though, this flirtation with self-indulgence may lead us into markets that are already mature or have nonexistent potential. Our NPOs give both board members and staff a chance to experiment a little recklessly with no personal financial consequence.

Sometimes our board and staff leaders direct us toward a market that simply does not exist. "Ghost demand" was a phrase used by Aubrey Wilson and Bryan Atkin (1976) to describe a situation where consumers have the desire and even the need for a service but lack the resources to attain it. Neither is there any financially feasible way to satisfy their wants or needs. In this case there is simply no market. Of course, a consumer can pay in nonmonetary terms with waiting time, volunteer time, and gratitude, but for most NPOs to exist, someone has to pay the bills with cash.

Even if we ask the potential consumers what they would like and then create and offer it, our success is in no way assured. Seeking to relieve the nation's backache, the YMCA developed the Y's Way to a Healthy Back, a program that has yet to live up to its potential despite the high level of need and proven effectiveness of the program. Business marketing can have this same problem, though not based on the same motivations. Seeking greater profits, Ford Motor Company developed the consumer-researched Edsel and suffered financial humiliation.

4. *Formulating good program strategies is more difficult for NPOs.* Rather than offering consumers quick comfort and immediate pleasure, NPO program staffs are often trying to recruit volunteers to do something unpleasant. We are trying to get them to give up smoking, work with a pack of twenty challenging children, go to exercise class for situps and pushups, or get a physical checkup.

When we do have an appealing program, we may be too slow in introducing it to the market. Seeking broad acceptance of new ideas dulls the timing of our market penetration until we don't dent the market at all. We wait and watch too long, thereby paying a high price for entering crowded markets. Recreation departments, YMCAs, and Jewish Community Centers that added racquetball courts to their facilities in the late 1970s did so when the demand had already peaked. Yet consumer demand has to be close to peaking for some NPO leaders to recognize that significant demand does indeed exist. The solution is to use market research to discover people's unmet or insufficiently satisfied needs. The same market research can help you to discover obstacles that keep consumers away and to understand how your current services are perceived.

Most NPOs have a program range that is too wide. They try to be too many things to too many people. They feel that there is a mandate not to turn anyone away. Even when consumer demand shrinks to a pitifully low level, killing a tired, old program is usually not worth the grief we anticipate. Even nonusers and previously uninterested parties are likely to complain.

There are situations where program volume does not have a significant bearing on an NPO's success. For some NPOs, their ability to attract third-party customers such as the United Way determines their financial health, not the number of consumers. Hence the emotional appeals that lace otherwise rational reports to the United Way, government agencies, foundations, and sustaining members. NPO managers who don't like what the numbers say usually do not report them frequently or prominently. They substitute emotional stories for hard statistical facts.

5. *NPOs have fewer opportunities to use pricing as an effective marketing tool.* In some cases, the programs are given away, or the low fee charged has no relationship to the true costs of delivering the service.

Volunteer boards of directors typically do not treat the NPO as a business. When making pricing decisions, for example, the board will frequently let the lowest fees prevail. The board seeks to serve more people with the lowest rates, rather than trying for a better return on investment or even much protection of the assets (including staff). Many NPO boards do not allow annual fee increases to keep pace with inflation.

Low margins mean there is not enough revenue for overhead staff—people who could be doing the market research, analysis, and training. Low prices can also dampen an NPO's ability to provide competitive staff salaries.

When there is not enough support staff to whom we can delegate tasks, we end up doing the jobs ourselves, either by working longer hours or abandoning the more complex, management-challenging tasks. Highly productive NPO managers who cannot increase the size of their staffs or otherwise profit from the high revenues they produce need some incentive, usually a higher salary, to keep up the fast pace.

Fees are often kept low by the program staff because they are the promoters (sales agents), and they reason that it is easier to enroll their quota at lower prices. They do not anticipate any appreciable personal benefit from helping the overhead support staff increase in size.

What a predicament! The complexity and cost of NPO management is increasing. Yet there exists tremendous pressure both inside and outside the organization to keep management costs low. Despite these constraints, NPOs can use some of the promotional pricing strategies that I describe later. By investigating the full value of your services to others and what your competitors are charging, you may show your board and staff some good reasons for changing the pricing and subsidy policies.

6.   *Channels of distribution may be harder to control.* Volunteers leading group programs away from the watchful eyes of the professionally trained staff may deviate significantly from the program protocol. Programs run by nonprofit social agencies in community schools are vulnerable to the changes in school scheduling and janitor moods each night.

Lack of control can affect programs in many ways. In most NPOs, there are few or no financial incentives for greater achievement or productivity. You don't get rewarded financially if you risk and succeed, but neither are you penalized much if your project fails. Facetiously, we used to tell staff that their "reward" was being able to keep their jobs if they reached enrollment goals and balanced their budgets.

Few nonprofit supervisors truly demand results; they request them. They pose issues to committees and list their concerns. They make suggestions for improvement, but seldom do they demand results. This absence of orders permits an appreciable amount of weak performance. A metropolitan unit executive explains a branch unit's sloppiness, high maintenance needs, tardiness, and unambitious goals by saying, "They are that way. We've talked with them many times, but they just don't seem to care." This is simply an effort to transfer the responsibility for management onto someone else's shoulders.

A friend of mine, Dick Rahal, worked as a branch executive for the San Francisco YMCA. Later, he took a job as a district manager of European Health Spas in Seattle, where the pressure to produce was much greater. Dick once told me that there were two major differences between the YMCA and European Health Spas, both of which were in the health enhancement markets at that time.

First, the Spas made it clear to all employees that membership sales were their lifeblood. Everything depended on being the very best at attracting and enrolling adults.

The second major difference related to demands and discipline. The YMCA treated its staff as professionals, with much trust in the relationship, little accountability for frequent reporting, and a modicum of tolerance when production goals were underachieved.

Contrast that with Dick's experience at the Spas: five days a week, Dick's six facility managers in the Seattle area would call his office with a statistical report of their sales progress. They called at 9 A.M. with a long report and at 4 P.M. with an abbreviated report. They had to tell Dick the number of sales made, amount of cash collected, their projection for the end of the day, the number of guests at the Spa, how many they were able to enroll, and their plans to get more guests tomorrow. Dick made a daily statistical summary of the six reports and called his boss in the regional office in San Jose, California. All units across the nation followed this same discipline.

Nonprofit managers may think of themselves as tough managers but wouldn't dare put such daily pressure on themselves and their employees. Without such extreme tightness, they may feel better but get paid less for their efforts. They also keep their jobs longer. Persistent pressure to produce against high goals often results in high employee turnover.

Comparing the two organizations, I felt the YMCA professionals could benefit from some of the enrollment discipline required of Spa staff. From a marketing point of view, it would make their jobs much easier. Memberships in the YMCA, too, have been its lifeblood. A good marketing plan would communicate to all staff the importance of meeting the needs and wants of customers, clients, and members. It would stress the value of attracting and keeping more supporters. Effectively communicating the plan after drafting it is one way to influence staff and focus them on what counts most.

7.   *Communications strategies are often more difficult for NPOs to carry out.* A low budget does not permit much paid advertising; many NPOs are thus at the mercy of the newspaper editor or station manager who receives their public service announcements. Rarely does an NPO, even a large one, have a budget that permits pretesting consumer reaction to a flyer or poster that is going to get wide distribution. However, this does not condemn you to ineffectiveness. You can still perform limited communications effectively, as I show in Chapter Seven.

8.   *NPOs are sometimes unsophisticated in marketing and management sciences.* The small NPOs, especially, can seldom afford staff specialists, and they therefore more easily miss opportunities.

Some NPO volunteer board members may not accept sophisticated marketing for their favorite organization because they feel that marketing has a bad image or is inappropriate. They may vocalize their distaste for creating expressions of consumer need where none were expressed before. They may say, "This is not appropriate for hospitals" (or churches or whatever). It is amazing to me how these board members apply different standards and strategies to an NPO. Conversely, things they would never do with their own businesses get their OK for the NPO. I have had that experience with key marketing executives as they helped set YMCA strategy. Board members need to realize that if we do not get more astute with our marketing, the NPO's very survival will be threatened.

9. *An NPO's results are more difficult to evaluate.* Although evaluation is difficult, it is not impossible. And the better you become at understanding your market, the more you will learn how to attract and keep various market segments. As I show in Chapter Seven, NPO managers can even engage in controlled price testing without too much complexity.

To evaluate a marketing program, NPO managers must, of course, be able to define convincingly what they mean by success. We run a risk of creating more demand than we can fulfill. If we turn over our meeting rooms every afternoon to senior citizens' social activities, are we able to cut into the after-school children's program to provide more space and time to meet increased senior demands? When raising money for camperships throughout the community, can we turn deserving youths away simply because we have not raised enough? What if the leaders of the swim program for people with disabilities request more pool time, and it results in less service to our own members and costs us money? Paying more attention to our marketing priorities can help us to allow for contingencies and to focus on areas we must succeed in.

Alternatively, we must avoid the darker side of marketing, which starts with an NPO's need for survival, not relevance. "We have a need; let's see how we can get the public to fill it for us" (Torrens, 1980, p. 6). The entire health care industry is damaged, for example, when a hospital's primary objectives are simply to fill empty beds, keep the hospital open, and provide jobs for the staff. Misdirection not only dismays new volunteers but also invites government intervention.

Our marketing objectives ought to be to satisfy consumer needs through a coordinated effort of staff and volunteers, while simultaneously achieving the organization's goals.

The Marketing Plan

The purpose of this book is to help nonprofit managers meet their marketing goals, in spite of the typical barriers and the added challenges facing most NPOs.

The first step is to acknowledge the mission of the organization and express that mission in contemporary commercial language; that is, affirm what business (or businesses) the NPO is in. The mission guides the focus of the marketing plan and gives direction to every staff member and volunteer. The marketing plan itself is intimately linked with the NPO's survival. Simply put, a planned, coordinated approach to the market enables an NPO to meet community needs for a longer time.

The marketing plan coordinates four major elements: goals, program, human resources, and budget. These areas need constant attention because they are so fluid. The marketing plan also helps to ensure a proper mix of all the support services. The plan usually includes pricing strategies and a tight time schedule that weaves the four major elements together. The goals specify the desired number of service transactions (sales). They also include the expected benefits derived by the community at large and by individual consumers. The program defines the service and establishes quality standards for performance. Because the work of most NPOs is labor-intensive, the marketing plan must carefully spell out how the NPO's precious human resources will be organized. Finally, the marketing budget details all the costs needed to carry out the program.

The breadth of the typical marketing plan is widening. Marketing is increasingly permeating more of the organization and having greater universal application. Not many years ago, an NPO market-ing plan would simply have been the public relations and promotion plan. Now the plan sticks its nose into the personnel and training function and the program development arena, and prods the main-tenance staff and telephone receptionists.

In the following chapters I will examine key areas particularly as they relate to increasing membership and support. I will show how to conduct economical market research, promote to target markets, and increase volunteerism. I also discuss the practicalities of target marketing in NPOs, and I show how to conduct audits to identify an organization's market strengths and vulnerabilities.

You pursue this path in search of greater success. But what does success look like in your NPO? I once asked fifty executive direc-tors of Girls Clubs (now Girls Inc.) on the West Coast how they would describe success. For some, success was a balanced budget or a large surplus at the end of the year. Others talked about program participation volume with the largest numbers signifying the great-est success. It might have been getting a new van, a new desk, a new office, or a new building. Some measured success by the lives of specific children changed for the better. Others mentioned their salary increase as proof of their progress. Among fifty NPO leaders, there were at least twenty-five different definitions of success.

Successful for-profit businesses have very clear annual objec-tives. In this respect, NPOs need not be any different from busi-nesses. You are on your way to improved marketing when you define your mission, goals, and objectives clearly. The next chapter will offer you ways to define what business you are in and help you define specific marketing objectives, always with the primary focus on the most important people in your organization—your cus-tomers, consumers, and supporters.

Chapter Two

What Are You Selling?
What Are They Buying?

Some of us have been in our jobs too long. We have forgotten why we are doing what we are doing. Immersed in the everyday details of the job, we lose sight of the bigger picture, the very reason for our hard work. We forget our mission, or, in marketing terms, we lose sight of what business we are in.

It is no wonder then that it is hard to enroll someone, recruit someone, or get another gift. When we are obsessed with the details of management, it is downright difficult to avoid discussing those details with potential customers. We mistakenly assume that merely providing more information to the customers will enable us to make the sale. So we tell them more about our campaign organization structure, the size of our pool, or the expert training of our staff. These all may be important attributes from our point of view, but they are of little value to the customers unless they can clearly see some personal benefits accruing to themselves.

Look at your brochures. Listen to your speeches. Listen to your telephone receptionist. Stand in the lobby and watch prospective members get their questions answered. Too often we provide facts and discuss the features of our program without tying in related benefits to the customer. Matching benefits to features is a critical step in the marketing process.

Tie Benefits to Features

Look at it this way: people don't need quarter-inch drills—they need the quarter-inch holes the drills provide. If a better way to make quarter-inch holes is ever found, the sale of quarter-inch drills will plummet.

Headache sufferers don't need aspirin—they need relief from the headache. That is why ibuprofen and acetaminophen have been able to take away a significant part of the aspirin market.

Our communities don't need Boy Scouts as much as they need the benefits the Boy Scout program provides. If someone else seems to do a better job of providing those benefits, or provides them more cheaply or quickly, customers' loyalty will shift. Competitors will be in our line of business even if their actual program is unlike ours.

Benefits are what customers and consumers derive from satisfactory use of the service. *Features* (the characteristics we most often talk about) are the distinguishing facts about the service that are true whether the service is ever used or not. Features are easily provable characteristics that are not debatable. They are the elements you can see, taste, touch, smell, and measure.

Staff who base their selling strategy solely on a description of the program's features are hoping the prospective customer will bridge a conceptual gap and convert all the features into personal benefits. Professional salespeople and marketers know, however, that the typical prospect, no matter how well educated, has neither the time nor the inclination to convert all the features into benefits. Professionals also know that no sale starts without the prospect anticipating some benefits.

You must persuade potential customers that use of your service will satisfy their needs and interests. Associating the customer's interests with your program takes thoughtful staff work before the presentation is given, the encounter is scheduled, or the publication is mailed. For example, the Society for the Prevention of Cruelty to Animals (SPCA) pushed a pet adoption program by selling the attributes of cats, which they had in oversupply. The SPCA staff anticipated the concerns of people considering a dog or a cat. They pointed out that cats are wonderful companions who do not bark, need a leash, or poop on the sidewalk. The SPCA described them as self-cleaning dogs.

Often people know what they should do, but they don't do it. People know full well they should stop smoking, lose weight, get more exercise, floss their teeth, cross with the light, and do a lot of other things that would provide them with benefits galore, but they delay positive action. Our task is to move people from good intentions to action.

Our task is not easy, because there are some mighty strong opposing forces standing in the way. The media choke us with messages telling us to enjoy life now, buy now and pay later, consume more delicious fattening foods, and so on. Our programs don't seem nearly as attractive as the commercial alternatives. Our NPO advertising looks bland—crammed with information about the organization and printed in one-color ink on newsprint. Compare it with the four-color, slick-paper advertisements of the commercial product companies.

We may be selling a lifetime of fitness and good health while national advertisers are selling liquor, instant warmth, and potential good feeling. Our programs present a big enrollment hurdle to prospective customers when they perceive that the benefits are only attainable by a lifetime of sustained effort. These social marketing situations make it particularly important that we know our potential customers well.

Rather than engaging in expensive primary market research, we can make some fair assumptions from others' research. For example, a study of 120 people who started an exercise program at the Central YMCA of Sacramento, California, found that the major factors influencing the consumers to enroll were a desire for self-improvement, peer influence, and the desire to prevent health problems (Baugher, 1978). Some of the benefits these people sought were to get in shape, lose/control body weight, feel good, improve physical skills, prevent a heart attack, enjoy fellowship, and retard the aging process. There were other motivations. Although most people were seeking the benefits already mentioned, others were pursuing slightly different goals. It is wise for a salesperson or marketer to refrain from simply citing a long litany of memorized related benefits. Try to discover and focus on those that meet the interests of the individual customer. The Sacramento YMCA staff also found that some people started a formal exercise program to relax, relieve an ailment, or just have something to do. After the San Francisco Jewish Community Center found that single Jewish women joined to get the benefits of meeting people (38 percent), to use the pool and sauna (36 percent), to relax (33 percent), and to have Jewish fellowship (28 percent)(Rotwein, 1981), the staff were able to redirect their membership enrollment program. Artwork and photographs in various promotion pieces promised the benefits the targeted groups desired.

Staff at the Franklin Institute Science Museum in Philadelphia surmised that the two major benefits sought by people visiting the museum were education and entertainment. Adult visitors wanted information about science in general or about a specific subject for their children or themselves. At the same time they wanted to be entertained with positive societal values themes. One of the primary benefits of becoming a museum member is that one doesn't have to wait in long lines to gain access.

Pick Benefits for Different Groups

Staff are not always the best people to decide what benefits to feature in our presentations, because there are often benefits that staff want from a program that differ from those desired by the customers and consumers. To solve this problem at the Northwest YMCA in Minneapolis, we made lists of benefits for each program from three different perspectives: that of staff, customers, and consumers. Table 2.1 illustrates the example of the day camp.

If we had felt it necessary, we could have identified the key benefits for other groups. The counselors would probably seek benefits in addition to their leadership experience, including pay, something to do, and a chance for a better job later. Customer groups such as the United Way and other program funders would predictably seek benefits different from those held most dear by

Table 2.1. Day Camp Benefits.

Staff (Professionals)	Customers (Parents)	Consumers (Eight-year-olds)
Capacity enrollment means I can keep my job.	Children are safe.	Have fun.
Meeting ACA standards is proof I run a good camp.	Children are busy.	Opportunity for adventure.
	No fights, dirty jokes, or accidents.	Learn new skills.
	Freedom from worry about the children.	No boredom.

parents. Overanalysis can kill the chance of getting the task done, however. Simplified approaches get us started toward greater marketing sophistication and make us feel good at the same time.

How do you find out what the customers may want? Simply ask them. Ask questions using the words *why, tell me how, what, where,* and *who.* Then carefully listen to and observe the customer's response. It is amazing to me how often prospective customers will reveal exactly how you can sell them your services and memberships.

Knowing exactly what benefits to talk about depends on the prior analysis of your programs and your appraisal of the customers. Figure 2.1 is a model that you and your work team can apply to each of your major program lines to derive the key benefits related to program features. From the benefits in the third column you can derive some other benefits that may be more important to mention in your promotions. Because your services will probably have more features and benefits than are shown in this figure, you should expand the model when applying it.

Another way to identify what people want from you is to have all the staff (and volunteers too, if you can get them) list all the features they can think of for each service or program. Tie one or

Figure 2.1. Features and Benefits.

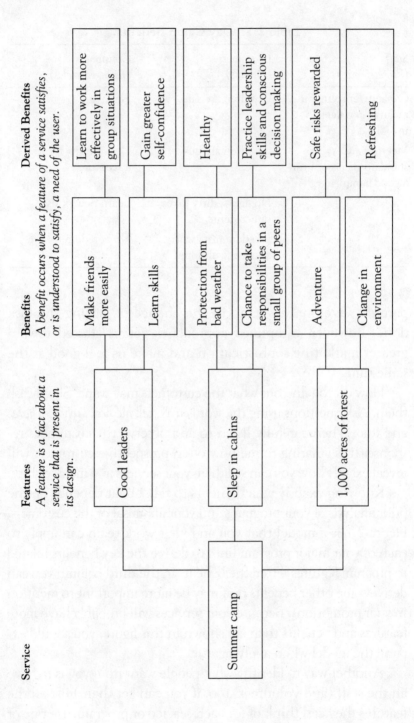

more benefits to each feature. Ask of each feature, "What is the value of that to anyone?" The transition phrase I use most often to tie benefits to features is "Our program has [describe a specific attribute of the service], and that means to you . . . [tie a desired benefit to the attribute you have just mentioned]." An example of the results you might get from this brainstorming activity is shown in Table 2.2.

There are many wonderful ways to discover important benefits of our programs. The nine-box matrix in Figure 2.2 can enable you to look afresh at old programs that may be taken for granted. Using the matrix is one way to find better brochure headlines, for example. Nine specific benefit areas can be derived by comparing the prospective customer's assumed motivations (the experience they seek, the image they want to create or maintain, or the problem they want solved) with their personal focus (primarily toward self-enhancement, seeking other's approval, or nonspecific). The nine-category matrix is especially useful in situations where work teams are drawing up lists of key benefits but are overlooking prospective customer motivations or orientation.

In addition to identifying benefits people expect, benefit analysis can identify the unique characteristics of your programs. Determining your programs' unique benefits is vital when promoting in a community where programs similar to yours exist. In the city of San Francisco, for example, there are at least forty-one major organizations offering services to senior citizens and competing for funds to keep up the good work. Carefully defining the benefits of your program is a way to make your organization stand out from the rest. Setting aside the list of program benefits that are similar to those of other providers, an agency can focus on actual or perceived consumer needs and desires, thereby capturing the consumers' state of mind in an expressive phrase.

Mention the safety features, for example, in a community where concerns for personal safety are felt but perhaps not expressed much. The benefit of safety may not be directly attributable to a specific program offering, but the fact that the program site is in a

Table 2.2. Derived Benefits.

Service	Feature	Benefits
Capital funds campaign	Gifts will build new buildings and rehabilitate existing units.	Thousands of deserving people will get wholesome programs. You can use the new facility.
	Large gifts are encouraged.	You will make a significant impact.
	A prominent plaque will list all major contributors.	More prestige will accrue to your family or company.
	Staff will give sacrificially.	Community will have more evidence of how much we care about them.
Fitness center	Open 7 days a week, from 6 A.M. to 11 P.M.	Available when you are.
	Four professional staff members.	Expert guidance to help you achieve your goals faster.
	We have been here since 1902.	Plenty of experience with quality service.
	Variety of facilities.	Avoids potential boredom from a fitness routine.
	Lounge with TV and newspapers.	Chance to relax.
Volleyball league	Play every Thursday.	A predictable schedule that you can count on.
	Three skill divisions.	Have more fun playing with people at your level.
	Tournaments.	A chance to win.
	Regional playoffs.	A chance to travel with the team and have fun.
	Final banquet.	A chance to celebrate the season with teammates.

Figure 2.2. Matrix for Identifying Nine Benefit Areas.

	SELF-ORIENTED	OTHER-ORIENTED	NONSPECIFIC
EXPERIENCE	(Camp Program) "Go to high adventure camp and experience the thrills of wild river canoeing."	(Fundraising) "Campaign for us and enjoy working with top community leaders for a worthy goal."	(Exercise Program) "Exercise to jazz music in the pool because it is a special experience. "
IMAGE	(Fitness Program) "Join the YMCA's fitness class—you will soon look like tiger."	(Volunteer Leader) "When you become a Scout leader, children and their parents will look up to you."	(Program Volunteer) "Volunteer with the art museum because interesting people are there with the attractive exhibits."
FUNCTION	(Weight Loss) "Join the hospital's weight-loss clinic—you will soon be able to wear your daughter's clothes."	(Skills Program) "Learn lifesaving skills at the Red Cross, and others will appreciate your improved response potential."	(Child Care) "Use JCC day care services because they do it better."

heavily trafficked, well-lighted, and well-supervised area may help alleviate the unspoken concerns of potential customers.

You open yourself to criticism when you promise benefits unrelated to reality. Be realistic about benefits and be prepared to provide proof that your claims for program performance have a basis in fact. That is one of the values of saving goodwill letters from satisfied customers. Also keep research reports handy.

After you have made the largest list you can of all the benefits your program provides, expanding the number of features and related benefits, pick just a few of those most relevant to consumers. Use these for your advertising and sales pitches. Store the leftovers in a file for reference.

Promise Benefits They Desire to Deliver Benefits They Need

Crime and the criminal justice system are currently growth markets. There is no need to market the services of prisons and jails. But there is a critical need to market the benefits of halfway houses. After incarceration, felons are frequently referred to halfway houses for supervised reentry into the community.

In most American communities, citizens shun halfway houses in their neighborhoods. Even shelters for victims of domestic violence sometimes have difficulty locating in a neighborhood. Typically the citizens readily recognize the need for shelters and halfway houses; they just do not want them in their own backyards. When there is an insufficient supply of halfway houses, people paroled from prison are allowed to find accommodations anywhere in the community. Unsupervised and more loosely monitored, parolees have more opportunity to steal a lawn mower or a television from neighbors to pay for their drug habits. If someone could convincingly elucidate the benefits of halfway houses, neighborhoods would be safer.

Often we must promise the public some of the benefits they want in order to give them some of the benefits we think they need.

That is the situation of churches today, for example. Many have broadened their line of activities to attract more members.

With 16 percent of the population moving each year, church leaders have to work constantly to attract new members, recruit new volunteers, and keep the collection plates full. Suburban church leaders have found it is easier to achieve these goals when they promote the benefits of their churches as places to make new friends quickly and develop community ties, as well as to worship. The church gives newcomers a place to meet like-minded people and provides an element of continuity in their lives. "Nearly everyone who comes to us is in the midst of an adjustment crisis," said Rev. Stanley M. Tozer, pastor of the Presbyterian Church of Palatine, Illinois (Ingrassia, 1977). "The wives have no friends, the husbands have new jobs and the kids are changing schools. They're hungry for instant intimacy, and we try to give it to them," he said.

Posted on church bulletin boards will be sign-up lists for the seasonal retreat, a poster advertising the coming brunch, another that tells about a film festival or play. Often there is a bulletin board displaying the pictures of new members. At Sunday services, new-comers are asked to identify themselves and sign the guest book (so follow-up calls can be made).

The coffee hour that follows the service at many churches is an important way of assimilating visitors and cementing relationships among regular attenders. At the Quaker Meeting in San Francisco, the coffee hour is busy with city newcomers seeking inexpensive apartments (the old-timers just smile and wish them well), amateur musicians seeking someone to play with, and people just celebrating the joy of being together.

To foster ties among church members that go deeper than the casualness of the coffee hour, many churches have developed small fellowship groups. Some call them *Koinonia* groups, which is Greek for Christian fellowship; others use different descriptive names, but the purpose remains the same: to help this country's mobile population and the unaffiliated to cope better with their rootlessness.

A few theologians question this modern role for the church. They are concerned that running a youth center, a day-care center, a community food shelf, and an information and referral service is very draining of the clergy's energy and may be distracting them from some of the more serious problems of our society. But it is not macro community changes that individuals are buying these days, and the local ministers know it. That is why they offer everyday benefits to the consumers. With the advantages that come from greater corporate strength derived through these activities, churches can attack the larger problems next.

"Our job is to give people what they need now, today," said Jude Nicoletti, a veteran Red Cross professional in Portland, Oregon (Nissen, 1979, p. 33). That means disaster victims get the added benefit of emotional as well as financial support from the Red Cross. Said one young wife who had just lost everything, "The insurance man just wanted to know how the car was and the housing guy just wanted to know how our house was, but the Red Cross lady asked how I was." A former civil-defense official said, "These people are professional mothers. They work mostly for love, putting on Band-Aids, breaking up fights, kissing everything to make it better" (p. 33).

Talk About Your Primary Business

The Red Cross's public image of self-sacrificing generosity makes the organization well accepted throughout the world. Other factors contributing to its success are its response time, lack of discrimination, and official endorsement by the government. None of these latter elements would make much difference to the public, however, if the primary benefit of human caring were not paramount in the organization's marketing program and in its actions.

A strong singular image is important because the public may get confused by the variety of messages emanating from a multiservice agency. For example, the Red Cross has many programs, including teaching swimming, conducting first aid clinics, and providing disaster relief. All of these services are marvelous, and they are all logical program extensions, but just what image do they present to the uninitiated? If you were only a casual observer, would you think of the Red Cross as primarily a youth organization or one for adults? Primarily for male volunteers or best suited for females? Would upper- and lower-income people feel comfortable in the Red Cross as volunteers with the middle classes? Is the Red Cross a good place for highly educated people and the very creative, or would they feel constricted by the organizational culture? Of course, the Red Cross would say they appeal universally and would be able to point to specific people from all walks of life who serve with them. Although there are marketing benefits to presenting a strong singular image, there is a drawback, too, for multiservice organizations. A single prevailing image often turns away prospective customers (volunteers, in the Red Cross case) who disqualify themselves. To show their inclusiveness, most publicly funded NPOs print pictures showing the diversity of their volunteers and staff. Without using a lot of words, the photographs give an impression of who is welcome.

Many commercial companies that diversified a few years ago have shed businesses not relevant to their central image and main business. The reason is that investors were hazy about what companies so diverse really did for a living, and as a result they did not buy their shares (Lynch, 1980).

Banks seldom offer services that are unique. The only advantage one bank may have over another is convenient location, and even that benefit has eroded with the proliferation of automatic teller machines throughout the community. To compete for business, some banks are adding more benefits (probably while they are simultaneously withdrawing other benefits, such as free checking and free safety deposit boxes). For example, the Bowery Savings Bank of New York decided that people's extreme interest in safety and freedom from crime and vandalism could be turned to some good marketing advantage. They held safety seminars at the various Bowery branches and gave away six hundred thousand whistles in a "Blow the Whistle on Crime" crusade, twice as many whistles as they had planned for. "You can't measure what this kind of thing does in terms of deposits, but it does have an impact," said Judith Gellers, an assistant marketing officer at the bank (Salamon, 1980). The safety education program of the bank did not confuse anyone about the bank's basic mission of providing safe financial services. It just added another customer benefit.

Hospitals have a marketing problem similar to that of the banks. They have a dual goal of promoting available services and also strengthening the community's trust and confidence in the institution. The latter is important because public confidence in the medical profession and health care institutions has declined. The single factor causing the decline was the rise in health care costs following the enactment of Medicare and Medicaid. Because of hospitals' origins as nonprofit benevolent organizations, most people felt hospitals were not supposed to be profit making. Some are and some are not.

The challenge for the for-profit hospital administrators was to make money while also regaining their historic image as benevolent institutions. The nonprofit hospital managers were charged with running organizations that at least did not lose money. The nonprofit hospital managers wanted the public to understand that their motivating force was compassion, not cost. But like their for-profit counterparts, they also wanted the public to understand the benefits of a hospital being operated efficiently and with good value given for the patient dollar.

From a marketing perspective, the basic mission of health care institutions is to satisfy the needs and wants of consumers, especially those in the target segments, in a manner that achieves the organization's objectives, through a coordinated systems approach that has satisfying services, appropriate prices, convenient locations, and promotional communications to inform the public and the targeted segments.

Every nonprofit organization should state its mission and its benefits to the public with succinct clarity. Considering that there

are over half a million NPOs in the United States that are dependent on philanthropy, the competition for understanding and
acceptance is great. Just what, in addition to the general assumed
benefits, are the specific reasons why individuals, foundations, businesses, and the government should support your organization?
What community or personal benefits make your organization
deserving of special attention in light of all the other NPOs?

Every NPO has a mission statement in its charter. However,
lofty language often disguises rather than reveals the organization's
reason for being. Whereas in the nonprofit field we talk about mission statements, the business schools get to the heart of the matter
by simply asking, "What business are you in?" The question may be
easy, but the answer is not, because there is no single right answer.
There are a variety of answers that shift with time and events, particularly during top staff changes.

I once asked my department heads at the Northwest YMCA
to state in one sentence the mission of their work. As chief executive, I used two sentences to describe the basic business of the
Northwest YMCA: "We are striving to create a community of love
in everything we do. Twenty-five thousand people, one out of
every eight in the area, is our service goal." Others had these
things to say:

> We will be the leading provider of an optimal lifestyle of health and
> exercise for all ages and sexes in the Northwest area.
>> —Dick Webster, health enhancement director

> With less government subsidies available next year, we will main-
> tain our current high level of detached worker staff and teenage par-
> ticipants to help prevent delinquency in the Northwest area.
>> —Frankie Francel, delinquency prevention director

> Our YMCA will continue to maintain high-quality family enrich-
> ment programs at their present level in spite of declining numbers
> of school-age children.
>> —Tom Carrothers, family enrichment director

Our camping will provide a unique outdoor experience to enrich the life of every camp participant.

—Bennie Loro, camp director

Our goal is to provide all of our program consumers with personalized, high-quality services throughout the organization.

—Deanna Dammer, consumer services director

Witness the variety of mission statements. One program director wants to be number one; two others are offering unique individualized services. Two are promising to hold their own in shrinking markets. These are clear messages about the intentions of their departments.

One way to force even greater clarity about the basic business of the organization and the benefits promised is to describe them in both formal and facetious terms. For example, formally a YWCA might say they are in the child-care business, while facetiously they might describe it as baby-sitting. The value of describing our mission and benefits in a facetious way is that very often the description contains a particular reality-centered truth that is absent from any of the formal statements.

Facetiously speaking, then, many NPO managers are in the cosmetics business. They are trying hard to make someone look good, usually their supervisors or someone higher up. Some executives act as if they are in the firefighting business, running around from emergency to emergency with no time spent on strategic planning and service pruning.

When we pause and accept (at least temporarily) the facetious descriptions as tinged with reality, we gain insights into tasks we should spend less time on and goals that require a more appropriate strategy for us to attain them. Although we may at times be in the cosmetics business, we probably are not doing an optimum job of making someone look good. If our work seems like a circus much of the time, we probably are not enjoying the circus as much as we could be. If we often seem to be in the employment business, are we spending enough time cultivating the job offers we want? If the main reason we are building a new unit in a weak market is to satisfy someone's need for a monument in his or her honor, perhaps we could substitute a larger-than-life-size statue that requires a lot less upkeep. There are plenty of ways of doing better when we recognize what it is we are trying to do.

Here is a good five-minute exercise that provides the basis for plenty of staff discussion. Simply make a list that formally and then facetiously describes your basic business. The following example was created by a group of employee publication specialists candidly describing the business of the editorial staff.

Formal	Facetious
Inform	Baby-sit
Entertain	Hustle
Educate	Management ego-gratifier
Build morale	Placater
Stimulate feelings of belonging	Pacifier
Company representative	Juggler
Recognize technical achievements	Manipulator
Management style setter	Slave driver

Under the umbrella of humor, staff will tell top management what management needs to know about morale and mission. Staff tell us how to keep their interests high. This is a wonderful gift. We can't build a great sales organization by losing good people.

Top managers are in business to serve those they supervise. If they are successful supervisors they keep their jobs. When the employees are unhappy, the supervisors lose.

I am in business to serve my leaders and my followers. As long as they are successful and satisfied, I get to keep my job.

That is facetious. Of course, satisfying community needs comes first. That is the primary business I am in. Which brings us back to where we started: What are you selling? What are they buying?

Part Two

Conducting Cost-Effective
Market Research

Chapter Three

Who Is Your Customer?

The Values and Techniques of Market Research

NPO managers use market research primarily for two purposes: to justify and to discover. Because these purposes are poles apart, in the interest of economy it is wise to decide right away just which goal is being pursued.

Under the guise of discovery motives, we often use market research to prove a point or justify a favorite course of action. The board or potential big funders of a project may balk until there is more evidence of the soundness of a proposed course of action. They want to reduce the risk of failure and get a good return on the investment of time and money.

Often, though, NPO executives feel that their experiences and observations of the situation are justification enough for the project to go ahead. Their intuition is that the present plan is right and that a research project is just delaying action. Appeals by others for more hard data are seen as impediments, as time-consuming hurdles. When that is the case, the true goal of the market research may be to spend the least amount of money and staff time to come up with an official-looking, impressive report that will justify the direction already outlined by the boss.

You should *not* do market research

- When the course of action is already decided
- When decision makers aren't likely to pay attention to the results
- When the cost of the research would exceed its value

- When the budget and time available is insufficient to do an adequate job
- When the research is politically motivated, or is designed to prove a point
- When the problem is unclear and the goals of the research are vague

Many times good market research is truly justified. What stops it is simply that average NPO managers consider themselves too busy to spend time with auditing and research. Such shortsightedness is bound to get them in trouble.

Research is a planned and organized effort to gather new facts and knowledge to help us make better market decisions. Research can tell us, for example, what kinds of customers we are presently getting, where they are coming from, who the heavy users are, what they think of us, how fair our fees seem to be, where we should promote, and what we should say. This knowledge is well worth the effort required to get it.

Research helps complete the marketing cycle (described in Chapter Twelve, Figure 12.1) by opening the feedback channel from present and potential customers to NPO management. Although research is definitely not a substitute for management decisions, it does help managers find problems, and tests the acceptability of possible solutions.

There are a number of good reasons for surveying your current consumers, clients, and supporters. You can use survey information to

- Develop a profile of current users
- Evaluate current programs
- Evaluate potential new programs
- Evaluate your performance
- Test receptivity to capital development plans
- Learn why members are not using the services

- Anticipate reactions to changes
- Discover new markets
- Uncover any needs for service improvements
- Find common key customer characteristics
- Discover a person's likelihood of making a donation

There are also good reasons to survey people who do not currently use your services. This research can help you to

- Learn why they are not members
- Learn what would induce membership
- Determine your image with the public
- Learn about the competition
- Learn why former members and supporters quit

Once you are convinced you want to go ahead with market research, make sure you cover the ten essential steps that I outline here. By anticipating and carefully planning each step you can avoid wasted efforts or unreliable conclusions drawn from the data.

1. Carefully define the questions you want answered or the problem to be studied. Get others' agreement at the very beginning.
2. Assign responsibilities and create a schedule.
3. Before launching your own study, find out what others in the field have been doing.
4. Select the type of survey.
5. Determine the sample size and who should be in it.
6. Prepare the questionnaire.
7. Conduct the study.
8. Process the data.

9. Analyze the data.

10. Prepare the report and present the findings.

The rest of this chapter elaborates on these ten steps, giving particular attention to types of surveys.

1. Carefully Define the Problem

It is very important to define the problem that is worth studying very clearly. Be specific. What do you really want to know? Drop questions that you are not going to do anything about no matter what the respondents tell you. Then seek staff and maybe even board consensus about the problem to be researched. The more people involved in the early stages and throughout the study, the more likely that the study recommendations will be accepted.

2. Assign Responsibilities and Create a Schedule

Avoid the common problem of having the findings of the research reported long after the management decisions have been made. Tailor the type of survey and production schedule to fit top management's need to make timely strategic decisions. Clearly define who has responsibility for each step of the program.

When my firm does fundraising feasibility studies, we tell the client that it will take them a full month to properly prepare for the first interviews. Our carefully worded instructions tell what they are expected to do and what we will be responsible for. We mention it will take us about four weeks to prepare the findings of our study after we complete our research. We also suggest that the board not take a formal vote to campaign the same day they hear our recommendations. They should mull over the various recommendations and implications before launching a bold campaign. In summary, then, approximately nine weeks elapse between an organization's choosing our firm to do the research and board decision making.

3. Find Out What Others in the Field Have Been Doing

Before launching your own original research, call or write to solicit other people's findings and suggestions. Discover what information has already been gathered that relates to your needs. Such secondary research is cheaper and quicker to do than original research and may help define your primary research goals.

There are two sources of secondary research data: internal and external. The internal sources are your own records, budget data, participation reports, donor records, annual reports, and so on. The external records commonly used by NPO managers include information found at the library and school district headquarters. Studies done by the United Way, chambers of commerce and other industry groups, foundations, health care providers, and national associations can become good reference points. A call to the national office of some NPOs may direct you to similar research done somewhere else in the nation.

There are six secondary resources I regularly read, clip, and catalog. They are as follows: (1) the *Wall Street Journal*—a Thursday column called "Business Bulletin: A Special Background Report on Trends in Industry and Finance" and a second front-page section titled "Marketing"; (2) *Sales and Marketing Management* magazine; (3) the *Journal of Marketing*, particularly the section on marketing abstracts, subsection 5.4 (nonprofit marketing) and subsection 5.5 (services marketing); (4) *American Demographics* magazine; (5) the *Chronicle of Philanthropy*; and (6) *Marketing News*, a publication of the American Marketing Association.

Most of us now have access to electronic resources for our research, but finding exactly what you need takes skill and practice. Helen Bergen, in a 1996 column for prospect researchers, said the Internet "is like Jell-O: just when you think you have a firm grip on it, it drips down your arm" (p. 6). Much of the secondary information found on the information superhighway has only marginal value for your market research. Rarely will the abundance of data provide exact answers to your specific questions or problems.

With a CD-ROM of a newspaper (available at libraries), you can search key words in texts. You can search for information on individuals, corporations, or topics. Once you have a CD-ROM in your hands you can take your time, unlike most other electronic research that requires you to pay for each minute of on-line time. Grant research is much easier using CD-ROMs and diskettes than it is if you have to search through books, newspapers, and foundation reports.

Many NPOs are adding home pages to the Internet, hoping Net surfers will find them and get interested. The depth of information about an organization that you can acquire for free on the Internet is usually much less than when you pay for a service such as Knight Ridder Information's DIALOG. You can access the DIALOG database through CompuServe, America Online, Prodigy, Microsoft Network, and probably others. A program called EDGAR offers corporate financial documents and annual reports for free. Bergen reports that PRSPCT-L is a popular resource for donor prospect researchers: "Anyone with an e-mail address can join the daily discussion on research-related topics and seek suggestions and help from others" (1996, p. 6).

When my friend Margery Williams joined the development staff at Lawrence Academy in Groton, Massachusetts, she got on the Internet and participated on a chat line. She asked her new fundraising colleagues on the chat line about the advisability of joining the National Society of Fund-Raising Executives. She received four full pages of advice. Now she regularly uses the chat line to communicate with other development officers and benefit from their experiences.

4. Select the Type of Survey

Each study method has its own set of advantages and disadvantages. Initially, you can choose between qualitative research and quantitative research.

Qualitative research has the advantages of being fast, inexpensive, and broad in scope. With personal involvement there is a lot of hands-on learning. The weaknesses are that the research is subjective and imprecise, and you can't make statistically valid projections from it. Examples of qualitative market research are focus groups, personal observations, volunteer audits, management interviews, and fundraising feasibility studies.

Qualitative research can prepare the groundwork for further quantitative research. After you have unearthed and probed the issues using qualitative research methods, you can find out how many people share certain opinions and preferences by using quantitative methods. You can propose a set of multiple-choice replies and ask a larger sample of respondents to choose among them.

Quantitative research has the advantages of being more precise and objective, and the data can be more accurately projected. The drawbacks are that quantitative research can be slower, more expensive, and too detached from the staff who will have to follow up on the study recommendations. It is usually narrower in scope. Some examples of methods used to carry out quantitative research are personal interviews, telephone surveys, mail surveys, focus-group interviews, lobby intercepts, work with the customers, and electronic screening.

Let us look now at the specific advantages and disadvantages of each of these methods.

Personal Interviews

With this method, you seek information in face-to-face situations. An interviewer asks questions that may or may not be shown to the respondent. Replies can be recorded either during or immediately after the interview. The interviewer is free to pursue a line of interest that emerges from the discussion and may ask questions not on the schedule.

I have used the personal interview method when talking to board members about their personal estates and any likelihood that they might include our NPO in their wills; when checking the interest of very wealthy individuals in a hospital's capital expansion plans; and when trying to find out why membership was declining in a women's health center.

There are many advantages to this method:

- You have better control of the interview.
- It permits a more detailed sharing of information.
- Concepts can be explained more easily using such visual aids as story boards, slides, videotapes, charts, and blueprints.
- Personal contact, empathy, and flexibility can elicit greater cooperation and more in-depth revelations.

The disadvantages of this method are as follows:

- It is more expensive than other survey formats.
- It takes more time.
- Unskilled interviewers can bias the information through improper phrasing of questions or by interpreting responses erroneously.
- Replies are difficult to tabulate and compare with others.
- If the interviewer spends a lot of time writing the replies, the respondent may withdraw or slow down.

Always thank respondents at the end of the interview or questionnaire. Even recalcitrant people should be thanked for their time. Understandably, some interviews are unpleasant because of the emotions aroused by the questions or because of the poor timing of the interview. Nevertheless, thank respondents several times at the end, and at the beginning, too.

Telephone Surveys

Some of the NPOs I have worked with hired professional market research firms to conduct telephone surveys of the community. The usual idea is to poll a good sampling of the community to estimate

mass opinion, rather than the opinions of a few selected individuals. It costs about $5,000 to interview enough people to deliver a
95 percent probability sampling about community interest. I have
known NPOs where the board of directors and other volunteers
have done telephone research themselves.

Telephone surveys work well when you are testing the community's receptivity to a proposed program or course of action.
The interviewers should be instructed to follow a well-defined
script, questionnaire, or outline. The looser the interviews, the
greater the difficulty in later tabulation. Because of the formality
of the structured interview, fewer personal or confidential questions are usually asked.

The advantages of telephone interviews are that you can get
quicker responses than you can with personal visits or mail, you can
contact a larger number of people, and you can easily cover a wider
geographic area.

There are also disadvantages:

- Some people, such as those who have two jobs or are constantly on the go, are difficult to reach. Persistent callbacks at
  odd hours can sometimes solve this problem.
- Most people are willing to give only a small amount of time to
  a telephone interview. Although it is surprising how many
  people will get interested in the survey and give twenty minutes or more to the interviewer, that is not the norm.
- The interviewer can comfortably ask only a few questions in
  the short time available.
- It is difficult to screen those being interviewed. Broad ranges
  of acceptability have to be set unless the list is small and the
  names carefully selected.
- The interviewer cannot see important nonverbal responses.
- It is difficult to forecast future consumer behavior on the basis
  of what people say on the telephone. Many people do not
  take telephone interviews seriously.

Professional telephone researchers reported that the average telephone interview time was 12 minutes in 1992. That is an increase from 8.4 minutes in 1986 (Schlossberg, 1992). Half of their telephone conversations occurred between 5:00 P.M. and 7:00 P.M.; only 15 percent were reported after 7:00 P.M.

Mail Surveys

Mail questionnaires are most effective when specific responses are sought to questions that emerged from personal interviews or focus groups. The main purpose of a widely mailed questionnaire is to gather a response from the largest number of people possible within the time and dollar budget.

The advantages of a mailed questionnaire are as follows:

- There is less chance of interviewer bias.
- You can reach a wide range of people for the lowest cost.
- Respondents can be anonymous if they choose, so you may elicit some of the most confidential information through this method.
- Because respondents choose the time to answer, their moods should be more favorable than during a phone call; 58 percent of people recently surveyed said they prefer mail contact, as opposed to the 18 percent who liked phone interviews better (Schlossberg, 1992).

Mail questionnaires have the following disadvantages:

- Respondents don't always understand what the questions mean or are unsure of how to answer.
- The responses received do not exactly reflect the attitudes of the survey population. Most questionnaire returns come from people who feel more strongly about the subject than do the nonrespondents.

- Perhaps 90 percent of the people you mail to will not return the questionnaire.
- The mailing list must be good.
- Many people are overly generous in their evaluations of a service. Positive response bias occurs when people feel they have no anonymity with their ratings, when they feel the job of a well-meaning employee may be on the line, or when the rating scale has no place for a neutral reply.
- Tabulating the returns takes longer than most of us think it will. Unless you employ a professional tab firm, the responses can sit on someone's shelf for a long time while more pressing work is done.

Some NPO executives I have worked with have sought to reduce the cost of surveying their membership by handing out short questionnaires as people came through the lobby. Avoid this very poor practice. It may make us feel good that we are surveying our membership, but we are getting feedback from only a portion of those who happened to show up during the survey. No valid conclusions about the total membership can be drawn from a sample like this. For accuracy and legitimate projections, you need to pay for the survey through the investment of time and project control or by using professional consultation.

Mail questionnaires have definite parts and a prescribed sequence. There is the introduction, which consists of a letter from the executive saying why the study is being conducted, an explanation of how to complete it, easy questions followed by the harder ones, personal identification, and thanks.

To get a higher response rate from your mailed surveys, consider making the envelope look impressive, interesting, and easy to respond to. Include a self-addressed, postage-paid envelope. Some researchers include a premium such as a new dollar bill or a chance at a prize drawing.

Focus Groups

Focus-group interviews demand the most skill of the person asking the questions. Professionals will run one focus-group interview of ninety minutes or so, analyze it, and write a report for $3,000 to $5,000. The cost per individual interview is a lot less than it is for one-on-one interviews, but the total price is higher because multiple groups are interviewed for the same product or program by the same researcher. You can try using your own staff as interviewers, but the conventional marketing wisdom is that you cannot easily obtain unbiased information from current users or potential customers. In a sense you know too much and may identify too much with the sponsor. Without saying anything verbally, you can send nonverbal signals that inhibit those being questioned.

A focus-group interview is most effective at the beginning stages of a multistage study. It precedes telephone interviews, individual interviews, or mailed questionnaires because it is such a good technique for uncovering the real questions and perceptions that need exploring. Capital fundraising firms use focus groups as a way of testing the community leadership's receptivity to a proposed large fund drive. One of the nation's largest fundraising firms calls them huddles, not focus groups. They claim the huddles are an effective form of philanthropic market research and charge the sponsoring NPO about $15,000 for a two-week study.

Focus groups and huddle interviews are part of qualitative research. Although they do provide useful information, they should not be used as scientifically derived, conclusive substantiation for a proposed course of action, such as proof that the community is willing to support a large capital funds drive. The small number of people in a group interview, usually ten to twelve, cannot adequately represent the general population. The potential for sampling error is so great that serious market researchers make no attempt to project from the group discussions how the rest of the population is likely to respond.

A word of caution: when it comes to the subject of prices, what people *say* is almost always different from what they *do* (Leaming, 1991). Because the information provided in a focus group about prices they would likely pay is unreliable, Leaming says that the best way to estimate potential customer reaction to new prices is to observe behavior. Study what they do or have done under actual, rather than hypothetical, conditions.

A focus group can be used to get reliable information after a test market price has been offered to a sample of the public. Focus groups can help explain unexpected reactions to price in your test markets. Focus groups can also help determine both buyer and non-buyer awareness of prices. But great care must be taken in making conclusions from the focus-group information alone, because some people in groups (and those who respond to individual interviews) may want to appear to be above price considerations; their responses can throw off your pricing decisions significantly.

The value of a focus group is in its ability to explore a subject in luxurious depth. The interviewer must be highly skilled to maintain the group's interest in the topic. Nowhere in real life would a group of married career women talk for two hours about their reaction to child-care brochures. Yet the essence of these group interviews is to focus the group's attention for a prolonged period of time on a lot of little items that may influence their buying, donating, or volunteering behavior. Participants influence each other's comments, and that triggers new thoughts and enables the discussion to proceed beyond where a person being interviewed alone would be likely to take it.

There are a number of practical considerations in arranging for and conducting focus-group interviews. The sponsor of the study should not be revealed. Disclosing the sponsor would introduce a bias into the comments of the participants. Participants are generally paid for their attendance and given refreshments. If they are all members of a club, a contribution of perhaps $200 can be made to the club treasury instead of paying individuals $25.

Do not pay the participants or their club with checks with the NPO's name on it. Although giving premiums to participants at the end of the interview is nice, make sure the premiums do not identify the study sponsor. Word can get around as to who the sponsor is before the last focus groups have had their chance. This is another good reason for using outside market research firms. They are more able to resist pressures to reveal the sponsor, and they will supply a moderator who can lead the discussion without disclosing the sponsor.

Most NPOs have the ability to recruit volunteers for the study in place of paid participants. Yet for a good survey, we may need the opinions of people who are not predisposed toward volunteering. Besides, if we recruit them, they will know who the sponsor is.

Best results are obtained when at least three focus groups explore the same subject. Getting church groups and clubs to commit the attendance of fifteen people is much easier than anonymously recruiting fifteen unrelated, randomly selected individuals from a target group. Recruiting fifteen ensures you will get the dozen you really need, and if they all show, that is still not too many. The people in attendance must have also given prior commitment to staying the entire two hours, or as long as stated in the invitation. You cannot have anyone leave partway through the process.

If the leader of a church or other group is hesitant to help because he or she doesn't know who is behind the project, the researcher should say that it is a local nonprofit organization. Explain that if the participants know who the sponsor is, they might say only things that are complimentary. This could impede the purpose of the talks, which is for participants to offer freely their opinions on a variety of related topics. They should be assured that their comments will be completely anonymous. The ultimate goal, they should be told, is to bring about better services to the community.

The discussion leader should welcome individuals as they appear and then welcome the group as the members gather for the formal discussion. She should identify herself and her research company. Next, she should make a brief statement about what a focus group is. She tells the group that there are no right or wrong answers, only different points of view. She encourages everyone to speak out, even when that person holds a minority point of view. She assures the group that she has no vested interest in the programs about to be discussed, only an interest in finding out what the participants think and feel about the subject. The interviewer also assures them that the focus group is legitimate market research. It is not a disguised sales technique to get them to join, donate, or volunteer.

Tape recorders and two-way mirrors are used during focus-group meetings so others interested in the research can monitor them. It is important that observers not be seen, because they can easily inhibit a group's responses. However, at the very beginning the moderator does explain that the session is being tape-recorded for analysis later. Therefore it is important that only one person talk at a time so that the sound is not garbled. The moderator assures them that their comments are treated anonymously. She then tells them where the restrooms and the refreshments are. Individuals are encouraged to take their own breaks, rather than to rely on the discussion leader.

The interviewer works from an outline. She is coached and knows well the program being discussed. But after she introduces the subject, she keeps her comments to a minimum. She asks questions to guide the group or to draw out individuals.

When the session ends, the moderator will have notes and a tape recording for you to analyze. Listening to the tapes, try to catch any themes that have surfaced. Pay attention to any emotional reactions to the discussion and to observers' notes about significant nonverbal body language. See if there are any groupings of opinions, such as users versus nonusers, young versus old. Don't ignore the minority opinion perhaps expressed only once and meekly. There may be some good material worth pursuing, even if it did not interest the total group at the time.

Here is a sample focus-group outline for a group gathered to explore the topic of youth camping. After discussing what focus groups are and the other preliminaries, the moderator says, "Tonight our topic of discussion is, as promised, children's leisure-time activities and opportunities in our area. I would like you to begin by writing a few things on the pad in front of you. Think about all of the leisure-time activities, not school programs, that expose your children to groups of others about the same age. Please list what your own children have been doing and also write the reasons you have chosen those activities. In a few minutes we will talk about what you have written."

The moderator then discusses the activities and reasons, listing salient points on a large pad of newsprint. Next he probes for any needs that are not being well satisfied.

The moderator attempts to establish a priority listing of children's needs and another priority listing of the parents' needs.

The discussion then proceeds from general to specific questions, such as: "When I say 'children's camping opportunities,' what comes to mind?"

The moderator also uses sentence-completion exercises: "As far as I am concerned, the most competent organizations running camping experiences are . . ." "The things that make them particularly good are . . ."

The moderator then moves into a discussion about group members' awareness of the sponsoring organization, talking in detail about their awareness of the sponsoring organization (without identifying it, of course) and of specific programs, their impressions of the fees charged, the perceived value in comparison to the fees, and the differences between the parents' reactions to the sponsor's camp and the children's reactions.

Finally, the moderator presents them with an exercise: "Imagine that you are the manager of a local children's camp. What would you do to make it more successful in attracting and keeping people like yourselves?"

Lobby Intercepts

Ninety percent of market research companies use mall intercepts (Smith, 1989). Their techniques could easily be adopted by zoos, theaters, community centers, city recreation centers, and others.

Lobby intercepts enable the researchers to interview a large number of people in a limited time. Visual material can be tested, and face-to-face interviewing allows for better probing. It is less expensive than door-to-door interviewing because it eliminates travel time and not-at-home situations.

There are several significant drawbacks to lobby intercepts. They are not well suited to probability sampling. People entering the NPO are not reflective of the general population. Usually they are in a hurry to get to their destinations and are apt to respond carelessly.

A Philadelphia science museum used lobby computers to gather information from general admission visitors and others. They were attempting to identify and convert visitors into members of the museum. The touch-screen computer was placed in an area past where visitors entered and paid general admission fees but before they could see the museum exhibits. Visitors were asked to enter data to receive future program and special exhibit announcements. A monthly prize drawing was an incentive. People were asked to give the computer their name, address, and age.

Work with the Customers

Shoppers at a Northbrook, Illinois, grocery store were surprised by the large number of questions directed at them by the men and women bagging their purchases. They were asked if they had noticed certain ads, why they selected particular brands, and how frequently they used coupons. The super-friendly and inquisitive baggers were really advertising researchers working incognito in an unusual effort to learn more about some typical customers. Relying on statistical profiles was not enough.

The researchers noted that the typical customer was a woman in a jogging suit with two children in tow. Most of the people in line were buying out of habit, they said, rather than in response to recent advertising. The researchers concluded the store needed to run their ads much more frequently if the ads were to get noticed and acted on. This observation is interesting. I have long noticed that staff get tired of an advertising theme long before the public recognizes we have one. Staff tire of repetitious messages before they have truly caught on with the target audiences.

Electronic Screening

In the last decade, several fundraising firms have added electronic screening to their list of client services. Basically, what this means is that an NPO shares all the names and addresses of its donors and/or prospects with a fundraising firm, which compares addresses with demographic data in the fundraising firm's file. The firm looks at such characteristics as age, household income, occupation, home-owner or renter, mail-order responsiveness, and education. This process works best for organizations with large files to share. For NPOs, the use of an electronic screening firm may help identify other communities or lists to whom they should send their appeals, because these others may share many characteristics in common with present donors. From an electronic screening of your member-ship, a researcher can also list some prospects' real estate values and tell you if they serve on corporate or foundation boards. Information on the compensation and holdings of prospects who are officers and directors of publicly held corporations can be obtained for free through the Security and Exchange Commission's EDGAR files.

5. Determine the Size of the Sample and Who Should Be in It

Consider three areas when determining sample size: cost, accuracy, and confidence. Understandably, the larger the survey sample, the more accurate its predictions of market behavior. However, you can achieve your desired level of confidence by sampling fewer than most of us would first expect. With a sample of two hundred quali-fied respondents you might find that 25 percent of them would likely use your new service. At the 95 percent level of confidence (a common standard), your estimate of users for the new service is accurate within 6 percent. You could then say, "I am 95 percent confident that between 19 percent and 31 percent of the target market will use the new service." That would be based on the 25 percent plus or minus a 6 percent margin of error.

If you increased your sample size to eight hundred qualified respondents, the margin of error might be reduced to 3 percent, so you could be 95 percent confident that 22 percent to 28 percent of your target market would respond favorably to the new service introduction.

A college textbook on statistics can help you determine the number of people you would need to survey in order to make reliable predictions of the preferences and opinions of a larger population. The number is surprisingly low in most cases. Witness the national opinion polls that survey just a few thousand individuals to project the opinions of more than 200 million others. The key is to pick individuals with characteristics in common with the larger population. An unrepresentative sample would bias the projections.

I have conducted many feasibility studies over the last five years to help NPOs determine how much money they can raise in large capital campaigns. Frequently the client is trying to determine if the NPO can raise at least a million dollars. The sample we take is usually between thirty and fifty individuals. From that we have projected campaign goals that turned out to be within 6 percent of ultimate achievement. The secret is in surveying the right people.

Frequently with a capital fundraising program, just 10 percent of the donors give 90 percent of the money. Many of our capital campaigns have three hundred to five hundred donors. When we can meet and personally interview the top thirty to fifty potential donors, we can fairly accurately predict the ultimate campaign accomplishment.

To get a good sample for testing fundraising potential, we want to interview people who can give away the largest gifts, if they want to. We don't prejudge their interest in the project nearly as much as we weigh their gift-giving potential.

In our fundraising feasibility studies in the past, we would include community opinion makers such as educators, clergy, politicians, and chamber of commerce executives. But we found that although their opinions about others might be interesting, they did little to increase our understanding of the giving potential of wealthy individuals, corporation presidents, and foundation executives.

It is fairly easy in most communities to find out who has money. What an NPO should not presume is these prospects' level of interest in the project. The best way to find that out is to talk with the people with the wherewithal to commit the largest gifts.

Potential interest in the project and ability to give are the major factors determining who should be included in the fundraising survey.

6. Prepare the Questionnaire

Talk to a lot of people about the problem you are researching. Only after you have a good grasp on the issues and the questions you want to ask should you and your staff develop the first draft of a questionnaire. Then administer it to yourselves before launching it on the public. It is normal to go through five to ten drafts before settling on the final tool that will work well for you.

The ideal questionnaire doesn't exist. It is best to make your own to fit the needs of your organization. Don't simply take the questionnaire used by your sister organization in another city and drop it on your people.

When preparing your own questionnaire, write it as a conversation, not an interrogation. Start and end friendly. Ask very easy questions at the beginning. Help people start comfortably. Write the questions so that respondents can run right through the first third of the survey thinking, "This is easy."

Arrange the sequence of questions logically. Write simply, removing words and ambiguous meanings from the earliest drafts. The experts tell us that no question should contain over twenty words. The words ought to be simple, and they should correspond to the level of education and experience of your respondents. Words that are ambiguous, such as "quality," should be tested at least ten times before trying them with the public. Repeated prior testings will cut confusing wording or structure that could spoil the survey.

At the beginning of each questionnaire or major section, explain why you are asking for that information. People want to know why you want to know.

Don't allow for "don't know" answers. By providing that category you are allowing respondents not to think very hard about the subject. People will write "don't know" in themselves if they really don't know.

If you are giving respondents a rating scale to check on various items, you may want to use one with seven points, with the extremes of opinion at opposite ends. Seven points allow people to take clear positions; more than seven choices is probably more calibration of response than most of us need.

How do you feel about . . . ?
Delighted ☐   Pleased ☐   Mostly satisfied ☐   Mixed ☐
Mostly dissatisfied ☐   Unhappy ☐   Terrible ☐

You can also identify the ends of the seven-point scale and allow the respondent to imagine the meanings when they check a particular spot on the scale.

To what extent does _____ currently meet your needs?
Extremely well ☐   ☐   ☐   ☐   ☐   ☐   ☐ Extremely poorly

If you are using anything much larger than a three-by-five-inch card for your survey you ought to provide an example of how to fill out the questionnaire. Here's a sample.

"Please rate your NPO. The more you feel a word describes your feelings, check a box closer to that word. For example, if you feel [the NPO] is mostly a place for families, you would check a space closest to that phrase. If it is mostly a place for individual adults, you would check close to that phrase."

Mostly for families	☐	☐	☐	☐	☐	☐	☐	Mostly for adults
Well managed	☐	☐	☐	☐	☐	☐	☐	Poorly managed
Uncomfortable	☐	☐	☐	☐	☐	☐	☐	Comfortable
Liberal	☐	☐	☐	☐	☐	☐	☐	Conservative
Always the same	☐	☐	☐	☐	☐	☐	☐	Changing
Convenient schedule	☐	☐	☐	☐	☐	☐	☐	Inconvenient schedule

You can make your questionnaire more interesting by using more than one format. Try some yes and no questions with an opportunity to explain, if the respondent wishes.

Are there any programs or services that need major improvement?
Yes ☐   No ☐   Explain _____
Are there any new programs or services that you would like us to offer? Yes ☐   No ☐   Explain _____

The goal in most questionnaires is to get information that is easy to tabulate and list in a few groupings for comparison.

How do you feel about the annual membership fees you pay?
Very low priced ☐   About right ☐   Slightly low priced ☐
Slightly high priced ☐   Very high priced ☐

Wanting to please you, respondents may say on the questionnaire that they don't have any problems with you. People often give different answers when they report on the opinions of others, so it is informative to ask them what they have heard others say. The following question shows a way to do this:

How do you think residents in your community would rate [your NPO] according to the following scale?

1 = excellent   2 = good   3 = fair   4 = poor

Condition of facilities ___

Variety of facilities ___

Cleanliness of parks ___

Attitude of maintenance staff ___

Helpfulness of recreation program staff ___

Effectiveness of management staff ___

Remember, the easy questions were at the beginning, which means, of course, that the hard ones must be at the end. The hard questions are the personal ones about age, income, education, and employment. The first-time questionnaire writer may want to put these questions right at the beginning to qualify respondents quickly. If you do this, you won't get many respondents. Amazingly, however, after people have spent considerable time completing a survey, they will tell a stranger very personal information. It is related to their investment. The more time they have spent on the project, the more they take ownership of it. So at the end you place questions such as the following:

Please tell us a little about yourself:

Sex: Male ☐   Female ☐

Age: ___

Under 17 ☐   17–20 ☐   21–24 ☐   25–34 ☐   35–44 ☐ 45–54 ☐   55–64 ☐   65 or over ☐

Approximate yearly household income:

Less than $24,999 ☐ $25,000–$49,999 ☐ $50,000–$74,999 ☐ $75,000–$99,999 ☐ $100,000 and over ☐

What is your occupation? _____

What is your marital status? _____

Do you get resistance from anyone in your family when you spend money on yourself? _____

Are you active in any type of volunteer work? About how many hours a week (or month) do you spend with volunteer activities?

Always thank respondents at the end of the questionnaire, just as you would for an interview.

With both telephone and personal interviews, a researcher can reach beyond the constriction of prepared questions. After administering the questionnaire, the researcher can add important notes about the proclivity of the interviewee to join, help, donate, support, antagonize, compete, block, and so on.

7. Conduct the Study

Follow the guidelines previously discussed in this chapter's section on survey types. Make sure you are collecting the information during a relatively short period. As new events occur over time, people are likely to change their opinions and invalidate your study.

8. Process the Data

This is often the most challenging task. It is not much fun, so it is best to tackle it right away or get a commercial tabulating company to do it. They will quote you a fee over the phone.

When we do fundraising feasibility studies we try to summarize the questionnaire information at the end of each day. As days pass and we conduct more interviews, the first information becomes stale. To summarize the information from a forty-five-minute personal interview properly takes about fifteen minutes. So on a day when the interviewer conducts six interviews of forty-five minutes each, summarizing the information will often consume another hour or two after dinner. This is work. Well-constructed questionnaires of the types mentioned earlier will take less time to summarize.

9. Analyze the Data

It usually takes an experienced market analyst to draw valid conclusions from research data. This professional weighs many factors.
For a fundraising research project, the factors considered most are
timing, leadership availability, community receptivity, goal achiev-
ability, and campaign strategy.

The numbers and opinions alone will not tell you what to do.
It does little good simply to say, "In response to question 4 about
the proposed site, Person X said this and Person Y said that." For
each question and response level there is a variety of possible
meanings that can be drawn from the volume of answers. The
implications of the data are best derived by an expert in the field
being studied.

Even so, researchers have had great difficulty predicting accurately what sales or enrollment results will occur on the basis of
attitudinal data they have gathered. Because of this difficulty, many
organizations see market research as very important for million-
dollar fundraising campaigns but not absolutely essential to the promotion programs.

The research issue today is not about capturing more data but
rather about effectively manipulating the data to derive more man-
agerial implications and value. There is plenty of information available on customers and consumers from external sources (household
income, education, employers, and so on). This can be appended to
your own information about your members, clients, and supporters
to paint a picture of their lifestyles. The use of consumer/customer
behavior data greatly enhances your capacity to explain their past
actions and to predict future behavior—what customers and
prospects are likely to do.

Every NPO probably has a group of best customers and consumers who account for a disproportionate amount of revenue or
service use. By gaining a greater understanding of what these people actually do, as opposed to what you might infer they will do
through a survey, you can more accurately predict their reactions

to changes your NPO initiates. Admittedly, behavioral data is a look at the present or past, not the future, which is what most managers are interested in.

When we use market attitudinal research from a very broad marketplace to seek new customers and consumers, we may be taking more predictive risks than necessary. It is well worth an equal amount of effort to get a better understanding of the customers and consumers right under our noses—those already in the family. The challenge then becomes to find more people like those we already have. A search for people who look like our customers is more a matter of selecting from a known universe than trying to predict who might be converted to us in the future.

10. Prepare the Report and Present the Findings

A report is usually presented to the people likely to be affected by its recommendations. For an NPO this may include reports to the board, staff, trustees, donors of record, members, and those interviewed.

The people interviewed during the study can be sent a letter from the executive director summarizing the report's recommendations and inviting further feedback.

Seldom is a board prepared to take action on the report's recommendations when they are first presented, so it is best not to have a media reporter present. When the report is first received there is usually no decision at that meeting to move ahead on all or any of the recommendations. That is done at subsequent meetings. Revealing the information to the public too soon may serve to back the board and staff into an uncomfortable decision-making corner.

In our campaign studies, we present two reports in person, one to the board and top staff and another to just four or five members of the top leadership. In the report to the bigger group, we give all the data and our recommendations for campaign goal, timing, leadership, the case for support, and strategy, but we omit references to specific candidates for campaign leadership roles or possible big gifts.

With the smaller group we mention names of potential campaigners and leaders that were identified in the course of our research.

With fresh, new information provided by the research, you can feel better about the choices you make in fulfilling the mission of your organization.

Chapter Four

Target Marketing to Reach Your Best Customers

"A twenty-nine year-old woman was so hostile to me," said the Girl Scout professional staff member, who was probably twenty-two years old. "She was feeling anxious because I was unencumbered. She felt tied down with job and kids. She was blaming me for being young."

"Do you know your typical thirty-one-year-old volunteers intimately?" I asked.

"No," said the staff member. "I look too young, like I'm nineteen. Sometimes it is hard for me to relate to how busy they are with their families. And some of them even go to school. When I tell them how to improve their volunteer work, they say 'I can't do this. I don't have the time.' I think they should just manage their time better, and even though I don't say it, I am sure that message comes across strongly from me to them."

"There are differences among the Girl Scout staff, too," claimed the twenty-two-year-old. "I try to make Girl Scouts fun. I encourage leaders to enjoy their jobs. Older staff are always pushing increased enrollments. Young staff push quality. Older staff push numbers."

This Girl Scout example illustrates an everyday problem. Age, economics, and value differences can seriously impede the interpersonal effectiveness of professional nonprofit managers as they try to relate to their major market segments.

The purpose of this chapter is to help you get a better understanding of your key customers, their demographics, lifestyles, and pressures. By gaining greater sensitivity to key customer groups, you can get a better return on your recruitment efforts. Target marketing and segmentation are your essential tools.

The Value of Segmentation

Alfred Goldman (1982, p. 10) wrote, "It has become increasingly difficult for a single brand of wine or liquor to be all things to all consumers. Marketing efforts which attempt this usually lack clarity and say nothing in particular to anyone. The trend toward market segmentation already has begun, and it's bound to accelerate and become more deliberate and sophisticated." More than a decade later, Goldman's prediction has obviously come true. It is easy to see in hotel chains. They have created all-suites, extended-stay suites, luxury economy hotels, economy luxury motels, courtyard properties, and others.

Today, all large profit-seeking corporations are doing market segmentation studies and analysis. Segmentation is a standard business strategy. When AT&T enjoyed the advantages of a monopolistic situation, it did not have to learn much about its customers. Now competition has forced it to adopt a sharply defined marketing approach to sales and service. Salespeople are going out to visit customers instead of waiting for them to call. The company has researchers determining future customer needs and developing services to meet those needs.

Using an approach similar to that of IBM, AT&T marketing staff segmented the business telephone users market into three groups: (1) industrial, (2) commercial, and (3) government, education, and medical. Each of these major groupings was subdivided into specific industries. A separate marketing plan was then drawn up for each. Contrast this strategy with that of a typical multiservice NPO with only one marketing plan that is supposed to fit all the varieties of service and customers equally well.

Market segmentation has at least eight major benefits:

1. It helps you focus on the different interests and needs of groups of consumers and helps in the design of appropriate responses.

2. It leads to a more precise definition of the market.

3. It helps the manager do a better job of developing program services and supervising to attain higher levels of consumer satisfaction.

4. It helps management keep abreast of changing consumer interests.

5. It multiplies customer service options.

6. It clearly identifies the most likely future customers and enables a manager to direct staff energies to them.

7. It results in more precise market penetration objectives and measurement of accomplishments.

8. It allows more negotiation among both volunteer and staff managers and encourages greater discussion of the organization's focus. Which groups should receive priority attention?

To segment a market you must understand the specific service to be marketed and its users. You need to pick target markets and acknowledge a wide diversity of human motivations. You need to know how particular services help people solve their problems.

You already know that some of your programs appeal more to certain groups than they do universally. You need to find out what those heavy users have in common with each other. What makes your program appeal more to one population segment than all the others? What do the noon-hour basketball players have in common? Why aren't a lot more people coming to use the gym at noon? Why do some families love your child-care center, whereas others drive to less convenient locations to solve their child-care needs? Why do people use the public library when the local college library with greater resources is also open to the general populace?

You want to find the answers to these questions so you can choose advertising media more wisely and budget your promotion resources for greater impact. By focusing more attention on the interests and needs of your regular customers, you are likely to get a much better response.

When you are more sensitive to key customer segments, your promotional timing should improve. Better results come when promotional efforts are massed in the weeks and seasons when selling resistance is lowest and responsiveness is highest. For example, experienced YMCA managers follow this dictum: promote fitness classes in January (right after the weighty holiday season), summer camp during students' spring vacation (when parents start worrying about keeping children safely occupied all summer), and child care in July and August (when parents are looking for a place for the preschooler in September).

Defining Your Customers

Each NPO has different key customers. While conducting sixty marketing workshops across the country, I discovered that for many NPOs the thirty-one-year-old mother was the most typical customer for a variety of programs. She was the one who made the buying decisions about whether her children enrolled in day care, day camp, resident camp, preschool activities, gymnastics, youth sports, Y-Indian Guides, Brownies, Blue Birds, Cubs, swimming classes, movement education, music lessons, and a host of other activities. She also enrolled herself in fitness class and encouraged her husband to participate in more activities with the children.

Focusing on one age and lifestyle is particularly hard for most NPO managers. We usually strive to be more inclusive, not exclusive. It is even downright distasteful, racist, ageist, and sexist, some managers feel, not to include more people in the target market group.

When selecting my target customers, I focused on a specific age rather than on an age range because I had noticed that when staff looked everywhere within an age range they often got confused. The wider the range, the more blurred their vision became. Focusing on a single age helped them see customers much more clearly. Once we knew what our typical customers looked like, we were freer to generalize about others in the range. Getting a better understanding of our present key customers does not preclude promoting to everyone. Yet in each situation, if we can choose a specific target market and do a demographic lifestyle analysis to sharpen our approach to that group, our overall marketing will benefit.

I once chose fifty-year-old male Rotarians as the prime target for my YMCA's financial development efforts. As members of a Rotary Club, these people are prequalified as prime prospects for financial development efforts. I didn't have to spend much time judging whether the time spent in cultivation would pay off. Rotarians are supposed to be the leaders in their vocations in a particular community. The fifty-year-olds also make good targets because they are in good health and do not see retirement for a long while yet. In addition to their ability to give generously themselves, they make good volunteer solicitors during annual support and capital fund drives.

Of course, there is a wide variety of potential financial development supporters for an NPO. The target market of volunteers to run a successful money-making special event might be primarily young females who belong to clubs. The target market for pooled income funds to benefit your NPO might be fifty-six-year-old couples.

People who are closer to retirement might seem to be outstanding potential customers for gifts to the NPO, but my observation is that no matter how much money they have, at this stage in their life they get much more conservative. They worry that the value of their stocks could fall. Something could happen to them so that they would not have the energy, time, or financial resources to cope successfully. Therefore, I feel the best time to get included in a person's estate plans is when the person is on top of the world, with good income, good health, and plenty of time before retirement forces the person to conserve. This situation occurs around age fifty.

Whether your key customer is a thirty-one-year-old mother, a fifty-year-old Rotarian, or some other type, the principle of focusing on key customer types is still the same. It pays to have a thorough understanding of your best current customers.

In an earlier chapter, I distinguished between customers, those who make the buying decisions that affect your program, and consumers, those who use it. The customer and the consumer can be the same person, but may not be. Customer definition is complex. There are nonapparent customers who have very powerful influences on the readily apparent customers. At the YMCA I found this to be true of Father and Son Y-Indian Guides, a program for dads and their six- to eight-year-old sons. In this case the invisible customer was the wife of the man who would ultimately make the buying decision. Typically the boy would come home from school with the YMCA's flyer, talking excitedly about the visitor to his classroom. The visitor let students wear a real Indian headdress and beat a drum, and said there was an organization meeting tomorrow night at the school. I found that it was frequently the mother who persuaded the father to go to the meeting. She was an important force in overcoming his inertia and apprehension about the awkwardness of meeting with a bunch of strangers. He didn't want to get sold on some new time commitments. Once he attended the orientation meeting, the father became the primary customer to be sold. The children had been presold.

To get into the classrooms to promote Y-Indian Guides, the YMCA needed the teachers' and principal's permission. This made them customers, too. In some communities, the school board and the superintendent of schools had to be persuaded that this was indeed a healthy program for the children and worthy of classroom disruption.

If any one of those key customers did not approve of the project, the lives of hundreds of children in the school district would have been affected. Knowing this, the pressure is always on the YMCA staff and board members to keep in good communication with the key customers. They have to know who these key customers are, what problems they see, and how YMCA programs can help these people solve some of those problems. That is the essence of good marketing.

Third-party–funded programs make customer definition even more difficult. The third party is neither the consumer who uses the program nor the parent who buys. It is the individual or organiza-

tion that pays for the program. Without the third party's participation, there may not be a program offered. Some typical third parties are the United Way, individual benefactors, service clubs,
foundations, corporations, and government agencies. It is not
enough simply to say that the United Way is one of your customers
and leave it at that. Who at the United Way is determining how
much money you will get? Is it volunteers or is it staff? Sure, formally, the volunteer allocation committee may make the decisions.
But how independent from United Way staff influence are committee members? If the staff are the key influence peddlers, which
staff person wields the most influence over your future?

Once you can pinpoint the key customer in your third- party–funded
program, it is wise to find out more about him, her, or them. What are this
customer's personal pressures? What relief can you offer? The Northwest
YMCA was able to get renewed Law Enforcement and Assistance Act
(LEAA) funds while other agencies were cut in the late 1970s because
the YMCA took good care of its key customer. The staff person influencing the allocations decisions had a problem common to his associates in
other cities. Many of the experimental projects LEAA funded did not
work. Some were even financial embarrassments. But whenever federal
auditors or important visitors appeared unannounced, our LEAA grant
customer could call on us and we would show the auditors a high-quality,
effective program. This made our funder look good, helped him keep his
job, and made him promotable. Although he and I never spoke of it as a
contract, he knew that he could call our YMCA at a moment's notice
and get a model program to show. Is it any wonder that this YMCA's
funding was renewed while others' funding was cut?

Program directors at an NPO have many different customers to
please. They have to take care of the program participants who want
fun, no hassles, easy in-and-out processes, and good leadership.
They also have to meet their supervisor's needs for more and more
volume. The top executive of the NPO may want from program
staff more income, less expense, lots of praise, and no complaints.

In a way, part-time staff reporting to the program director are
also customers. If they are pleased and well directed, they make the

program director's life easier. So the needs of the part-time staff for good pay, recognition, and improved working conditions need to be met. Volunteers are customers who need recognition in exchange for their support.

Even potential employers can be seen as current customers. They need to be aware that you personally exist and are a hot item. Your published writings and your participation in conferences, special events, and your professional society might draw the attention of a prospective employer to you.

Springfield College in Massachusetts recently identified distinct customers whom they could divide into internal and external audiences for the school's messages. The internal audience included students and their families, faculty, staff, faculty and staff family members, alumni, and trustees. The external customers for the college included prospective students and their families, local community leaders, legislators and government agencies, the print and broadcast media, the campus neighborhood, the general public, foundations and other donors, colleagues and competitors, and suppliers and vendors. You can imagine how hard it would be to develop a message that would please all of them.

Researching Target Markets

There are many ways to segment a market, to divide it into parts permitting systematic study of basic characteristics. The easiest and most reliable segment variables are those that deal with demographics. Although psychographic segmenting is a stimulating process, the information is less reliable than demographic data. Here are typical categories in each kind of segmentation.

Demographic Segments	*Psychographic Segments*
Geographic region	Lifestyle
Community size	Personality types
Population density	Heavy users of the service

Age
Gender
Family life cycle
Family size
Income
Race
Nationality
Occupation
Religion

Type of users
Loyalty to the brand
Marketing sensitivity
Benefits perceived
Attitudes

A good marketer will do both demographic and psychographic analyses because each has its special advantages.

Demographics

"Dirty demographics" is an expression I use to describe rounded numbers that are easy to remember and to apply to get rough estimates. Here is an example of dirty demographics applied to ages. Of every 100 people in the general population:

7 are age 5 or younger
8 are between the ages of 6 and 10
8 are between 11 and 15
9 are between 16 and 20
8 are between 21 and 25
8 are between 26 and 30
7 are between 31 and 25
6 are between 36 and 40
6 are between 41 and 45
6 are between 46 and 50
6 are between 51 and 55

6 are between 56 and 60

5 are between 61 and 65

4 are between 66 and 70

7 are over the age of 70

You can use these estimates to make calculations of market potential. For example, if you were a Girl Scout executive seeking women volunteers ages thirty-one to thirty-five, you could conclude from the chart that about 7 percent of your community were in that age group and that half would be female (3.5 percent of the total). If there are one hundred thousand people in your area, then you have about thirty-five hundred women to choose from. Twenty-eight percent in that age group say they do volunteer work. That theoretically reduces your market potential to 980 women. Now, how many of those do you need?

Many market segment numbers do not need estimation. They are readily available from free local sources. The Boy Scouts get enrollments from each school every fall. The number of boys enrolled in Boy Scouts each year is divided by the total available boys to determine the Boy Scouts' penetration level. This gives the organization two good indexes to manage by: the enrollment numbers compared with previous years, and the saturation level. When the gross enrollment numbers are declining, Boy Scout leaders are less apt to worry about the appeal of the program as long as the penetration level remains high. There is nothing they can do about shrinking numbers of boys in the community, but they can affect the relative percentage who sign up for the Scouting program.

Psychographics

Never assume in advance that any one method of segmentation is best, warned Daniel Yankelovich in his classic *Harvard Business*

Review article on segmentation (1964). Your first job is to muster various market segments. Then choose the most appropriate market segments from your list. Yankelovich argued that demography is not always the best way to segment markets. Of equal importance are psychographics: differences in buyer attitudes, motivations, values, patterns of usage, aesthetic preferences, and degrees of loyalty. You can guess somewhat accurately at people's values by looking at how they dress and groom themselves, what kind of car they drive, where they live, what they do for fun, how they spend weekends, and who their friends are. By studying the behaviors of your best customers and consumers, you can much more accurately predict the likely response to a promotion aimed at a wider population.

What your key customers may feel is good, right, and normal relates to when their values were established. Expectations programmed at an early age continue when the child becomes an adult, unless a significant emotional event occurs to change them. Matching your NPO program "story" to the values of the listener will get the most favorable response. That person's values were imprinted before he or she reached seven years old, we are told. By age twenty-one their values are firmly established, unless a significant emotional experience takes place. There are many factors that influence a person's value system, including his or her family, religious upbringing, school, and friends. People's values are also influenced by social changes that occur while they are growing up, the textbooks they read, and the music, radio, and television programs they grew up with.

Table 4.1 shows some of the influence factors for different generations of Americans. We must know the age-group differences as they apply to staff, volunteers, customers, consumers, and third-party funders. Pay particular attention to the values of people in their fifties and sixties. They are our religious leaders, our mass communicators, our board of directors, our power elite, our benefactors, and our most influential NPO executives. They make policy decisions that affect us all.

Table 4.1. Influences on Values.

Age in the 1990s	When Values Programmed	Influence Factors	Values
70s	1920s	World War I Close family Flappers Model T *Saturday Evening Post* covers Men were breadwinners Willing to do any job to earn a living	Patriotic Close family
60s	1930s	Great Depression (No food to eat) (Walked miles to school) "The Green Hornet"	Save for tomorrow Security
50s	1940s	World War II Mobility for the men Moving to different community Family life changes as men went overseas to fight Heroes: G.I. Joe, Superman	Commitment to win Get the job done
40s	1950s	Affluence Indulged kids Dr. Spock Charles Van Doran, "$64,000 Question" Elvis TV: "Leave It to Beaver" Length of hair was an issue	The good life has arrived They think superhighways are normal Permissiveness
30s	1960s	Space exploration Civil rights Scruffy hippies on TV John Kennedy shot Vietnam War, computers TV: superclean kitchens	Bad guys can win in movies Husbands should share housework They think jets are normal Ride bicycles

Table 4.1. Influences on Values. (Cont.)

Age in the 1990s	When Values Programmed	Influence Factors	Values
20s	1970s	Jaded expectations Watergate Joe Namath and his girls President resigns TV: "M*A*S*H," "One Day at Time," "Starsky & Hutch," "Emergency"	Kids think divorce is normal Liberated women

Lifestyle Analysis

One way to get a better fix on your typical customers is to do a leisure lifestyle analysis. Use the outline in Exhibit 4.1 to conduct some in-depth interviews. Discover common threads. Let the outline carry you into information areas you might not have planned to explore.

Those in leisure-time industries are competing for a share of the customers' and consumers' valuable time. Rosen (1982, p. 16) estimated how a typical adult's week is broken down in terms of time allocated to the "necessities" of life (including working and traveling to work, sleeping, eating, watching television, and reading) and time available for all other activities. Rosen determined that this typical adult had ten hours available each week for shopping, visiting family and friends, housework, and so on.

Typical Adult Time Allocations

One Week

45 hours:	Work and travel to work
56 hours:	Sleeping
20 hours:	Eating
27 hours:	Television viewing
10 hours:	Reading
158 hours:	SUBTOTAL

168 hours:	Available (7 x 24)
-158 hours:	Allocated
10 hours:	Available for all else (running, shopping, quarreling, helping with homework, visiting family and friends, doing laundry, going to a sports event or a movie)

In the following pages I offer two examples of market segments: the middle-aged male business executive (of whom my fifty-one-year-old Rotarian is one), and women between the ages of eighteen and forty-nine (of whom the thirty-one-year-old mother is one); this latter group is further segmented into four major subsegments. These examples are intended to give you information about major market segments important to many NPOs.

The Middle-Aged Male Executive

The fifty-and-over age group has been largely ignored by advertisers, who are busy focusing on the elusive youth markets. NPOs should not overlook the middle and older age groups. They have power, money, and time—all resources that NPOs badly need. A 1995 study by Roper Starch Worldwide for *Modern Maturity* magazine found that fifty-plus consumers are going through the major life events—retirement, major diet changes, death in the family, divorce—that provide fertile ground for marketers of social services.

The forty-five-to-sixty-four age market has the highest incomes in the nation—about 20 percent above the national average. This age group has over half of all the discretionary income in America.

People fifty and older today are more self-indulgent than the generation before them, and they don't feel guilty about it. They are also less gullible to advertising claims. Word-of-mouth advertising is very important to them, but they do not yield easily to peer pressure. It is fairly safe to assume that the majority of them

Exhibit 4.1. Leisure Lifestyle Analysis.

I.   Name of your program

II. Demographic traits of the typical customer or consumer
  A. Age
  B. Income level
  C. Residence
  D. Family size
  E. Marital status
  F. Education
  G. Employment
  H. Transportation
  I. Other

III. Comment on that typical person's recreation
  A. Use of games and toys (frequency, places)
  B. Vehicles (tricycle, bicycle, snowmobile, motorcycle, skates, wagons, aircraft, boats, canoe, car, other)
  C. Dolls and stuffed toys
  D. Sporting goods and game equipment (video games, table games, camping, guns, golf, baseball, football, basketball, tennis, bowling, hunting, fishing, skiing, racquetball, weight lifting, flying)
  E. Athletic shoes and clothing (jogging, swimming, hiking)
  F. Alcoholic beverages (beer, wine, whiskey, gin, vodka, rum, cocktails) (Name the chosen brands if you can)
  G. Travel
    • In own community
    • In the United States
    • Foreign travel
  H. Reading
    • Books
    • Magazines
    • Newspapers (favorite section?)
    • Comic books
  I. Home entertainment food and drink
  J. Radio, television sets, VCR, compact discs, camcorder
  K. Favorite radio stations
  L. Favorite television programs

M. Favorite musician(s)

N. Flowers and garden

O. Vacation place

- Amount spent on vacation

- Lodgings while on vacation

P. Spectator events

- Favorite movies

- Theater, opera, concerts

- Auto shows, exhibits, art galleries

- Professional sports (baseball, football, soccer, hockey, horse and dog race tracks, college football, basketball, wrestling, boxing)

Q. Commercial amusements (billiards, bowling, dancing, pinball, riding, shooting, miniature golf, regular golf, instruction, private flying, theme parks)

R. Clubs, fraternities, social organizations

S. Pets

T. Hobbies

U. Dining out for pleasure (amount spent?)

IV. When does this person have time to pursue his or her interests? (time of day, day of week, season)

- Have their basic necessities out of the way.

- Have children who are grown and whose educations are either provided for or completed.

- Have some money in the bank, some investments, and more disposable income than ever before.

- Have a feeling of comfort. Physically and mentally they are doing fine.

- Have the prevailing attitude that now is the time for some self-indulgence.

- Are heavy users and purchasers of

  New luxury cars

  Securities worth $10,000 or more

  Foreign travel

Dinner parties

Domestic plane travel

Fine china and sterling silver flatware

- Regularly read the following:

Reader's Digest

National Geographic

TV Guide

Time

Better Homes and Gardens

Affluent consumers express a far stronger commitment to print media than do consumers in general. A large majority report daily readership of newspapers ("The Affluent Market," 1982).

Of those in the age group of fifty and older, it is the business executives who receive the most attention from NPO managers. Business executives provide the fodder for our boards, advisory committees, and campaign teams. Those NPO managers who do not live the same lifestyle or enjoy the same annual incomes as do their board members should study rather intensely this target market.

A study of two hundred executives in six major U.S. cities reported by Ernst & Whinney Executive Tax Service more than ten years ago revealed this profile of the typical executive (Winter, 1981, p. 25):

- Personal finances:

Saves 20 percent or more of income

Uses investments to keep ahead of inflation

- On the job:

Loves the job

Works fifty-one hours a week or more

Does not want children to follow the same career path

- Off the job:

Works on company business fewer than five hours a week

Prefers golf for leisure activity

The executives surveyed reported a surprisingly large amount of weekend leisure time. A third of them said they had more than twenty-five hours of leisure each weekend, excluding chores. Obviously, that one-third does not do a lot of house painting, lawn work, plumbing, or automobile repairs.

A combined study of 824 chief executives of businesses conducted in September 1981 by the *Wall Street Journal* and Gallup revealed that, contrary to the office situation where delegation prevails, the bosses did not mind doing things themselves around the house. They took their turn at grocery shopping, writing checks to pay the family bills, running errands, and doing other household chores. Most did not believe in flaunting their economic status.

One in ten took regular lessons from a sports pro, usually in golf or tennis. Most executives did not take time for long vacations. They typically stayed away from the office no more than a week at a time.

Golf was their favorite form of recreation (26 percent). Eight percent indicated that reading was their favored activity, 7 percent chose boating, and another 7 percent chose gardening. Six percent watched sports. Only 2 percent said jogging was their favorite pastime.

Compare the top executive's recreational pursuits with yours. It is little wonder that your paths do not frequently cross after work hours.

While on top of the world at work, the middle-aged male executive is frequently going through some difficult tensions at home. He may find himself out of phase with his wife. Typically, the successful male executive has been working his tail off for more than twenty years. That is how he got to the top. Now he wants to relax and enjoy some of the fruits of his labor by spending more time with family. This inward move comes at the very time that his wife and children are bursting outward with their own career excitements.

Time together becomes an issue for these couples. They do have more family income when the wife is employed in significant jobs outside of the home. With this they should be able to purchase better vacations and higher-quality time when they are together.

Two other concerns of middle-aged executives include too-frequent business travel, and promotions that would uproot their families or disrupt a comfortable lifestyle (Klein, 1982).

To reach these people with higher incomes and greater purchasing ability, advertisers select media that will match the executives' interests. Data General Corporation used lifestyle marketing information when it channeled a few million dollars into television advertising during golf and tennis programs rather than during bowling, baseball, and all-star wrestling shows (Abrams, 1981c).

Middle- and upper-income executives are divided into three categories of values and lifestyles, according to the Stanford Research Institute (Gigles, 1981). There are (1) the belongers, those motivated by a need for greater acceptance; (2) the emulators, those trying to appear like the rich and successful; and (3) the achievers, the hard-driving success-oriented (including those already successful).

Paying astute attention to such different values and lifestyles, the advertising agency of Young & Rubicam decided to change the "bullish on America" campaign for Merrill Lynch to a new theme line, "a breed apart." The "bullish on America" campaign appealed to traditionalists and belongers—patriotic flag wavers. However, the heavy investor that Merrill Lynch wanted to attract saw himself more as an individual achiever, not so much a member of a group or herd of safe people. The "breed apart" campaign connoted innovation, action, resourcefulness, brute strength, and finesse.

My previous supervisors and my key volunteers were often in the third category of achievers. They were fast-moving hard workers who always wanted more. Because those few individuals influenced so much of my happiness and future opportunities, I considered them a market to satisfy.

Sometimes I would spend hours or days creating written pieces for their consideration. The subject matter ranged from campaign schedules, to annual report drafts, to newsletters, to strategy documents.

Imagine my dismay when they did not spend much time reading the words I had labored over.

It took me a while to learn an extremely useful fact about middle-aged executives. Their eyes deteriorate, with increasing astigmatism, long before they admit it. Macho managers shun bifocals. They will even keep an extra pair of reading glasses concealed in a suit pocket and spend the day fishing them out and returning them. The apparent lack of interest in my written materials was caused by the fact that the executives simply could not read them comfortably! Now my materials contain large photographs (not collages) and ten-point type (large enough to be read without glasses).

There are several other good rules to remember when writing for older managers. They happen to be the same as the guidelines for advertising to the elderly, an entirely different market (Dupont, 1982, p. 1).

- Keep the language simple.
- Present a clear, sharp picture. Many seniors have trouble seeing, even with glasses.
- Be single minded. The ability to assimilate information declines with age, so a single sales message is advised.
- Relate new information to something familiar.

These adaptations to your target market will often make the difference in whether your written material is noticed and read, let alone heeded. The kinds of lifestyle concerns described here should be part of your ongoing plans for gaining supporters among the people with money and power to affect your NPO's future. In marketing workshops, I used to ask, "To sell refrigerators to Eskimo, do you have to know more about refrigerators or Eskimo?" The class would always correctly reply that we need to gain more information about Eskimo: why and how would they use refrigerators. Yet it seems that many of us are loaded with more product and program information than understanding of the customer and his or her values. The real payoff comes when we adapt our services to better fit the pressures and aspirations of the service users.

Four Groups of Women

The women's market is complex. Not long ago it was popular to make simple assumptions and approaches to housewives in the eighteen-to-forty-nine age group. Media advertisements clearly revealed some basic assumptions. Her motivations as the prime purchaser for the family were to win husband's and children's approval of her competence. She was out to do a more efficient, more effective job than her neighbor. She could fool everyone into thinking she had done things the old-fashioned, high-quality hard way when in fact she had wisely taken commercial shortcuts.

The depiction of women by advertisers has changed from that of wonderful mother and wife to new levels of exaggeration reflecting what they think will sell today. We still see warped role interpretations of the superwoman: brain surgeon by day, great lover at night, winning athlete on weekends, with a sprinkling of gourmet cook and dance contest winner—and all the same woman! We can better focus on the new roles of women and the opportunities they present by segmenting the mass market of women.

The women's market can be divided demographically into two major segments, homemakers (H) and women working outside the home (W). Among homemakers, there are those who plan to stay at home (SH) and those who plan to work outside the home sometime (PTW). There are also two segments of working women: those who consider their work just a job (JJ) and those who consider it a career (C). Each of these segments can be further divided into two more segments: those women who are married and those who are not (Bartos, 1978, 1981, 1982). For most NPOs there is not much value in analyzing the intermediate levels—those planning for divorce, separation, or marriage. NPOs in the counseling business may find such further segmentation worth the effort.

All segments mentioned so far can be further divided into two groups: women with children and those without. This segmenting process produces a total of sixteen market segments, as illustrated in Figure 4.1.

Stay-at-Home Homemakers

According to research done by Batton, Barton, Durstine & Osborn Inc. (BBDO) of New York, stay-at-home women were happy with their choice to remain at home with their children ("Ads," 1981). However, nearly 70 percent of the three hundred women surveyed nationally said they felt societal pressures to go to work outside the home. Those who felt the most pressure were the most educated. It is interesting to note that the pressure came from outside the home. Only 7 percent of those studied indicated that their husbands wanted them to go to work. Married, stay-at-home homemakers perceived themselves as the unifying force within the family circle, and more than half cited child rearing as the determining factor in their decision to stay home.

There is now a rapidly growing national organization of stay-at-home mothers called MOMS Club. It appeals especially to large numbers of baby boomer women who have left the workplace to tend children full time. Mothers join MOMS Club hoping to meet other at-home mothers with whom they can socialize, find playmates for their children, and talk about their experiences of staying home all day.

According to BBDO's research, stay-at-home women were not envious of modern career women. Two-thirds of those studied saw themselves as more fun loving, sexy, and romantic than their wage-earning counterparts. They were not particularly sympathetic to women who had to cope with the demands of both an outside job and the home front. They considered themselves to be as busy, energetic, and intelligent as their career-minded neighbors. They did have the lowest formal education level of the four primary seg-

Figure 4.1. Women Divided into Market Segments.

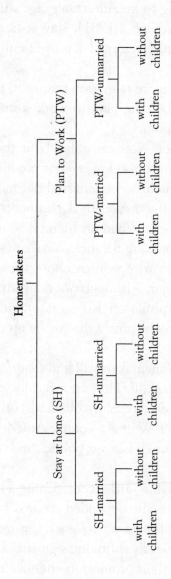

Homemakers

Stay at home (SH)

Plan to Work (PTW)

SH-married · SH-unmarried

PTW-married · PTW-unmarried

with children · without children

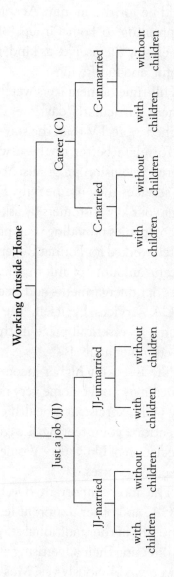

Working Outside Home

Just a job (JJ)

Career (C)

JJ-married · JJ-unmarried

C-married · C-unmarried

with children · without children

Source: Adapted from Bartos, 1978, 1981.

ments, however. Stay-at-home women felt working women were more fashionable, materialistic, and self-confident. The biggest reason they would be tempted to join those in the workforce, though, would be for the money. According to an *Advertising Age* study ("Appealing to Four Groups of Women," 1981), stay-at-home women saw themselves as kind, refined, reserved, family oriented, faithful, and fun-loving.

Full-time homemakers watched more television than working women, particularly daytime TV, but the plan-to-work women watched more TV than the stay-at-homes.

To relate better to these women, you can talk about their favorite television programs. You must also know what products and services they use heavily. Frequently you can find out more about your key customers by asking the marketing departments of the companies providing their products. When my friend Roseann Beutell worked for Formfit Rogers, for example, she could share significant amounts of information on why women chose various styles of undergarments and sleepwear. Although not relevant to YMCA services by itself, the information Roseann provided became an essential piece in the jigsaw puzzle that made up our key-customer analysis.

NPOs seeking higher-income homemakers will find that these women may not be home very much at all. They are typically very busy with exercise at a health center, tennis or golf, cards, other recreation, volunteering, League of Women Voters, American Association of University Women, Junior League, politics, and college credit courses.

The most important question for Girl Scout, Camp Fire, YMCA, and other nonprofit leaders who depended on heavy responses from the traditional stay-at-homes was, Were these agencies directing their advertising at a rapidly shrinking segment? The answer was obviously yes. Most of their promotion energies and limited recruitment budgets went toward increasingly difficult-to-reach markets.

Plan-to-Work Homemakers

Plan-to-work homemakers have more in common with women who work outside the home than with stay-at-home women. They model their behaviors on those of working women, and more than likely their mothers worked outside the home. They plan to join the workforce within five years. According to the *Advertising Age* study ("Appealing," 1981), these women see themselves as tense, stubborn, awkward, and affectionate.

"Just a Job" Working Women

The flood of women into the paid workforce is one of the most significant economic phenomena of our century. There are four basic reasons why women become employed (Bartos, 1978, pp. 73–85):

1. Economic need.
2. To supplement the family income. While not required for survival, a second paycheck enables the family to enjoy a higher standard of living.
3. For social stimulation and a sense of identity that comes from working outside the home.
4. For personal fulfillment and professional achievement, an opportunity to realize one's goals.

In the competition for the working woman's time, NPOs lose to her need to shop, rest, help her family, or be entertained in her off-the-job hours. Parent Teacher Associations have experienced dramatic drops in meeting attendance during the last two decades. Membership in garden clubs, Legion Auxiliary, and League of Women Voters is also down significantly in most communities.

Women who work outside the home complain they have very little time to socialize, and are very busy and tired when they come home from work. Their increased feeling of anonymity and isolation opens a way for NPOs to market services to these women. There is a widespread hunger for greater community ties, but that involvement has to be packaged as a convenience item without a heavy initial investment of time.

Career Women

One-third of women who work outside the home commit themselves to careers (Bartos, 1978, p. 78). They are most likely to be better-educated women. They spend less time planning shopping trips, which means their buying decisions are frequently spontaneous. First impressions really count. Career-oriented consumers may be more educated, but they do not take the time to read much about a program or product. They relate to pictures and headlines.

Career women are action oriented. They exhibit confidence and often seek the limelight. They decide quickly and seldom change their minds. Being the most decisive of all women, they are also most likely to set goals for themselves.

A study of twenty-four hundred women ages twenty to fifty (Nickles, 1981) revealed that women employed outside the home were less family dependent and domestic, but more aggressive, self-confident, and self-centered than stay-at-home women. The *Advertising Age* study ("Appealing," 1981) reported that career women see themselves as broad-minded, dominating, frank, efficient, independent, self-assured, very amicable, and affectionate. Their major focus was usually outside the home. They were also 80 percent more likely to be divorced or separated than women in general.

Appealing to Each Group

Table 4.2 shows how these four groups of women vary demographically, in the mass media they choose, in some consumer behavior, and in some family patterns. The variations have a direct bearing on how you should approach these groups and on what you must do to be heard in all groups.

Where Do We Start?

As is probably obvious by now, do less mass marketing and direct your efforts toward specific market segments. Target marketing becomes more important every week. The implication for NPOs is that we have to offer a variety of services to specific market segments. We have to do a better job of tailoring our programs to meet the needs of our clients and supporters. By pruning marginal services and programs, we can channel more resources toward the targeted groups, finding market niches of significant size and potential, and addressing them well.

Caution: do not become overzealous as you discover the values of target marketing. An overemphasis on a target group can lead to neglect of important secondary markets (such as the favorite programs of your board members or major contributors, or emerging new markets). Perhaps you can expand your services by convincing nonusers outside of the targeted group that you have something that might make life a little better for them, even though the service is not really aimed at them. For example, older adults who don't swim and people with disabilities can often benefit by exercising in a swimming pool originally created for children.

You can go too far in abandoning the urge to broadcast the market. Sharpshooting at well-defined and differentiated markets has distinct advantages: a potential savings of promotion time, money, and effort. But several times a year you need to tell your story to all kinds of people in the area, not merely those who at the moment happen to be your very best prospects. There are both potential users and supporters who need to know what you are doing to benefit the community and people like them or people they may know.

Segmenting the market is not always productive. This is particularly true when the market is small. If you are operating a child-care center in an apartment complex of two hundred rental units,

Table 4.2. Appealing to Four Groups of Women.

Demographic Differences

Segment	Education	Age	Young children	Affluence
Stay at home	(4)	(1)		(4)
Plan to work		(4)	(1)	
Just a job				
Career	(1)			(1)

Media Choices

Segment	TV	Radio	Newspaper	Magazines	School flyers
Stay at home	+	–(4)	+	–(4)	+(1)
Plan to work	+(1)	–	–	+	+
Just a job	–	+	–(4)	–	–
Career	–(4)	+(1)	+(1)	+(1)	–

Consumer Behaviors

	Impulse buying decisions	Style conscious	Miles driven	Travel
Stay at home	–	+	–	–(4)
Plan to work	+	+	–	–
Just a job	+	+	+	+
Career	+	+(1)	+(1)	+(1)

Family Patterns

	Husbands help with youngsters	Family teamwork	Husbands help with chores
Stay at home	–(4)	–(4)	–(4)
Plan to work	+	–	
Just a job	–	+	+
Career	+(1)	+	+

Note: (1) = most, highest, or most frequently of the four segments; (4) = least, lowest, or least frequently of the four segments; + = yes; – = no

Source: Adapted from "Appealing to Four Groups of Women," 1981.

there is little advantage in spending more than five minutes in market segmentation analysis. In an instant you could decide not to distribute flyers to the doors of people without children.

Some marketers have discovered that they had defined their markets too narrowly and needed to broaden their target segments. This process is called countersegmentation. Clearly, you can define your target market either too narrowly or too broadly.

No matter what you do, it is getting harder to reach your targeted customers because of their greater time pressures. Even though our promotional methods are expanding, the available time that customers have is not. To get their attention away from the increased competition, our approaches need to be much more marketing astute.

Fortunately, the advances in and wide distribution of computer technology make it easier to focus on our customers. Recording customer use patterns helps us find new ways of segmenting. This, in turn, should help improve our pricing, scheduling, staffing, promotion, and overall program. Our direct mail promotions alone can have a much better return on the investment.

Customer information stored in the computer can enable practically anyone on the staff with access to be more responsive to the needs and interests of individuals. And that's what marketing is all about.

Chapter Five

How Many Customers Do You Have?

Improving Your Market Share and Analyzing Your Competition

Just how big is your market? Some administrators assume that if there are ten thousand teenagers in the community, then the market for a teen center is ten thousand. They continue the error by dividing their teen center enrollments by ten thousand to find their market share. This approach is wrong because the market for a service is composed of everyone who buys it, not everyone who could buy but doesn't necessarily do so. By contrast, an NPO serving a community that has ten thousand teenagers could use the ten thousand figure to determine its penetration or saturation. Both the Boy Scouts of America and Girl Scouts USA do a particularly fine job of keeping such penetration statistics.

This chapter describes how to calculate your market share and understand your enrollment figures in relation to the strength of the market. It also suggests ways to analyze the competition and discover how you compare. Armed with that information, you are much better prepared to make adjustments that can increase your NPO's appeal.

The first step in determining your market share is the same as the first step in marketing: get an agreement on what business (or businesses) you are in. Finding the answer is a challenge for those in the nonprofit social service sector.

Physical fitness directors, for example, wrestle with this problem when they assess the market for indoor banked jogging tracks. Jogging is a strong interest in most communities. Could the fitness directors estimate the size of the running/jogging market by noting the number of participants in the most popular "fun run" in the community and multiplying it by some factor such as ten, assuming that 10 percent of the available joggers were at the fun run?

If you were in the fun run (three miles or more) business, then the number of available joggers would be worth knowing, especially if they had to pay an entrance fee in exchange for a number or a T-shirt. Yet jogging for most people is an activity for which the producer and the consumer are the same. No exchange takes place with an NPO. The market for the fitness director with an indoor running track is *not* everyone who jogs in the community. Rather it is everyone who jogs or runs indoors and pays some institution money for the privilege.

Similarly, a camp director should not assume that the overnight camping market includes people who camp on their own. The weight lifting market does not include people who lift weights in their own garages, nor does the crafts market include people who do crafts at home, unless, of course, your business is selling camping, weight lifting, or craft supplies.

When consumers produce their own service, thereby making no exchange with another party, no viable market exists. Of course, through promotion efforts, you can hope to stimulate a demand for your services. But that is a potential market, not an existing market. A business example: those who always bring their lunch from home are not figured in determining the size of the current restaurant-lunch-customer market. However, we should know how many choose not to eat in a restaurant at noon when we calculate the size of the *potential* market. This way we can estimate if it is worth the effort and expense to convert nonusers to users.

The most practical method of determining relative market share is to separate your NPO's services into basic categories. Call them businesses. Then identify three or four major competitors or other NPOs offering similar services.

Let's try an example. In a community that has ten thousand teenagers, there are one thousand who go to teen centers at least four times a year: five hundred attend the recreation department's teen center, two hundred attend the YMCA teen center, two hundred attend the Jewish Community Center teen center, and one hundred attend the Salvation Army teen center. Thus one thousand teenagers make up the total teen center market. If your NPO were the Salvation Army, you would have 10 percent of the teen center market.

Gather Good Information

Getting accurate facts from others can be a challenge. The biggest stumbling block to determining your market share in comparison with other NPOs is that we all count differently. Why is this? Can't you simply get the figures from the United Way, an organization to which many human service agencies report? No.

The United Way is the biggest single customer of many NPOs. It pays the largest sum of cash in exchange for services to consumers of the agencies. Thus it makes sense for the agencies to please their biggest customer by giving what they believe the United Way wants most—simply more. The unreliability of comparative market share figures, then, comes from some agencies that are adding 10 percent to last year's enrollment figures. After all, not many of the agencies truly require accurate, auditable enrollment figures for themselves. Estimates are often good enough.

Too many NPOs manage on the basis of faith and trust. NPO managers do not demand and get accurate numbers except for the financial statement, which is legally audited. Here are some reasons why accurate enrollments are not always reported:

- *Atrophy.* Leadership does not use the figures to make management decisions. If accurate enrollment numbers are not deemed essential and useful, after a while the staff will not bother to collect data or post timely updates.
- *Lack of desire.* Managers do not really want to know. They choose ignorance because they are afraid or ashamed of the facts.
- *Accountability.* Managers do not want to take responsibility for what the figures say, so they duck the issue.

- *Cost.* The cost of collecting the information seems to exceed the benefit. Who really wants to hassle field staff? And who wants to go out into the field or office and count each enrollment card to audit the reported figures?

- *Lack of relevance.* The figures may seem to have little relevance to the prosperity of the agency. Resources appear to accumulate more by telling wonderful human interest stories than by boasting about market penetration. (But the fact is, both passionate stories and evidence of excellent management are needed to continually acquire large financial resources.)

Another example of problems we have with counting differently is that enrollment numbers do not attribute a value to the quality of the participant's experience. The penetration figures of the Boy Scouts are definitely helpful, but they are inadequate because they count a boy who attends only once, and they count him in the same way as a boy who participates all year long. The public's assumption is that the penetration statistic represents those who have attended most of a year.

Many more consumers now choose short-term experiences over long-term commitments. The market demand is for quick in-and-out experiences. Character development youth agencies, on the other hand, want long-term opportunities for the program participants to develop and mature. Theoretically, the quality of the experience improves over time. In making interagency comparisons, the challenge for study teams is to define equal or comparable units of service and weigh them accordingly. This is hard.

Focus on the Best Figures

There is still another explanation for the reluctance to count and report program service figures accurately. Almost everyone in this society wishes to be regarded as successful. Thus we describe our efforts in terms that lend evidence to the assumption that we are definitely on the right path. After all, the prevailing social attitude is that bigger is better, and growth is a must. The tapeworm is seldom satiated. Our San Francisco YMCA raised 15 to 20 percent more each year in voluntary contributions for three years in a row, but instead of relaxing and basking in that accomplishment, 15 percent growth became the standard. Our hungry eyes fixed on a target of 25 percent annual growth in fundraising.

"Small is beautiful," wrote the late British economist E. F. Schumacher (1973). That may be particularly true of the nonprofit service field, where enthusiastic staff unencumbered by policy and procedure manuals can work with flexibility to meet the interests of the local market. On the other hand, the enemy of consistently good customer service is staff discretion, according to Theodore Leavitt (1969) of Harvard Business School. He is probably right when we are dealing with large volume and delegating key responsibilities to receptionists and front desk staff. They are among our lowest-paid, least trained, and often least informed employees.

We have been taught since childhood that bigger is better. Yet there is value in choosing to stabilize at one size. Harvard Business School chose that tactic in the 1970s. Although there was great demand for the school's services, the administration chose to remain at a more easily manageable size.

The Girl Scouts of Orange County, California, dropped from forty thousand to twenty-two thousand members in six years during the 1970s. Yet in the 1980s, they remained as one of the most successful Girl Scout councils in the country. The assistant executive director commented that maybe they were doing an even better job in 1980 than they had when memberships were almost double. She said, "During the boom years, we were all stretched pretty thin and gave less intensive staff service to the individual troops and volunteer staff."

Market share statistics are better for good marketing management than are simple growth or decline figures. The *Wall Street*

Journal and *Fortune* magazine report market share statistics along with growth rates when describing a company's progress or plight. Unless you make similar comparisons, you can be misled by some statistics and make wrong management decisions.

Let's look at an example. Imagine that you manage Fair Oak, a community center with multiple services. The physical fitness director glowingly reports enrollments growing at an annual rate of 20 percent, whereas the camp director laments that day camp enrollments are about the same as they were five years ago.

It is not unusual under such circumstances to reward the fitness director for her exciting contribution to the center's health and punish the camp director with a threatened loss of employment because he cannot move a static situation. Yet if we look at market share figures, we may reverse the reward and punishment given.

Figure 5.1 shows that the number of people seeking exercise classes has tripled during the last five years. This means that in the first year, Fair Oak had 50 percent of the available exercise market, but now, although Fair Oak has grown, it has not been at the same pace as the market. In fact, the two hundred Fair Oak participants are now only a third of the market.

YMCAs with handball courts in medium-size markets experienced this loss of market share during the 1970s. At one time, many YMCAs, with their two handball/racquetball courts, had 100 percent of the market. But racquetball boomed across the land. If a YMCA did not add more courts (because it saw itself in the health and fitness business, not the racquetball business), it lost market share. By the time a YMCA board and staff decided to enter the racquetball business and build more courts, the market usually had peaked in the program life cycle. Their lag response was both very expensive and loaded with risks of failure.

Conversely, your Fair Oak camp director may have been witnessing a declining youth population. My experience at the Northwest YMCA was that all agencies offering day camp services experienced declining enrollments and were getting out of the business. That left just the YMCA offering the same day camp to

Figure 5.1. Fair Oak's Market Share.

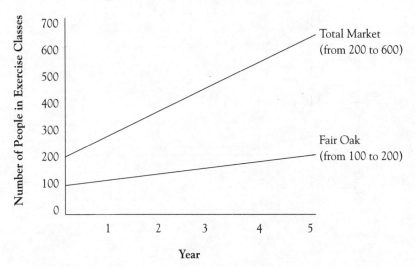

fewer children than in the past, which meant that the YMCA's market share had increased. See Figure 5.2 for an illustration.

The YMCA was doing very well just by standing still. The total available children of day camp age was decreasing 6.5 percent annually, and yet the YMCA's share of the day camp market increased from 22 percent to almost 100 percent.

Despite the problems described here that you must watch for, there are several quick and effective ways of getting accurate figures from other agencies. You may be able simply to ask your colleagues in other agencies. I have found them to be quite candid. The candor increased the farther down the hierarchy I went. By polling individually, not collectively, at a council of agencies meeting, I got reliable data. In situations where information is not readily disclosed, our staff visit the enigmatic facility, or even the parking lot, to make sight counts and estimates. If you use this method, make several visits so that your count is not warped by a special event or an interim of low attendance between seasons or classes.

To get accurate program data within your own NPO, take the reporting process out of the hands of the person who cares the most about the figures. At the Northwest YMCA, I had secretaries, not

Figure 5.2. Day Camp's Market Share.

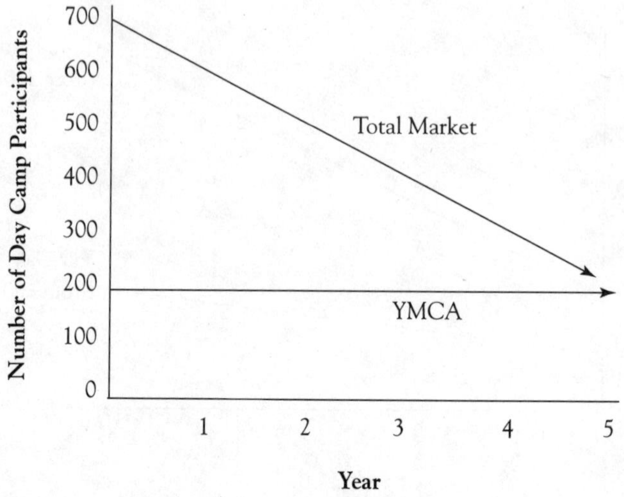

program directors, report the card counts of enrollments weekly. Two sides of one piece of paper were used to report the enrollments of twenty-six thousand participants in every program and membership category. Secretaries signed each report, attesting to its accuracy.

Occasionally, I would ask to see a stack of enrollment cards for a particular program. Yes, I would find discrepancies, but not many. The embarrassed secretary would explain that the program director said fifty more people were in the activity and promised their cards soon. But promises were not supposed to count. People attending programs who had not yet completed an enrollment card did not count either. If there had been no exchange of a completed enrollment card for our services, then there was no enrollment.

Competition

It's not nice for nonprofit organizations to compete. It is downright distasteful to some board members that charitable groups should be competing. After all, they lament, there are plenty of social problems to solve. There is room for everybody. When consumer interests change, the NPO should adapt, pull in, or simply disappear.

Recent experience shows that NPOs have a momentum that keeps them going even when their original impetus disappears. When polio was successfully stopped on a national scale, the March of Dimes found another cause, birth defects. When the Vietnam War ended, Clergy and Laymen Concerned About the War regrouped to become Clergy and Laymen Concerned, with broader peace issues as their reason to be.

There are plenty of social problems to solve; plenty of interest in artistry, history, and community improvement; plenty of souls needing solace; and plenty of healing needed. The needs and interests are abundant—it is the resources that are tight.

Although overall philanthropy has outpaced the Gross Domestic Product growth rate, many NPOs do not get enough gifts to pay the bills. Volunteers continue to be generous with their time, but the amount of their uncommitted time is decreasing. At the same time, donors, volunteers, and potential clients are growing ever more sophisticated, asking for more real value from their investment of time, energy, money, and creativity. Our job is to help them get that value.

Our job is also to help our NPO prosper. This can be done by identifying the competition, listing the comparative advantages each has, selecting two or three of our NPO's comparative advantages that are also important in the customer's eyes, and then promoting those factors. There are two forms of competition to consider: similar services and substitutes.

Similar Services and Substitutes

First, list those NPOs that look like you, the similar-service providers. If there are many, limit your list to the top five, perhaps those in your neighborhood, those with the largest volume, or those whom potential customers would think of when asked to list providers of the service.

The second form of competition is substitution. If people do not choose any of the similar-service providers, where do they go or what do they do to satisfy the same basic needs? If a problem perplexes them and they don't seek professional counseling, then advice from a friend, coworker, or bartender might suffice as a substitute. There are advantages to each choice. The substitute for exercise class three days a week could be jogging in the neighborhood on weekends, strict dieting, or buying larger clothes, depending on the benefits desired deep down.

Substitute competition is often right under our noses. A primary group is the do-it-yourselfers. Former members or clients may have switched from participating in your NPO to doing it themselves for a number of reasons:

- The level of expertise required is within their ability.
- They have the physical capacity to do the activity.
- They have the time available to do it.
- There is an opportunity to save money.
- There are psychic rewards, such as self-satisfaction.
- There may be greater flexibility—more options.
- They can exercise more influence working with outside contractors.
- The risk level seems acceptable.

There are many examples of this type of substitution: the do-it-yourselfer might replace paid child care by having an older child look after the younger one. Instead of participating in an American Camping Association (ACA) certified family camp program, a family might spend a vacation week using city parks. A fitness center membership for an adult member of the family might be replaced with home exercise equipment. Season tickets to live theater productions could be replaced with rentals from the video store.

Here are three options for NPOs who want to convert do-it-yourselfers to being consumers of the NPO's services:

1. Help them do it themselves. Be a facilitator.

    Provide newsletters

    Sell or rent equipment

    Distribute maps and instructions

2. Tell them how they would be better off by not doing it themselves. Sell your benefits better.

3. Add value to their substitution by providing valuable supplemental services.

    ACA camp referrals

    Child-care listings

    Personal counseling services

    Baby-sitting course for potential baby sitters

    Swim instructions for backyard pools

Perceptions of Reality

When comparing your NPO to your competition, consider possible differences between reality and perception. Do potential clients perceive your fees to be higher than the competition, for example, when they are not? Have you recently lowered your prices or has the competition raised theirs, and few people are aware of the fact? Do they think your program center is crowded when in fact it is only the lobby that is too small, whereas the rest of the facility is truly spacious (but potential customers don't see or recall it)?

The worksheet in Exhibit 5.1 can help you compare your organization with facts and perceptions about both similar services and substitutes.

There is still another set of questions to consider when creating your competition strategy. When brand-new competition emerges, seek top-staff agreement on an appropriate response.

Exhibit 5.1. Service Comparison Worksheet.

Attribute	Competition			
	Similar Service		Substitute	
	Fact	Perception	Fact	Perception
Cost of switching from us to them: high/low				
Cost of switching back to us later: high/low				
Price comparison				
Program quality: high/low				
Convenience of parking: high/low				
Cleanliness: high/low				
Ability to focus on the needs and interests of any particular age group (identify which): high/low				
Easy payment plans: yes/no				
Easy trial use: yes/no				
Professionally guided facility tours: yes/no				
Staff with sales skills: yes/no				
Describe your NPO image among:				
users				
nonusers				
donors				
Customer service: high/low				
Top management pressure to produce:				
Surplus/profit: high/low				
Volume: high/low				
Quality: high/low				
Recent profit/surplus history: good/bad				

Facility advantages

Favorable location: yes/no

External sign: yes/no

Where do we have decided advantages that mean much to our present and potential customers? Answer this question taking into consideration the elements just reviewed. Which two or three advantages should we exploit in our promotions?

Answer These Questions When Competition First Appears

1. Can we retaliate vigorously?

   Staff determination

   Board willingness

   Enough resources to fight back (cash, unfilled spaces, downtime, parking, caseload)

2. What is the growth rate of the local market? Can the community easily absorb a new service provider without negatively affecting our financial performance?

3. Shall we impede the competition's entry by offering significantly lower prices?

4. Are there advantages we should exploit because of our being here first?

5. What marketing strategy are we going to pursue for the next five years? Don't get so obsessed with the competitive threats that you reduce your attention to a long-term strategy. The very appearance of a competitor on the horizon dictates that you pick a strategy that will work well for a long time. Choose just one from among three classic options.

   We will be the low-cost provider.

   We will be known for offering services unique in the marketplace.

   We will be widely recognized as the best at focusing on one particular market segment.

6. Do potential consumers have full information for comparison purposes?

7. Have our current users gained power because of the threat of competition?

8. Are the traits that differentiate us from the competition truly important in the potential consumer's eyes?

9. Who now dominates the local market? If it is not us, what are they likely to do with the increased competition?

10. Will any bold competitive moves on our part negatively affect our biggest financial backers?

11. Just how loyal are our current users?

   What is their level of satisfaction?

   Should we test it very soon?

12. What will the competition have to do with their prices and volume to get a good return on the investment of their resources?

13. Could we easily lose some good staff to them? How can we prevent this?

14. What are the barriers preventing us from dropping unprofitable programs and unproductive staff?

15. What does the competition appear to believe about their relative position?

   Program quality

   Technological sophistication (computers, equipment)

   Sales force

   Advertising

   What do they see as their strengths and weaknesses? (training and skills of the sales force, breadth and depth of program line, location, cash flow, cash available, depth of management, leadership of top manager, flexibility of management)

16. What is the competition's capacity to respond quickly to any moves we make?

17. Will the competition pay much attention to our competitive moves?

18. How will we gain more information?

19. How much time do we have?

By answering these questions and completing the comparison worksheet with a group of interested staff and/or volunteers, you will find your response to any competition much clearer.

Benefits of Competition

A word of caution is now necessary. Although it is important that a manager identify and understand both the direct and indirect competitors, it is also important not to overreact. Some forms of competition are good. In fact, many times it is better to have some competition than to have none.

The appearance on the scene of a new or growing competitor can force you to improve your staff, programs, or facility for the benefit of all your consumers and the greater community. Competitors also can serve a segment of the market that you really don't want to deal with, but would have to if you were the only provider.

Healthy competitors can make it harder for others to enter the marketplace and erode your position. If people are satisfied with the amount of child-care services offered in the community, it is harder for a new, large child-care agency to enter the market. You and your current competitors may have the market already sewn up.

Newly emerging competitors also can help reduce public resistance to price increases. With only one service provider, the public can argue that the fees are unfairly high, but when more than one provider charges those fees, the public begins to accept them as fair.

New technologies and new services are easier to introduce when the competition is making moves similar to yours. Nautilus exercise machines, although they looked like instruments of torture, were readily accepted by the public when they discovered that more than one fitness center had them. Similarly, aerobic dance classes proliferated when the public perceived aerobics as the thing to do. The fad faded not because there were so many service providers—so much competition—but because after a while the public got bored with jumping up and down to music.

Some of your perceived competitors may not be real threats. They may merely be offering services similar to yours but to a different neighborhood or market niche. The presence of two performing theater groups and a college theatrical production company in the same community may be helpful to all three organizations because they expand the number of people actively pursuing the performing arts. It is likely the two community theater groups would pick special niches in the marketplace to avoid head-to-head competition.

So look before you leap at the throat of a competitor. Do your market research to check initial assumptions. A frontal assault is rarely the best strategy anyway.

Chapter Six

Strengthening Your Marketing Practices with Internal Audits

The thought of an audit of our strengths and weaknesses is scary for some. They feel they should improve performance first, just as a person may want to get in shape before seeing the doctor for a checkup. The people who are physically unfit already know it. They feel they don't need an expensive doctor to tell them the bad news. The people who welcome a doctor's feedback are those who are feeling really sick and also those who are healthiest. The healthy people want to stay that way, so they go for regular check-ups. I recommend similar action for managers and their NPOs.

Not in the shape you want for your organization? An audit can quickly help you make the right moves to get in shape. Preceding corrective action with an audit can save money, time, and stress. An audit enables you to get beyond the symptoms of problems and directs you to the causes. Since you can't simultaneously change everything that needs to be corrected, you can rely on an audit to help sort out the priorities needing your attention. Hasty moves may prove detrimental in the long run.

The benefits of conducting regular audits of strengths and weaknesses and doing periodic formal market research are that we can anticipate problems before they get out of hand and can seize new opportunities long before the competition does. By constantly testing the quality of our services, we can make nontraumatic fine adjustments and keep things going well.

Without regular service audits and market research we are prone to making errors. Management experience and enthusiasm alone are not enough to keep us up-to-date with the changing interests of our people. It is unwise, for example, to locate a new facility on land a private donor or the government has given to us free, without first doing some very careful research.

Unlike for-profit businesses where there is a clear economic bottom line to define success, an NPO's bottom line is more elusive. It needs to be carefully defined in each case. Simply to say, "We are touching the lives of several hundred people," or "We are responding to the obvious needs of others" is not good enough. Peter Drucker, in his excellent self-assessment tool for nonprofit organizations (1993, p. 39), says, "The discipline of thinking through what results will be demanded of the nonprofit institution can protect it from squandering its resources." He goes on to say, "The Salvation Army is fundamentally a religious organization. Nevertheless, it knows the percentage of alcoholics it restores to mental and physical health and the percentage of criminals it rehabilitates. . . . In the church, the first measurement may be the level of new membership and the church's ability to hold them and keep them coming and becoming more involved as unpaid staff."

The Bloomsburg, Pennsylvania, public library was able, with my company's help, to raise sufficient capital contributions to double the size of their facility because of the well-recognized contribution the library was making to the quality of life in the county. It was easy to see there was no room on the shelves for more books. Each new book purchased meant another book had to be relegated to the sale conducted annually by the Friends of the Library. However, the greatest stimulus for the million-dollar campaign was the popularity of the children's story hour. Library director Hal Pratt enthralled the little children with his weekly tales from library books.

In 1994 the library board and staff audited the operation. They knew how many children were attending the story hours, but was that good enough? What about the children whose parents couldn't or wouldn't bring them to the library? They solved that by having Pratt conduct story hours in schools and day-care centers. Their easy audit quickly showed a need to make the place much more accessible to people with disabilities; they needed more space for the popular children's program, and they needed to catch up to the electronic age. Loaning books and tapes and telling children's stories were not sufficient as a service strategy. Town manager and library board member Jerry Depo wanted the library to help more teenagers and senior citizens use information available through the Internet.

Depo's strong desire to add a well-equipped computer center for library patrons was not embraced by all fifteen board members. Several of them just wanted to maintain the existing programs in larger spaces. They were not necessarily shortsighted. Perhaps Internet access was already being provided by the schools and the senior center. A good audit not only identifies service gaps but also can help one purposely avoid an area or delete a program. An audit of other service providers may find they are more ready to handle a program that you should drop.

Suzanne Walker, executive director of the YMCA in Northampton, Massachusetts, once audited the memberships of her women's health center the hard way. It was also a mighty effective way, but many of us would rather assign someone else to do it. On the other hand, anyone assigned the responsibility would likely take shortcuts to avoid personal embarrassment. Walker simply sat for a full day in the health center locker room and requested that each person show Walker her up-to-date membership card. Her audit of the women's health center users revealed a significant number who had successfully gotten past the downstairs membership control desk. As a direct result of Walker's audit, membership transactions increased. Many transgressors explained to Walker that they were not aware their memberships had expired, or that they were unaware a nonmember had to purchase a guest pass to use the facilities. There was a control point in the center that should have caught these problems, but only Walker's audit revealed the large number that somehow were getting through in defeat of the policy.

An audit is good not only for the management team but also for potential donors. Large commercial donors are interested in how many of their customers and employees use the NPO's services. Their gift may be in proportion to their vested interest. More and more companies are asking for employee participation numbers prior to making a large capital donation. Levi Strauss, for example, usually limits its largest capital gifts to communities where the company has plants and employees likely to benefit from the capital development program.

Companies also make large capital investments where they have some key staff on the NPO's board of directors. The regional manager of a very large insurance company told me that his company's $50,000 capital contribution was due mostly to his serving on the board of directors. Once his term expired it was unlikely the NPO would get a similar-size gift from his company.

Some foundations want information about the diversity of an NPO's board of directors before they commit a large gift. They are also more interested if the NPO board has representatives of the constituency being served. Many national organizations request this information annually from their constituent chapters.

Several years before launching a major capital funds effort, you should audit the board roster for evidence of inclusion. At the same time, you should insist that the staff responsible for gathering membership enrollment information have all blanks completed. Listing employers of everyone in the household is a step frequently missed. The rationale may be that noting the employer of the person enrolling is sufficient, but listing employers of everyone in the household increases your fundraising marketability.

Potential donors are interested in the results of an NPO's efforts, not just its activities. Don't assume potential donors can easily conclude from your list of programs what effect the programs have on people's lives.

This chapter is for the manager who wants to get a grasp of some audit techniques before launching a significant change in service or prior to conducting a large fundraising campaign that needs the support of outsiders. This chapter gives you some practical tips on what to do in your situation. You will also be wiser when employing someone else to do studies for you.

Basic Audit

When, as is often the case, I am restricted to a one- or two-day visit to an NPO to analyze their marketing situation, I take the following steps. You can follow these same basic audit steps yourself.

Step 1.   I mail a questionnaire to the executive director and ask that it be returned completed so that I have more time to ponder how I can be most helpful to the organization. Here are some of the questions I have submitted in questionnaire form in preparation for a fundraising and marketing audit. Note that the questions get quite personal at the end. Candid answers, however, steer us into a more helpful consultation mode.

Your Case for Support

What are the major social problems and concerns of your community?

What makes your organization deserving of special support?

Who has said you are good?

Who will benefit from the money you raise?

How important is that to the community?

List your top five programs/services with the most appeal to donors.

Volunteers

Number of board members?

What is the average attendance?

How many board members do you consider affluent?

How many board members control large contributions?

What concerns have consumed the most time at board meetings during the past year?

Budget

What were your revenue, expense, and net income figures last year?

The year before that?

How have any losses been covered?

Donors and Prospects

How many donors are on the computer file?

What months were they mailed to last year?

How many times in a year do you ask them to contribute?

Who are your major competitors?

Do you have a list of your one hundred top donor prospects?

Do you have the time and interest this year for a top donor prospect research and cultivation program?

Assessment

List your organization's particular strengths and weaknesses (planning, employees, board, facility, public relations)

If you had more revenue, which weakness would you try to improve first?

What are your aspirations as the leader of this NPO?

What do you plan to accomplish while executive?

What is likely to be your next career move?

Where would you like it to be?

How much longer are you likely to remain at this NPO?

Would you predict you will be here three years from now? Five years?

Step 2.   I take a tour of the facility accompanied by a staff member of the NPO. En route I dictate into a microcassette recorder my first impressions from a typical potential customer's viewpoint. I start the narrative report in the parking lot or sidewalk, noticing and commenting on the entryway and on every public place thereafter. The first-impression report is important because I will soon hear the reasons things are not as clean as they should be, or need repair, and I will accept the apologies. That is because I, too, was an NPO staff member and am sympathetic to the chronic problems of well-meaning NPOs. But a potential customer does not have to understand the reasons. Dirt is dirt, and they stay away from it when given options.

Step 3.   I meet with the executive and other staff members, individually. I ask them to define their typical customers and to describe their best programs and most responsive areas of the community. In these interviews, they are starting to segment their market and ascribe pertinent traits to each.

Step 4.   I gather the promotional literature of the NPO and quickly surmise how well each piece speaks to the key market segments identified by staff.

Step 5.   With some staff, I do a laborious card count of the membership to get a true count as a starting point for any new marketing program. Whether the NPO uses a regular hand tally system or a computer for its membership files, our card audit always emerges with significantly different numbers. While conducting the card count, we also can tally the members' age, gender, and type of membership. Later, we make profile charts from this data.

Step 6.   I interview representatives of the highest-volume membership categories or those categories with which staff are most concerned. Staff members arrange individual interviews scheduled every half hour. I fill out a two-page form while interviewing each person. Later the forms are tabulated and summarized.

Step 7.   I may enlist some friendly visitors, people who have never been to this NPO, to visit incognito, under the pretense that they are about to become new residents of the area. They note their first impressions and score the NPO on scales for friendliness, attention to customer service, and other items.

Step 8.   After my first visit, I send a twelve-page questionnaire about current marketing practices to the executive, who fills it out in consultation with the staff and sends it back to me. Just by answering the questions, the staff start getting a better handle on their problems and opportunities.

Probe Beneath the Surface

Do they have good marketing tools, and are they using them? A marketing tool may be as simple as current census data. Can the staff responsible for planning readily recite relevant figures beyond the gross of the total population?

Do they have computer software or a hands-on system for following up leads? Too many legitimate leads go nowhere when they are not followed up in a timely and skillful manner. Within three days after a person visits or calls, he or she should receive a phone call or visit from someone with sales and enrollment skills, someone who knows how to move to action anyone expressing interest. When more than three days have passed since the initial enquiry, a follow-up is frequently fruitless.

Audit by Walking Around

You can regularly audit an operation just by wandering around and observing what is happening. Walking around a facility, you can see if classes start on schedule, if the place is clean, if the bulletin boards are up-to-date, and if the staff look good.

An outside consultant or a colleague from another unit can also do this wandering around. The advantage of using outsiders is that they are likely to be critical of poor existing situations. An insider's advantage is his or her greater understanding of the problem and the implications of various solutions.

One major branch of a large city YMCA was having severe budget difficulties, running over $200,000 in the red. The manager of the afflicted unit asked his colleague in a more successful branch to visit for a day and diagnose the problem. His peer chose to spend that ten-hour day observing from behind the membership desk, where he discovered that the problem YMCA unit was turning away business, membership income they could not afford to lose. Management policies and procedures were the barriers. For example, the YMCA refused to cash checks drawn on out-of-town banks. Therefore, new residents who had not yet found a local bank couldn't easily join this YMCA. Furthermore, the membership office was open only from 10:00 A.M. to 7:00 P.M. It was closed an hour for lunch and on weekends. A potential member could join only when the membership office was open, and office hours did not conform to the average person's free time. There were plenty of staff doing other member service chores at the key times, but they refrained from processing new memberships or renewals because the systems were so complex. The suffering YMCA was probably turning away a thousand dollars of business daily.

There are many ways for a top executive to find out what is going on in the shop. One way is to rely on the chain of command for accurate and timely reports. But often the assistants tell their leaders what they think the leaders want to hear. They protect the leader from "unnecessary" worries by filtering the information, and they protect their jobs by harboring information rather than sharing it. Thus they remain essential to the smooth functioning of the entire operation. At least 15 percent of the information received by the chief executive should come from personal observations and investigations. Part of each work week should be devoted to getting firsthand information from the employees and members at the places where the service is delivered. Instead of asking unfocused questions such as "How's it going," seek specific information with well-defined queries.

For example, I used to meet parents in the lobby as they picked up their children after sessions. I would walk down the hall with them and enquire about their child's experience. This routine check usually yielded replies of satisfaction, but when there was some unhappiness expressed, I could follow up on it. If I had not done this, I would have had only the staff's verbal evaluation of the program and a written summary of the parents' end-of-session evaluations.

Study Board Meeting Exhibits, Annual Reports, and Other Material

Early in any audit, conduct an analysis of current and previously used materials. Ask for the written evaluations of previous campaigns; frequently they are available but staff forget to mention them. Get copies of the long-range plan, earlier market studies, records of board and staff retreats.

My friend Diane Ward is a museum membership marketing specialist whose first steps with a client involve a thorough study of the data already on hand. She said many museums are spending a lot of money and staff time on marketing, but they don't understand it. So she takes their membership data and searches for ages, household incomes, and length of memberships. Using some mathematical proportionate analyses, she will create marketing models for the staff: "If you do this, the outcome is likely to be. . . ."

Very busy staff may accept some simple marketing statistics, but Ward digs deeper. In her own analysis of membership renewal rates, she finds big variations between young members and older members, between first-year members and ten-year members. Her rules of thumb are that first-year members' renewal rate may be 51 percent on average. People who have held museum memberships for three or four years typically renew at the 70 percent rate. Those who have held museum membership cards for ten years almost always renew. Such figures are important for an auditor who is looking for any deviations from the norm.

Information that management provides the board of directors can be useful in assessing the performance of an NPO. Most NPO reports discuss the service efforts and activities. Ideally, they should also provide some measurement of the service accomplishments, but unfortunately, this information is usually hard to come by. Similarly, information on the efficiency of the NPO is more available than information about its effectiveness. There is no universal agreement about what to count and how to compare data. Much of the NPO information will not be quantifiable.

Board and annual reports should provide information that helps the organization's supporters make rational decisions. Insist on consistent historical numerical data. The figures needed to judge each organization's effectiveness will differ, but it is important to measure the inputs and the processes (what the NPO is doing) to gain some understanding of both its efficiency and effectiveness.

Inputs are such resources as money, time, personnel, equipment, facilities, and contracted services. For a college the inputs would include the number of faculty, number of library books, buildings, and square footage of floor space available for various activities.

Quantifiable *outputs* would include credit hours, degrees granted, reports published, and attendance. The results of all this could be expressed in terms of the number of students who go on for higher degrees, the number who were successfully placed in jobs, and the number who joined the alumni association.

The outputs of a human service organization might be the tons of clothing picked up and distributed and the number of people with disabilities employed in the process. The quantifiable results might be the number of people who found employment after rehabilitation.

A hospital would measure its efficiency by including such items as the number of nursing hours worked per patient-day or the hours per treatment. *Efficiency* is the relationship between an organization's efforts and its results. When personnel hours are multiplied by hourly wage rates and then divided by the number of days of care, a unit cost is produced. That quantifies efficiency.

There is a lack of trend information in most NPO reports. Seemingly we include trends and related historical data when they suit our purposes and omit them when they do not contribute to the case we are trying to make. There is no accounting rule that says one must include past seasons' enrollments when reporting on the current season. I urge managers and volunteer board members to seek comparative statistics for five years or more.

Cost-Benefit Assessment

Managers of NPOs are not in agreement about appropriate ways to identify and measure results of their service. Thus it is practically impossible to get agreement on the comparative effectiveness of different NPOs. The costs of acquiring measurable information for comparison purposes seems to exceed the benefits. This holds true for NPOs of all sizes. Comparative effectiveness has to be a matter of faith.

The costs of using outsiders for auditing and formal market research depend on frequency and extensiveness, as well as on method. A rule of thumb about formal research costs is that they may easily approximate 1 to 2 percent of your annual operating budget.

You can significantly reduce the costs by asking fewer questions, thereby simplifying the process of acquiring data, tabulating it, and preparing reports. Asking questions that give the responders limited choices makes tabulating much easier.

Easy processes, questions, and answers make us feel good. Unfortunately, they frequently fail to give us the information we need. Difficult situations give us a headache, but they are more likely to provide the answers we need for the long run. We can start simply and add complexity when we are ready. The important task is to *start*: start asking questions right away.

The Timing of Audits

Clearly, you should conduct an audit to discover strengths, weaknesses, opportunities, and threats as soon as you take a new job. It is wise to get an accurate assessment of the current situation so you can measure the effect of your efforts. Planning expert John Bryson (1995) points out that gathering information about strengths and weaknesses is usually a process directed inwardly toward the organization. The assessment of opportunities and threats is usually external and future oriented. The distinctions between internal and external, present and future are fluid, Bryson says, and people should not worry too much about whether they have made them properly.

Periodic careful assessments of external as well as internal organizational factors are necessary because the jobs of most managers preclude paying much attention to external events. Most of their jobs demand a rather intense internal focus. Except for a weekly service club meeting, NPO managers may spend very little time outside their place of employment. Without some good external monitoring devices, they are vulnerable to being blindsided and victimized by external developments.

One of the benefits of belonging to a national organization is the external environmental scanning reports they usually provide. Newsletters and electronic message boards give legislative updates on government deliberations. The parent organizations frequently provide periodic demographic information and synopses of potentially relevant market studies. Consultants use newsletters to do the same. For example, in the mid 1990s some of the fundraising trends I noted and reported to local groups were the following:

- Government institutions were competing more frequently with private NPOs in the philanthropic marketplace. Examples include the John F. Kennedy Center for the Performing Arts, the National Archives, and state colleges.

- Increasing government regulations were having a negative impact on some NPO budgets.

- For-profit businesses in related sectors of the economy were pressing for NPOs to pay taxes.

- Local governments were looking everywhere for more tax revenue, and NPOs were no longer exempt from their consideration.

- There is a growing number of NPOs, and most were established since 1960. This has put competitive fundraising pressure on the traditional NPOs.

- Ninety percent of large companies have formal programs encouraging employees to volunteer. About 13 percent of employees did volunteer work.

- Cause-related marketing continues to grow as corporations seek more positive public relations in exchange for their donations.

- Donors are looking for more proof of an NPO's effectiveness and integrity. There is less trust.

- There is more pressure for individual board members to be better fundraisers.

- United Way funding for the traditional agencies decreased as a percentage of their total income.

- The United Way is losing exclusive control over workplace fundraising. Other federated campaigns have gained access to payroll deductions.

- Donations are shifting from social service agencies to projects for the homeless and hungry.

Taking his university's strengths, weaknesses, opportunities, and threats into account (called a SWOT analysis by planners), Mark Lloyd devised a marketing plan for Bloomsburg University, Pennsylvania, in 1995. He prepared the report six months after joining the administration, which is important because he still had the fresh view of an outsider. His document started with three pages of background information serving as an inarguable audit. Establishing an undebatable assessment of the current situation in his academic setting was a very important step for Lloyd to take before launching into his prescription. Mark's audit mentioned that university sales (meaning enrollments) were down 5 percent over the past four years, the number of applications had dropped by 11 percent, and the retention rate of enrolled students also seemed to be on the decline. He quickly explained the plight (decline in the size of the applicant pool, a national fall-off of interest in business disciplines among young people) and plunged into a SWOT analysis. The elements discussed as institutional strengths included student placement rates, student-faculty ratio, leadership, facilities, and pricing. The weaknesses he cited were a lack of marketing culture, a diminishing price advantage, financial pressures that diminished flexibility, diffused responsibility for marketing, and undifferentiated services. The opportunities Lloyd saw for the university were favorable demographics, partnership opportunities, and centers of excellence. Threats included a decline in reputed quality, more choices available to area residents, and a decline in federal support for education.

If you are not yet ready to create your own marketing audit and plan from scratch like Lloyd did, then consider using *The Marketing Plan Workbook* by James C. Makens (1985). It is a good place to find plenty of audit and planning forms to start the process. The forms have to be adapted to fit NPOs, but that is not difficult.

Measuring the success of any NPO's marketing program is particularly difficult, as I have mentioned earlier. A college audit can track the number of applications, number of students, faculty salaries and those of the competition, alumni support, and appearances in the press. But those figures have to be carefully weighed to determine their true value. The college may have been mentioned twenty times in the press last month, but if they were all in the local paper and the school draws from a much wider area, the twenty mentions are of less value. If the stories were negative reports of campus activities, that is even worse.

As you approach the audit, consider the recommendations of Robert Rubright and Dan MacDonald (1981). They said audits should be conducted every year or so, and written check-off lists should guide the process. Audits are best performed by people independent of the organization. The auditor's report should include his or her recommendations following the data and analysis, and the audits are to be completed prior to the development of any marketing plans.

James Hardy (1984) writes that an annual review and update of an organization's corporate goals and planning process are essential to continuity, renewal, improvement, and relevance in planning. Reviewing and evaluating performance against annual and long-range goals are parts of the auditing process.

The objectives of an annual review of corporate or department goals are to make adjustments in light of internal and external changes that have occurred and to identify any weaknesses in the planning system that may require corrective action. Hardy (1994) says that ideally the entire board of directors as well as key staff members should be involved in an annual review and update session lasting an average of four hours (p. 198). It is the CEO's responsibility to direct the process of gathering essential information and presenting a summary of organizational performance in response to each goal. In his book *Managing for Impact in Nonprofit Organizations* (1984), Hardy provides useful forms for assessing progress toward specific goals. He also suggests forms for periodic performance evaluation of individual units comprising the organization, staff work performance reviews, and a special review of the chief executive's annual performance.

Studying recent records of the various formal reviews will provide you with powerful insights into the health of the organization. Organizations that are without any such records of recent formal performance review are vulnerable to criticism. If they don't have formal written audits of personnel and corporate performance, perhaps they have no well-defined goals. If they have not drafted goals and objectives within the last year, perhaps they are not focusing enough attention on the outside environment, the external factors that have an impact on internal functioning.

Bryson (1995) says one should always try to get a strategic planning team to consider what is going on outside the organization before it considers what is going on inside. "Attending to the outside is crucial, because the social and political justification for virtually every organization's existence is what it does, or proposes to do, about external social or political problems" (p. 102).

Audits of organizational strengths, weaknesses, opportunities, and threats (SWOT analyses) provide the basis for good group discussion. Bryson (1995) warns there is a human tendency to focus too much on the weaknesses, which he labels "action inhibitors," rather than focusing discussion on strengths that serve to facilitate action. Focusing more on positive attributes turns a group away from its tendencies to assign blame and avoid action. It is important to turn weaknesses into challenges to be overcome.

Part Three

Successful Marketing Strategies

Chapter Seven

Promotion, Publicity, and PR

Effective Ways to Get More Customers, Members, and Donors

Your very first step in promoting and advertising your services is to write a good description of the one, two, or three typical customers you want to reach. List their salient demographic characteristics, lifestyle patterns, purchasing behaviors, and frequency of use or support of your NPO.

As described in Chapter Four, sharply defining your key customer types is important to achieving efficiency in a promotion program, yet most of us feel we know intuitively or through experience who our targets are. We skip the seemingly laborious and unnecessary first step. But our choices of message, media, budget, timing, color, paper stock, print size, type style, and placement should be dictated less by experience of what we have done before, and more by what will work best with our ever-changing customers.

Once you have adequately described whom you want to reach, you need to do some further thinking about these target audiences. Seek staff consensus about what customers are thinking about your organization, your program, and their other choices (your competition). Decide which existing positive attitudes you can build on, whether there are some negative attitudes you must overcome, and whether some new attitudes need to be created.

When planning a campaign, you should define your goals in detail. Answer the following four questions as specifically as possible.

1. *What do we want to accomplish?* Set enrollment goals, income goals, desired changes in actions, desired attitudinal changes, and new levels of contributions.

2. *What is our assessment of the marketplace?* How is the economy? Where are the new developments? What adverse news concerns the public? What is our competition doing? What regulatory or government action is pending?

3. *What do we want to say?* What are a few key thoughts we want people to have about us? What simple sentence would we like people to say about us in comparison with similar service providers? What are our major selling points?

4. *How are we going to judge the effectiveness of our promotion program?* Through enrollments, donations, phone calls, increased allocations from present supporters, independent research to measure attitudes, or some combination of these?

An effective promotion uses the least amount of staff time and money to achieve the objective, yet once again most of us simply resort to the most familiar methods. The purpose of this chapter is to examine the comparative benefits of different promotion, publicity, and advertising methods, and to suggest ways to get greater persuasive power from them.

Initial Considerations

Consumers are barraged with advertising messages and promotion efforts. The average consumer receives between two thousand and six thousand advertising messages every day (Sloan, 1987), so you have to be very good to get your message noticed and favorably acted on. The competition for people's attention intensifies every year. For example, in 1979 the Catholic churches in the Delaware River Valley spent $70,000 for a twelve-week evangelizing campaign designed primarily to improve Catholics' self-image. In the early 1980s Christian churches throughout the nation began buying advertising to attract and keep more churchgoers. They paid significantly more money each year to get their messages off the religion pages of the newspaper (where they felt they were only speaking to themselves) and into a mainstream where they were more likely to gain attention. Public service announcements were not enough. Ads were aimed at a variety of markets: newcomers, backsliders, the lonely and disheartened (Yao, 1979). By 1995, church ads on radio and TV had doubled over the past decade, and billboard advertising had tripled (Housewright, 1995).

Facing an aging congregation in a city fighting economic decline, a synagogue in Perth Amboy, New Jersey, offered $2,500 in 1996 to families willing to relocate and help revitalize the community (Sharn, 1996). Other orthodox synagogues have had to employ marketing methods unorthodox to them. Jewish families who moved in 1996 to the Edgewood Park section of New Haven, Connecticut, for example, could get $5,000 interest-free loans from the synagogue.

Colleges, too, have hunted aggressively for prospective customers (students). Administrators were frightened by demographers' predictions that the number of high school graduates would decline. With their traditional feeder markets predicted to shrink, colleges launched new marketing efforts to win attention and commitment from adults of all ages. LaSalle University promoted an open house by placing large ads in the *Philadelphia Inquirer* saying "Spend one day at LaSalle and we think you'll stay for four years."

Faced with an exodus of middle-income families and the threat of the voucher program that would enable children to attend private schools, public school administrators are now adapting the marketing techniques long used by private schools. A recent California law requires that all school districts allow children to transfer to any school in their district if there is space and the transfer does not upset racial balances. The motivation to use marketing techniques is not only to boost enrollment and the state aid tied to it but also to increase parental involvement, a proven factor in academic achievement.

Hospitals have used a wide range of promotion methods to attract patients. The techniques of hospital marketers have included radio advertising, public relations activities such as ten-kilometer runs and sports injury clinics, speakers' bureaus, one-on-one visits with physicians, newsletters, booths at conventions, mailings to every household in the immediate community, open houses, referral services, billboard advertising, and cooperative relationships with YMCAs and other fitness centers.

All of these institutions were trying to get people's attention amid the noise and clutter of the marketplace. But just getting attention is not enough. The prospect must be moved to action. There are several steps involved.

Moving from Information to Action

Initial awareness may spark some expressed interest, culminating in positive action. There are four general sources that can stimulate initial awareness of, and interest in, your NPO: (1) personal sources, including friends, coworkers, parents, children, and neighbors; (2) public sources, which include mass media such as radio, newspapers, and TV; (3) NPO sources, including advertisements, mailings, solicitations, flyers, speeches, and events for the public; (4) personal experience, which can take the form of facility tours, workshops, and telephone enquiries with staff.

During the initial awareness phase, our goal is to stimulate general good feelings about and acceptance of our NPO. We are communicating our existence to get people interested in us.

Publicity is usually directed to the general population. The purpose is more specific than simply to increase general public awareness. It is to increase everyone's understanding of the breadth and depth of the NPO's services and to suggest the value of those services.

Promotion efforts get a specific number of people to act positively for our NPO. The goals of promotion are to convince people that our service is as good as we say it is and to stimulate their desire to get involved, donate, vote in our favor, enroll, or whatever.

The San Diego Zoo has been marvelously successful at the first stage. It has a widely recognized image, but that is not enough to get attendance. People know the zoo is there and always will be, so a decision to visit can always be put off. The challenge for the zoo staff is to move people to the final stage of action. At this last stage, prospects should be considering the following questions: What do I have to do to get what is offered? What personal benefits will I get from a commitment to this organization? What is the price? How long will it take to get the benefits promised?

Once prospects have answered these questions satisfactorily, they will usually be ready for the plunge. We don't need total commitment to be successful at this last stage. Our long-term purposes can sometimes be accomplished if we get prospects to serve on a committee; try an abbreviated session as a sample; allow our staff or volunteers to visit their home or office; write the date of our special event in their appointment calendar; permit us to distribute flyers through their school, shop, or office; or meet us for lunch and further discussion (which presumes the ultimate sale).

Getting to that final stage is not easy. We can tell our story, but if the prospects are not listening, if we don't have their attention, our efforts are useless. Without success in the first stages of awareness and attention-getting, we will not be able to persuade anyone or move them to action.

Using Psychology

Draw upon some psychology as you plan and create your campaign materials. Keep the following points about people's behavior and interests in mind.

- People follow leaders whom they trust and have confidence in, so get some respected, well-known leaders involved in your program.
- People react best under the pressure of deadlines, so give them a specific and rather immediate time when action must take place. Don't let them easily put off deciding.
- People easily lose their sense of identity. Mobility and change in American communities create an opportunity for enterprising

NPOs to build a sense of belonging, even if the bonding is only through newsletters.

- People give incomplete attention to things. They notice only a small portion of your message, so help them remember it by keeping the message simple. Repeat it.

- People glance instead of read. They seek quick impressions so that they won't have to read the entire text. Therefore, carefully select type size, pictures, and colors. Ask outsiders to quickly glance at your promotion materials and give you their candid first impressions of the organization.

- People generalize about the whole organization from small fragments of information. They jump to conclusions based on little more than your letterhead, grammar, posture, and lawn. Who pays sufficient attention to those details in your organization?

- People are suspicious of perfection. You gain more trust by admitting a failure or a poor choice. You can lose by appearing too good to be true, whereas you can disarm someone by admitting to some imperfections.

- People respond best to emotional appeals. Where is the emotional appeal in your messages?

- People like their leaders and their organizations to have some dignity. That makes it easier for them to justify their support and involvement.

- People resist change from the familiar, so call the change something else, something less threatening to their security and pattern of doing things.

- People like it most when you address them as individuals. Personalized communications work best.

- People don't like strangers, so carefully introduce staff members, board members, and others by using newsletters, bulletin boards, and personal introductions.

- People like the feeling of power. They like to be on committees that really make things happen. They don't like to see those power-confirming sessions end quickly (though they may say they do). They like to be sought after for their opinions.

Preparing Materials

Seek to make all of your materials speak well to the conditions of those you want most to serve. Increase their comfort level with your NPO.

Magazine publishers have responded to the breaking up of the women's market into many different interests by electing to focus on one important aspect of a woman's life and covering it editorially better than anyone. The same principle has worked for magazines on both ends of the spectrum: *Good Housekeeping* and *Savvy*. As Cecelia Lentini stated, "Their common success seems to prove that although the traditional woman of twenty years ago may no longer exist, there's still plenty of room in the women's market for all types of magazines—as long as they define their purpose and fulfill it well" (1981).

Good Housekeeping's strength is its ability to provide better and more highly respected service than its competitors. The *Good Housekeeping* seal of approval has been a standard American criterion for product acceptance. Articles in the magazine focus on food, health, and diet. It also regularly runs stories on abortion, rape, justice for Native Americans, civil rights, and the right to die with dignity. The stories are usually told in the first person, with a chatty, informal tone. They are designed to appeal to the traditional woman.

Savvy magazine, by contrast, has found a comfortable market niche by appealing to an elite group of the top 5 percent of the female workforce. In its first year it reached an outstanding circulation level of 250,000, zeroing in on highly educated women whose work was the primary shaping force in their lives.

It is not just a career that separates the *Savvy* reader from the *Good Housekeeping* reader. The demographic differences are clear. Whereas the typical *Good Housekeeping* reader is age thirty-nine, her *Savvy* counterpart is thirty-four. The *Good Housekeeping* reader has half the household income enjoyed by the *Savvy* reader. But the main difference is in values. Working in the commercial market-place is the central focus of the *Savvy* reader but not of the *Good Housekeeping* reader. Each publication addresses the values of its typical readers.

Now, how about your NPO publications? Do they reflect their targeted readers' values through and through, or do they reflect the biases and personal judgments of the writers? More often than not, our publications are centered on staff values rather than customer values. What about your materials for the nonprint media? As we prepare all our messages for targeted audiences, knowing and reflecting their values and concerns become major assignments.

Both *Good Housekeeping* and *Savvy* are trying to stay in touch with what their readers want. It was easier for the younger magazine to assume a bold new stance than it was for the older one. *Good Housekeeping* changes have had to be gradual. Its editors felt that if they changed overnight they would lose a significant number of current readers, more than would be replaced.

You should know the values of your customers, consumers, and supporters. Each group's values may be decidedly different. Burger King's ads, for example, used to be directed squarely at children. Although parents decided when the family would go out for dinner, children exercised significant influence over where the family ate. Because the parents had to be happy once they got to Burger King, management decided to remodel the stores, replacing the plastic shrubbery with live plants and adding softer lighting. The kids got their interests met while the parents enjoyed the ambience more. Both sides were satisfied, and so was Burger King when large numbers visited frequently.

To make our advertising and promotion efforts more effective, we need to use more of what we already know about our customers. Now that we know there are definite market segments that need to be addressed, should we always draft a different brochure for each? That is probably both uneconomical and unnecessary. A single creative strategy will probably work as long as it builds on positive images and contains no put-down clichés. For example, all sixteen segments of the women's market can be addressed in one piece that warmly communicates a recognition of women's changing roles and the increased pressures they face. It may also be done with charm, a light touch, and contemporary style. Rena Bartos (1982), author of *The Moving Target: What Every Marketer Should Know About Women,* counsels that (1) all market segments of women have much more in common than we might have assumed, (2) housewives are not turned off by seeing ads portraying women who work outside, (3) we do not need to show working women in an occupational role to reach them, and (4) housewives as well as working women respond most positively to contemporary commercials and imagery and most negatively to traditional images.

This kind of information gives our NPO brochure and catalog designers clear directions. When we can show proper sensitivity to all the segments in one marketing piece, we do not have to design separate flyers, newsletters, or public service announcements for each segment.

Promotion

A promotion is a short-term incentive to increase purchases. Advertising and promotion use different types of vehicles. Advertising vehicles include TV, radio, print, and outdoor media. Promotion makes use of exhibits, sampling, coupons, sales, discounts, incentives, consumer education, demonstrations, direct mail, and specials.

Promotions emerged among NPOs when simple announcements of activities and services failed to get enough responses. When museum attendance and memberships did not pay the bills, museums launched special promotions. The most memorable have been blockbuster shows such as the King Tut exhibit. Similarly, theater groups have had to promote hard to stay alive.

The Boy Scouts of America (BSA) distributed detailed promotion plans to all local councils to fill its national High Adventure

Programs. A BSA workbook encouraged local Scout leaders to plan their promotions in detail twenty-one months before visiting one of six base sites. No price incentives were offered, however—only a reminder that capacity utilization of the camps would benefit everyone. High Adventure Programs could not become financial burdens to the national organizations, the local leaders were told. Assuming that everyone wanted the benefits of a high adventure program in Scouting but that the program wouldn't happen without special effort, a promotion effort was called for.

Promotion activities were needed to lure more paying customers to college athletic events, particularly football and basketball. For example, Wichita State's athletic director, Ted Bredenhoft, planned a turkey scramble in which a dozen turkeys were to be let loose on the football field—that is, until the Humane Society interceded. (Participants scrambled for a dozen frozen turkeys instead.) Said Bredenhoft, "We were the first school to bring in the Dallas Cowboy cheerleaders to entertain at a football game; we brought in a half dozen camels from California for a series of half-time races; and we had a hot dogs, apple pie and Chevrolet night at a basketball game—awarding a compact Chevy to one of the 58,000 fans" (Roessing, 1981, p. 48).

The University of Miami baseball team experienced a budget cut despite their winning seasons and College World Series experience. Coach Ron Fraser countered with a series of promotions that boosted attendance 77 percent. He had raffles, exhibition games with professional teams, international musicians, and even an "income tax night" on April 14. He also made a profit from the sale of sports-fan paraphernalia such as T-shirts, caps, jackets, and drinking glasses. There is little limit on the variety of merchandise that can carry a team's or other organization's colors and logo and be sold as promotional items: chairs, pants, skirts, hats, wildlife prints of the team mascot, coloring books, dolls, wastebaskets, and inflatable toys.

College coaches' and athletic directors' jobs have changed from the days when they could concentrate solely on strengthening the team, arranging schedules, and buttering up alumni. Now they have to promote and do fundraising to generate more revenue.

All game and performance tickets are for a perishable product. Unused seats cannot be stockpiled and sold at a later date when demand increases, so it behooves management to get the maximum volume at each opportunity. To maximize revenue, the price has to be sensitively set as high as the traffic will bear. For example, to test price receptivity, the Brooklyn Academy of Music sent two small and limited promotional mailings offering the same series at two prices—$20 and $25—to different mailing lists, then compared the responses. If they drew the same response, the higher price was chosen for promotion to a much larger mailing. If the lower price was chosen, those who responded to the higher-price offer got refund checks—many of which were returned as donations (Ricklefs, 1979, p. 1).

Art institutions have effectively used many promotional techniques. The Milwaukee Repertory Theater Company flooded the mail with 350,000 leaflets annually and thus sold ten times as many subscriptions as a year earlier. In Louisville, Kentucky, the Actors Theater used hundreds of coffee klatches to help increase subscriptions by 500 percent.

Although arts groups and museums reach the widest audience when they offer blockbuster shows, they can also target mailings with a well-chosen message to a small, selected group for a very good return on their promotional efforts. The Brooklyn Academy of Music, for example, sent flyers to its drama subscribers complimenting them as "among the most adventuresome people in town." Pleased respondents snapped up dance series subscriptions. A similar flyer was sent to its music program subscribers flattering them, too, as dance enthusiasts. These compliments to both the fans of music and the fans of drama effectively yielded more dance subscriptions.

The people who typically respond to promotions are seeking more for their money. They are intrigued by the chance to win a new car, get a dollar rebate, take home a teddy bear. A survey by

Frankel and Company of Chicago revealed the types of people who respond most often to promotional offers (Simon, 1984). They usually are on moderate incomes. They are cautious planners, bargain hunters who shop with a purpose and a list. They budget their expenses, usually shop once a week, and plan their meals for the entire week. This description fits the stay-at-home woman. Probably the career woman would be least likely to take time to respond to the average promotion.

Before picking a particular promotion program, seek agreement on its specific purpose; different purposes lend themselves to different types of promotions. For example:

To create community awareness of your services: try contests, sweepstakes, or drawings.

To attract new customers: offer a bargain, coupons, an open house with a premium, or a trial use or sample. For example, each person joining the National Arbor Day Foundation ($10) is offered ten free trees with planting instructions.

To keep loyal customers: offer a discount for re-enrolling, a special performance or party (exclusive special event), or membership privileges.

To increase sales to present customers: offer bonus packs (six programs for the price of two), discounts or premiums with multiple purchases, coupons, or discounts simply because customers are in our "family" (museum store discounts for members).

Caveats About Promotion

NPO advertising consists mostly of letting people know of our program. NPO promotion is a concentrated effort to get people to buy *now*. Compare your NPO marketing practices with that of profit-seeking industries. Businesses have experienced greater growth in their promotion expenses than in their advertising expenditures. Promotion is playing a progressively more important role for them.

More emphasis has been directed toward promotion efforts for three main reasons, not all of them positive. First, promotion stimulates immediate sales and improved cash flow; however, sometimes the quick fix comes at the expense of long-term organization growth.

Second, promotion activities turn customers' attention away from comparison (where there often are no discernible differences). Promotions hook interest by offering a premium, potential prize, or lower price through rebates, coupons, or packaging specials.

Third, promotions enable the staff to look good and improve their status long enough to get promoted. The long-term consequences of price discounting or the true promotional campaign costs are rarely studied thoroughly before a new staff star is given the opportunity to move up the ladder. Short-term successes get more attention and reward than long-term strength. A new program director is hired; he or she adopts an aggressive promotion strategy, achieves some early success, and takes another job before anyone analyzes the effect of his or her success on loyal, long-term members' satisfaction and the attendant budgetary consequences.

The cost effectiveness of promotions is usually not explored in depth. Managers often get caught up in the excitement of new promotional ideas. Financially analyzing proposals seems tantamount to throwing cold water on ideas. Our typical budgeting process is to ask, How much did we spend last time? How much do we have budgeted this year? How will we spend it?

To get approval to do what they want, some managers will exaggerate the potential of their proposed promotion program. An anticipated large response can get more money invested early in the promotion. Later, if the responses are not what were expected, the manager may switch attention to a comparison with his or her predecessor's results when no promotion occurred. It is not hard to figure out the cost of a promotion and assign it as a charge against the revenue the promotion generates. But too often this is not done. Attention is focused instead on inappropriate comparisons or the next big event.

NPO managers must bear in mind that promotions have limited value. They can give short-term jolts to the cash intake, but in general they contribute to long-term growth only under certain conditions (Strang, 1976). Promotions can induce a trial use and thereby are good for launching a new or improved program. Promotion can also speed up enrollments in a program where customer interest is already growing stronger. However, in a declining market, the program will most often continue its long-term slide despite promotions (Peckham, 1976). Table 7.1 illustrates this concept.

Evaluating Promotions

Promotion planning should have a long-term consideration. Managers should ask themselves, "If we discount membership fees or offer a blockbuster attraction now, will we have to do likewise in later years? Are tax authorities going to view our NPO as competing unfairly with taxpaying businesses and hold us responsible for fees in lieu of taxes? Are we jeopardizing our tax-free nonprofit status? Is the promotion going to solve the problem or merely postpone our addressing a larger problem?"

Managers have the most job security when production goals and budgets are met. It is no wonder, then, that they succumb to promotions to gain short-term benefits. This can be countered when top management modifies performance expectations for program directors and membership directors to keep them in the same job longer. Then we also gain the benefit of their experience.

You should set specific objectives to evaluate each promotion. It is not enough just to compare sales with the previous period or a year ago. Other factors that influence sales should be taken into account: weather, strikes, the newness of a facility, competition.

In addition, be aware that promotion tends to cause present users and supporters to buy or support more, or more often, rather

Table 7.1. Effect of Promotions on Enrollments.

Program with	Before Promotion	During Promotion	After Promotion
Declining trend	100	96	93
Stable demand	100	105	100
Increasing trend	100	110	107

than bring new buyers in. Increased sales to new customers are more likely when the copy introduces something new about the program, or when the message tries to change, rather than just reinforce, consumer attitudes (Potter, 1992).

Promotion campaign goals can be set at three levels: pessimistic, realistic, and optimistic. The optimistic goal is often suggested by the person with the greatest vision or enthusiasm for the campaign's potential. The realistic goal is simply what you have achieved in the past. The pessimistic goal is a correction point. When results hit that number you must enact certain remedies.

A promotion designed to bring potential customers to a service center can be evaluated by a questionnaire offered to people just before they are about to leave. This next-out-the-door method ensures that all people have an equal chance of being interviewed, and catches both buyers and nonbuyers. The questionnaire should reveal the demographic characteristics of people making special visits, what they liked and disliked about the promotion, and even their awareness of it. By interviewing everyone exiting you can also find out how frequently current clients use the services and what they did during this visit. From new visitors who enroll, you can find out what persuaded them.

What is the ability of the promotion to generate special visits or extra usage among current members? It is the net new enrollments, not the traffic volume of visitors, that enables you to judge the financial value of your promotion. The number of special visits or inquiries your promotion generates and the immediate conversion of those to enrollments are the figures most important to determine when evaluating the success of a promotion geared to increasing facility membership.

Table 7.2 presents a calculation showing how a facility promotion might be evaluated from questionnaire information. In this case, the promotion was not as successful as might appear at first glance.

By comparing the results of several promotions, you can identify the patterns leading toward success. For example: are contests with the lure of a giant prize more successful with your customers than those that offer many smaller prizes? Do seasonal promotions during the normal peak of interest do more for you than promotions during lull periods? Do bargain deadlines, such as "renew at the old price before midnight December 31," work? What is most likely to bring in new customers? Be careful when offering price breaks, however. You can overdo it. Consumers offered a significant price break promotion will usually delay further purchases until the next big price break rolls around, even though you assure them none is planned. They reason that when your cash flow is threatened, their stalling strategy will pay off.

Enrollment promotion generally includes a price incentive. Either the customers save money or get more for their money. When you shift marketing emphasis away from advertising to price promotion you are identifying price as your major marketing element. Price competition generally indicates problems in your marketplace. The logic is that you would not be lowering your price if you didn't have to. For a nonprofit organization, in particular, lowering the price temporarily during a promotion gives the impression that the regular price is too high—that not enough people are drawn to the service or program at the regular price. Even, perhaps, that those who pay the full price are paying too much.

Though I have shared with you the positive and negative considerations of price promotions, I strongly advocate that most, if not all, NPOs should avoid price discounting. It is like a lot of things that may make you feel good in the short run but are not good for you in the long run. It is better by far to run an organization with

Table 7.2. Evaluating a Facility Promotion.

Total people surveyed	1,000	100 percent
Number aware of promotion	700	70 percent
Number unaware of promotion	300	30 percent
Became new customers	120	12 percent
Already our customers	600	60 percent
Visited but did not enroll	280	28 percent
Made special visit to enroll because of promotion	120	12 percent
Promotion did not influence visit	880	88 percent
	1,000	100 percent
Number who made special visits to enroll		120
× Average membership fee		$20
= Additional revenue due to promotion		$2,400
× Average contribution toward overhead of a membership		80 percent
= Additional net revenue from promotion		$1,920
– Cost of the promotion		$2,000
= Net proceeds of promotion program		($80)

everyday fair prices and special arrangements for people who cannot afford the full fees.

Enrollment promotions will continue to increase sharply with all NPOs—zoos, the military, hospitals, dance troupes, and the like. Top management needs to be aware of the risks, the implications, and the best ways to make promotions effective in both the short and the long run.

Public Relations and Publicity

Publicity is the process of getting your story told by the media without paying for it. Your goal is to get stories told that boost your sales and support. The Salvation Army fundraising kettle campaign with volunteer bell-ringers during the Christmas season always receives local television publicity. The Red Cross receives lots of free publicity every time it responds to a national disaster. Similarly, food assistance programs and homeless shelters usually get publicized in the newspaper and on TV during times of pressing community need.

You can get free media coverage by publicizing new services, the opening of new facilities, entertainers and important guests, and innovative services to meet community needs. The American Diabetes Association (ADA), for example, got stories in lots of women's magazines during National Diabetes Month, a time event they initiated. In March, each state is rated by the ADA using a diabetes index of about fifty factors, and the comparative ratings are issued to the press. The ADA gets plenty of publicity because of interest in how states compare.

Try to cultivate specific people in the local media so that when you need their support they are favorably inclined. Make your friends before you need them. This can be done through a press conference, a background session for the media, lunch, visits in their shop, and attendance at their special events.

Profit-seeking companies invest large sums for public relations efforts in hopes of generating sales. Examine their promotion efforts to get ideas for your NPO. For example, Kenner Products created "Workshops for Baby-Sitters" in New York, Houston, and Los Angeles aimed at junior high school students. Kenner felt that parents wanted baby-sitters to do something more constructive than simply let the children watch TV. Their seminars covered topics of safety and first aid, how to play with children and keep them interested, and how baby-sitters could make personal savings goals for school and other needs. They told baby-sitters it would help if they took a bag of toys—Kenner products ideally—to keep the children's interest high.

The direct costs of the Kenner program were only $5,500 in each city. That included the lecturer's fee, creative concept time, preparing the lecture outline, and enlisting the support of the local boards of education. For that investment, Kenner generated free publicity about the seminars (and the Kenner company) that reached an estimated 2,000,000 TV viewers, 2,164,000 radio listeners, and 32,329,000 newspaper readers.

One of my predecessors in YMCA public relations management had a man wrestle a bear in the gymnasium. Three of the San Francisco TV stations covered the event and showed it that night. None, however, mentioned the YMCA, and no new memberships were attributed to the publicity. Public relations efforts should be linked closely to formal, written marketing plans of your organization. At events, program specialists should be on hand to support any generalists on the program. For example, a YMCA fitness expert should have been on hand for the bear wrestling to point out the advantages of being in good physical condition and well prepared for any emergency. A Humane Society official could take the bear's side.

Both advertising and public relations seek to place your message before a large audience. Here are some of the differences that will affect the content of your publicity and help you decide what to expect from your efforts.

Publicity	Advertising
Free	Paid
Goal: awareness	Goals: awareness, persuasion, and action
Little NPO control over way information is presented to public	NPO control of who gets it, when they get it, and media used
Usually can't ask people to join	Can ask for the order
May not result in increased demand	Should create greater demand

Although the focus of most public relations efforts is on a large audience, we must not lose sight of our best form of publicity: positive word-of-mouth spread by our own satisfied members and staff. A good public relations program will seek to keep our members and employees informed. No matter how large the organization, there should be an effort in publications to create a sense of family, of belonging to a warm and caring organization.

To achieve this familial goal we should seek to create a friendly, but not necessarily informal, atmosphere. Our publications and bulletin boards can introduce new staff to the membership and acknowledge the achievements of individuals. Staff can learn to say thank you more often: to new members for joining, to volunteers, to supporters. The executive director can write more letters of appreciation and congratulations. More telephone calls can be made thanking reporters for excellent articles and donors for gifts. The best public relations spring from expressing appreciation well.

It is easy to get caught up in the excitement of a publicity campaign. Indeed, any attempt to measure its results in terms of sales may be seen by the person who got the publicity as a lack of personal support. We're asked to be satisfied by the scrapbook of press clippings.

But a good publicity effort must be expected to meet specific goals. Someone should be held accountable for documenting its results. There should be specific, measurable goals for publicity alone. If you erroneously define the goal as increased market share, the goal would be indistinguishable from the total marketing effort. When you charge only direct costs, and conduct the publicity campaign prior to and separate from other marketing efforts, it is possible to quantify the results, as the following example shows.

Estimated enrollments due to publicity campaign	$10,000
Average contribution toward overhead of each enrollment	–2,000
Contribution margin from campaign	$8,000
Direct costs (only) of the publicity	–2,000
Net contribution toward overhead	$6,000

This example shows that an investment of $2,000 (not counting staff time) produced an additional $10,000. Supposing it costs $2,000 to serve the new enrollees, the net benefit—the publicity's contribution—is $6,000. When this is divided by the $2,000 investment, the return on investment is 300 percent. You made three dollars for every dollar spent.

When NPOs cannot get what they need through publicity and promotions, some resort to buying advertising. The advantages and strategies of advertising are explained in the next chapter.

Chapter Eight

Making Advertising Work for Your Nonprofit

Much to the delight of the advertising industry, a study in 1987 by the Ogilvy Center for Research and Development in San Francisco (Stiansen, 1987) found evidence that firms that advertise over a long period do better than their competitors. Studying over seven hundred consumer businesses, the Ogilvy Center found that consistent advertising improved the public's perception of a brand's quality. When the quality is judged superior, people are willing to pay more and show more loyalty through repeat purchases. The profits of well-advertised brands are better in the long run because of greater public acceptance.

Churches buy TV, radio, and newspaper ads not only to reach their three target audiences of newcomers, the lonely, and the disheartened but also to retain more of their backsliding members. In addition, they are battling their competition. If some church groups did not advertise, they fear they would lose many prospective members to charismatic TV evangelists.

Mainline churches say that TV substitutes lack the greatest benefit a church provides—a warm, caring community of fellow believers. But that benefit may not be as important to some TV churchgoers as the benefit of convenient conscience salving. Nevertheless, local churches persist, continuing to advertise on local cable TV and other places in the effort to catch the attention of nonattenders.

As the competition for people's attention and participation increases remarkably, more NPOs are paying for advertising. The average NPO manager does not claim to know much about the relative efficiency and effectiveness of ads, yet he or she is increasingly persuaded to invest some of the NPO's precious resources in them.

Larry Rosen, president of the Los Angeles Metropolitan YMCA, believes that while some NPOs, such as museums, symphony orchestras, and zoos, must advertise, others, such as YMCAs, should resist the temptation to advertise and rely more on strong, positive word-of-mouth from their members.

"The urge to advertise is largely reflexive and unexamined among NPO leadership," Rosen wrote to me in June 1996. The urge is, however,

> strong enough to overwhelm good judgment and ignore tepid cautions. The strategy of inside-out marketing—creating value, converting users into members, converting members into co-owners and coproducers of the organization and its programs, retention tactics, organizing the operation from the point of contact first (and administration last)—involves concepts that are now drivers of our market-centered approach. Instilling these concepts, making them the core of our marketing behavior, is the essence of the organizational change many of us are trying to create.

Rosen is absolutely right. It is a far better strategy to build a large cadre of committed members, volunteers, clients, and staff who sing your praises and spread the word throughout their individual spheres of influence than to pay people to print your message.

The aim of this chapter is to arm the NPO executive who feels pressure to advertise. Considering that the money you may be investing in advertising is not your own and that you have to justify your expenditures, it is prudent to know a little about what works best. Moreover, do not place your trust solely in the advertising expertise of people selling radio or TV time or print ads. Usually they have had no formal marketing training, and their recommendations to you are based on their observations of what others are doing. I have seen them give ineffective advice. Their goal is to sell space or time, and they will advise you to buy what they are selling. Even media people serving on an NPO marketing advisory committee will most frequently recommend the media they know best—their own. Although politically hard to do, at times you must seek more objective opinions on what would be best for your NPO.

Sometimes NPOs receive pro bono assistance from advertising agencies. To minimize difficulty with an ad agency offering pro bono work, your very first question to them ought to be, "What type of media do you suggest for us?" Their answer will tell you a lot about the agency. If they suggest free radio and TV time, ask how they will get the public service announcements (PSAs) distributed and aired. With about two thousand organizations going to the networks, most PSAs are never aired (Johnston, 1988).

Often, solutions offered pro bono by ad agencies are ineffective because the agencies have an inadequate understanding of what the client needs. Pro bono work is usually given to junior creative people who may be more interested in expressing their talent than learning much about the client and the client's audiences. Frequently the pro bono creatives offer only one solution to the NPO, which feels it must accept that solution. Production costs for execution of the creative ideas can be costly, much more than the NPO expected.

This chapter provides some information that will enable you to make better advertising choices, particularly when supervising a designer or instructing a creative team.

Two Key Questions

Getting your prospects' attention is the first step and purpose of your ad. You've got to move them quickly into a stage of paying attention to your message. After they've heard or read the message, move them to some positive action.

The job of advertising is to convince more than it is to communicate. That is why we must be judicious when deciding the merits of advertising with, say, a chart as opposed to a close-up photo of a child. Not wanting to waste our money, we also need to know the difference between preaching and persuading, telling and selling. At the outset, we have to make some major choices. Knowing our target markets, we need to answer two key questions: (1) *What is the main objective of our advertisement?* Is it to arouse interest? To encourage people to act? To tell about a new service or about problems to avoid? To remind people about our services? To maintain a good level of support? To build up prestige? To show how up-to-date we are or how good we are? (2) *What is our main appeal going to be?* Choose the primary emphasis: health, safety, preparing oneself or one's children for the future, convenience, fun, efficiency, making friends, adventure, altruism, a bargain, being first to try something new, forestalling future problems, a way to avoid problems, or curiosity.

Pick a Campaign Category

Advertising campaigns fit into four categories depending on the result you expect: direct response, educational, image, and awareness. Each has a distinctive set of characteristics, so you should know which one you are creating.

In a direct response campaign, you want people to respond, to do something because of your ad. The copy length will be related to the amount of commitment you are asking for. The greater the individual response you want, the more copy you will have to use. The size of the ad will depend on what you have to say.

The size of an educational ad is usually big. The purposes of the ad and the long copy are to explain and to gain support.

Image campaigns usually require the biggest ads. The purpose is to improve your competitive position. You will notice this factor most easily in the Yellow Pages telephone book. People searching for the first time for a chiropractor or pizza parlor will most frequently pick the largest-size ads to call first.

Awareness campaigns have very short copy repeated over and over again. In an awareness campaign you will not sell much. You are simply making people cognizant of your existence. Because of the necessary repetition, awareness campaign ads are usually the smallest of the four categories, in order to save money. The goal is to get people to remember something, and memory is enhanced when the message is simple, short, and frequently repeated. A direct response ad changes; an awareness ad is repetitious. Don't try to achieve both objectives in the same ad. You will only weaken both thrusts.

Suppose you were designing the advertising strategy for a fundraising firm whose customers were NPOs. Which one of the four goals would you choose? Immediate sales would probably be your objective in order to pull in the cash to pay your staff and yourself. These ads would call for long copy, frequently changed, with a large telephone number and call for action at the lower right corner.

Remember the Forgetfulness Curve

Within twenty-four hours after we deliver our message, only 40 percent of the people will remember what we said. Two days after we deliver the message, 15 percent remember it. When three days have passed, just 5 percent recall what we told them. Therefore, use multiple identical ads to help people remember your message longer. Two repetitions spaced fifteen minutes apart improve the retention rate. Six repeats spaced fifteen minutes apart usually provide the maximum recall (80 percent). This explains why it is so easy for us to remember the repetitious ads on late-night television. It is also the rationale for placing similar ads in the same page quadrant on different pages of magazines.

There is disagreement about how many times—with what frequency—a person needs exposure to an ad before he or she will act. Obviously, we would all like multiple exposures until we are certain our prospects have our message, but we cannot afford to keep shooting. The trick is to figure the minimum number of times we need to send out our message to get the response we want.

Many of us using direct-mail promotions hope that one exposure will be enough. Indeed, one exposure can work. Research shows that at least two and possibly three exposures within a short time span are best. This issue is not a theoretical exercise for a manager. If our first promotion costs $3,000, are we going to do much better if we spend another $3,000? We must get more than $3,000 in enrollments from the first promotion to break even. To reach the break-even point after a second promotion, we must get a $6,000 net contribution toward overhead. Here are some guidelines that help in the frequency decision-making process (Ostrow, 1981).

- A simple message requires less frequency than a complex one.
- If the message is truly unique from all the others, it requires less frequency of exposure. If it looks like them, then multiple exposures will be required.
- When the message is always in the same time, place, or format, it may wear out. Prospects grow so accustomed to it that they won't notice it any longer. The less a message is worn out, the less often it has to be released.
- Well-known NPOs offering new programs will require less frequency because the awareness and acceptance level of the organization is higher than that of an unknown NPO.
- The greater the brand loyalty (such as churches have), the less frequency required.
- If the goal is to beat the enrollments of the competition, then a strategy of higher frequency is appropriate.
- Multiple media use requires more frequency than if you restrict your promotion message to one or two media.

A three-exposure rule of thumb says that the first time people see your message they think, "What's this?" The second exposure prompts some recall: "I've seen that before." The third time, ideally, prompts them to think, "Now what? What do you want me to do now that I've got your message?"

Because recognition is important in acceptance of the message, many organizations take advantage of the "umbrella" concept to tie together several different programs. Weak programs do much better when they are attached to the promotion of stronger, better-accepted programs (Abrams, 1981b). Under the umbrella technique, the strongest programs are advertised prominently, and the introductory or weaker programs are purposely given subservient status. The latter are then purchased more than if they were promoted on their own merits, because they have come in under the umbrella of the winning programs. It is normal practice for symphonic orchestra performances to include with a well-known attraction some much less known pieces that few would pay to hear by themselves. Live theater series subscriptions usually have some plays unfamiliar to the general audience sandwiched in with traditional favorites and crowd-pleasers.

Prepare Good Copy

Keep your copy for printed advertisements simple. Assume that one-third of America is illiterate and probably another third is too busy or distracted to read much. Simple, common, familiar words are easiest to comprehend and result in fewer reader misunderstandings.

Recognize that most readers approach reading in three distinct stages. The purpose of the initial quick scan stage is to determine if the reader should invest any more time. If sufficient interest has been aroused in the scan stage, the reader will move into a confirmation stage. There the goal is to review the material to determine if reading is truly going to be worth the effort. During this second stage, the reader is still scanning, but now there is a quest for a "read more" or "don't bother" decision. The third stage of commitment is reached when the reader is satisfied that further reading may be worth it.

You can see that your copy has special challenges at each of the three stages. You have got to do something to catch each reader's attention, to lure him or her into considering your message. Then you have to maintain that interest long enough, promise the reader enough benefits, to get him or her locked into reading further. Finally, your copy has to get some commitment to action: to call, to attend a meeting, to support, or to donate.

Your copy will start with a headline that has a dual purpose: to draw attention to the subject and to pull the reader into the beginning lines of text. The headline is the most important part of the copy, because if it does not do what it is supposed to do, the reader is unlikely to go further. Here are three examples of headlines that encourage the reader to go further: "98 Reasons to Buy Season Tickets Within the Next 3 Days," "How to Cut Your Waiting Time in Half," and "Genealogy Research Center Open Free to the Public This Week."

A headline can best achieve its objective by giving news, by promising a benefit the reader may want, or by arousing curiosity. Check all of the large ads in today's issue of the *Wall Street Journal*. Note how the headlines of those professionally created ads give news, promise a benefit, or arouse curiosity. Next, look at the largest type used in a weak brochure. You may find that many of those headlines look as if they were carved in stone. "Summer Schedule," for example, offers little to stimulate people who are only casually interested.

Write a number of headlines for your copy, perhaps ten. Then share the list with your colleagues to see which they like best. They are unlikely to pick your favorite. You can always do whatever you choose after hearing their ideas, but without their opinions you are poorer.

The first paragraph of your copy has to be the grabber. Some wordsmiths say you should limit your opening paragraph to a maximum of eleven words. They advise using short sentences and short paragraphs, and avoiding any words that are difficult to understand, at least until the reader is thoroughly hooked. Don't get choppy, but don't be afraid of occasionally using one-word sentences to get your point across. Here's an example of a good opening paragraph: "Everyone needs room to grow. We all need to strengthen our bodies . . . enlighten our minds . . . nourish our spirits."

The first paragraph of Chapter Seven instructed you to start your strategizing with a good description of the people you want to reach. Keep them in mind as you write your copy. Do not address your readers as if they were gathered in a stadium. When people read copy they are alone, so write as if you are speaking to one person, your targeted customer. Be sure you do more than tell the features of your offering. Emphasize related benefits the prospective customer might prize, as described in Chapter Two.

When you know and love the institution it is easy to fall into a trap of providing too much background information. In fundraising brochures, background information can be especially helpful to your volunteers and potential donors, but in ads meant to attract more service users, background information is seldom wise. Users want to know more about the program's benefits to them than about the organization's history, board of directors, long-range plans, and recent organizational changes.

Avoid the negative in both headlines and copy. Preferring pleasure over pain, most people would rather hear about solutions than problems. You can describe negative situations in positive, hopeful terms. You can show people what you and they can do together to solve significant problems.

Avoid making direct comparisons with another organization, implying that you are the best. Running down your competition will make you look bad. If you are the low-price leader you can simply include the price of your program in your copy. Readers will figure out the rest on their own.

Staff like corporate slogans, sometimes requesting a new one each year. Experts tell us corporate slogans are useless and detract from our main message. People rarely remember them, anyway. When they can recall the line they usually have difficulty tying it with the right sponsor. So skip the slogan unless you are using it to make yourself feel good.

Don't devote much space in your copy to overcome a long list of anticipated objections. Doing that introduces objections the average person has not even thought of until you bring them up.

You might address the single objection most often heard, but leave the response to other objections to your trained staff. They can talk with each individual. Besides, people who already have a long list of objections are unlikely to be reading your copy anyway.

Use testimonials of average people. Here's an example: " 'The scariest thing for me,' says Joy Swanson, 'was leaving my kids in baby-sitting. I started slowly, with one hour, and then I got to know the people. They take care of my children as well as they would take care of their own.' " Readers find the endorsements of people like themselves to be very persuasive. Celebrities catch readers' attention quicker but aren't as persuasive as someone readers see as more like themselves.

Use words and pictures that will help your readers form their own mental images. Stimulate imagery by using concrete words that define things the way a person would see, hear, taste, feel, and experience them. By appealing to the senses you can help your readers remember your message.

At the end of advertising copy, try to move readers to take some plausible action. It is easy for them to put your piece down, maybe thinking they want to mull it over awhile before doing anything. Your goal is to get them to act now while your full persuasive message is still fresh, so you will need to emphasize the advantages of taking quick action right now. Offer a time-limited deal or the ease of doing everything with a short phone call. Promise their money back if, later on, they reconsider and feel they have made the wrong choice. In other words, take away any potential penalty for acting right now.

Use Sentiment and Logic

Appeal to both the heart and the head. Some people see us as a bunch of well-meaning do-gooders, strong on zeal but not very smart—at least not as smart as they are. (If we were, we would be driving expensive cars and dressing better, they reason.) For them, use statistics and graphs and research findings to support your claims. Others don't care much whether you serve seven hundred or seven thousand or seventy thousand people; they just want to know how well you take care of individuals. So you give them passionate, warm, true stories.

The use of emotional stories and pictures is one of the best ways to reach people's hearts. True stories can help relate your work to the lives of the individuals whose support you are seeking through advertising.

Look at television ads today. Many of them use sentimental appeals to sell what were previously considered unemotional products: coffee, cotton, orange juice, telephone calls, towels, and hamburger. They show frisky puppies, doting grandparents, cute kids, and harried adults being soothed with the advertised product. Slogans talk about feeling, touching, sharing.

Sentimental ads are often used where logic is not a compelling selling point. Because most jeans are similar, you will notice the biggest advertisers have wrapped them with emotional music and visual messages. They don't say much about the strength of the fabric. As they cannot legitimately claim that their product is the best there is—their competitors would issue complaints to regulatory agencies—their emotional pitches effectively create a distinct personality and appeal.

Sentiment won't sell every product. It is not necessarily a better pitch than logic, and it can be overused to the point that people don't want to hear our story again. They find that it makes them too sad or that it is trying too hard to manipulate them. But used with care, sentiment is mighty effective for achieving many of our objectives.

Illustrations

Illustrations account for about 60 percent of the attraction in an advertisement. Attention-getting devices rank as follows, from most to least.

1. Color photos
2. Black-and-white photos and large headlines
3. Line art drawings, charts, tables
4. Body text
5. White areas

Until they have formed a sharp mental picture of your message, people will remember your illustrations more than your prose. A person's visual memory can last a very long time, so use pictures worth remembering. Ads with some form of illustration always draw better than ads without an illustration. Pictures can often get your point across faster than words.

Ads with pictures of people usually do better than those without people. Showing people interacting with each other is much better than a group portrait. Even implied motion does better than average. Fantasy pictures do well because they arouse curiosity.

Larger pictures are usually remembered longer than small pictures. Readership of the ad seems to increase in direct proportion to the size of the illustration Yet it is very difficult for most of us to choose one or two pictures to feature when we know we have many good ones. It is mighty tempting just to make them smaller so more can be included in the printed piece. However, experts tell us that when we use compelling pictures—those that hold the viewer's attention for at least two seconds—we stand a much greater chance of being remembered (Percy and Rossiter, 1982). This is why you will frequently see photographs that fill an entire page with one great shot. Excellent photographs of your NPO's program and leadership tell your story more persuasively than almost anything else. When we create endowment development materials, for example, we concentrate on showing photographs of people similar to those we are trying to enlist in our fundraising program. They are usually over age sixty and well attired.

Sometimes your NPO logo can appear discreetly in a picture, to remind everyone that your NPO is responsible for these good services. Overall, however, logos are not very important in an advertisement. They have neutral pulling power. If you are using one-third of your space displaying the logo, you are wasting valuable selling space.

Layout and Design

It doesn't matter how well your prose is prepared or how pretty your pictures look if the layout and design make it difficult for people to get the message. People glance. They try to perceive your message quickly, looking first at the illustration, then the headline, and next the copy. Most people will read the caption under a photo before they read the body copy. So consider a caption for each photo, even if it is set in tiny print.

With most layouts, the reader's eyes naturally focus on the middle of the page, move to the upper left side, then down the left side and across to the bottom right corner (where a call for action is often placed). Judge some of your pieces from that perspective. Does your layout help the eyes move in that path? When you give people a clear reading sequence to your page, you are likely to get 20 percent more readership. Anytime you deviate from the normal path people are expecting, you are asking them to work harder. You are forcing them to make decisions about the worth of proceeding further.

Some professional designers appear to be more interested in expressing their creativity than in creating pieces easy for your customers to read. Twenty-nine-year-old designers can have difficulty preparing readable copy for your fifty-nine-year-old donors. Beware especially of pieces that look beautiful but whose meaning is a chore to grasp. You can win the battles with your designers when you keep uppermost in your mind the person you are trying to reach. A super-slick design may impress your staff, but it is probably commonplace to your customers when you consider all of the advertising they see daily.

Use large type size and wider margins for older population segments. Make it easier for those with weaker eyesight to read, or else they won't. Use eleven-point type for audiences with a median age of forty-five, twelve-point type for those over sixty-five. When you use type that is two points off the optimum size, readership will decrease as much as 25 percent. When it is three points off, such as nine-point for those over sixty-five, you will lose 50 percent of your potential readers.

Anything in your ad that decreases reading speed, such as small type, reverse type, and polysyllable words (for example, "sixty-seven thousand, four hundred and sixty-four cardiovascular patients"), will tire people and cause them to quit reading. Borders and other graphic designs are neutral. Adding color costs 35 percent more and often has a neutral effect.

The most valuable advertising locations in booklets, newsletters, and catalogs, in order of descending importance, are the

1. Front cover
2. Back cover
3. Inside cover
4. First page opposite the inside front cover
5. Centerfold
6. First 10 percent of the pages

There was a YMCA in Connecticut that sold the first page of its program booklet to a furniture store to defray the cost of printing. The furniture store owner loved the arrangement. For about $100, he got his message distributed to several thousand prime prospects who might use the booklet repeatedly to get YMCA program information. The YMCA was giving away its precious opportunities much too cheaply.

To make it evident that your various advertising pieces are coming from the same organization, even though they may be designed by a variety of people, you should specify some common design features, such as where the logo should be placed on each promotion piece. All work should look and feel as if it is coming from the same NPO. This consistency is admittedly a difficult challenge for NPOs that have many people creating their own promotion pieces, but it will yield more.

Ultimately, potential readers must perceive that they will get more by reading your ad than they would if they ignored it and did something else. You use pictures, design, and copy to say "stop and take notice of my message." You promise some benefits and ask people to make a decision about the service you have described. You want them to call, write, join, think positively, stop in, give. Remember, so do several thousand other advertisers each day (Sloan, 1987).

Advertising to Children

To prompt children to persuade their parents, advertisers have most frequently chosen television to do the job. Children watch television most during weekday early evenings, even more than on Saturday mornings. Other family members are also present, so the same advertising reaches not only the children (purchase influencers) but also the parents (ultimate customers). However, parents have complained about TV advertising aimed at children, particularly that targeted for the under-twelve age group. Mothers accept and welcome commercials that teach children good hygiene and better eating habits. They complain about misrepresentations of products and attempts to get children to demand certain products from their parents, a strategy that adds to the tensions already existing in tightly budgeted households.

The advertising that most persuasively reaches children, according to William D. Wells of the University of Chicago, has four main characteristics ("Communication with Children," 1965, p. 2).

1. Children enjoy fantasy, except when it is unrealistically represented.

2. Advertisements for children are more effective when the product is individualized. One way companies do this is to

associate the brand with a personality the children admire, such as Bill Cosby or Michael Jordan.

3. Motion within advertisements is much more effective than static pictures or words.

4. Motivating scenes include demonstrations of someone wanting or enjoying the product or gaining new powers because of their use of the product.

When youth service NPOs direct their promotional efforts at children, they should heed what commercial advertisers have discovered about effective ways to reach targeted audiences. This means wrapping messages in a way that is attractive to children but not offensive to parents and other authorities, such as school teachers and principals. When school officials cannot see an evident benefit to all their students, they frequently forbid NPO leaders to distribute flyers throughout classrooms. When the school promotional channel is blocked, the promotional costs of the program significantly increase.

Promotion to Major Donors

Reaching major donor prospects with your message is particularly challenging because so many individuals and NPOs are trying hard to reach them at the same time. The prospects for large donations have been well identified. They fall into four classifications: wealthy individuals, foundations, governments, and corporations.

Once again, you need to fix your sights on narrow targets. A huge prospect file of names and addresses is not as valuable as detailed information about a few hundred carefully screened prospects. While raising money in San Francisco, I was elated when my file of prospective donors of $1,000 or more grew to thirteen thousand names. In my fifth year, I concluded I was on the wrong path. The file had grown larger than our organization was willing to mail to frequently.

There was no cultivation of the thirteen thousand prospects, and maintaining the list was an onerous task, as every year probably 20 percent of the people changed addresses.

Large donations are usually preceded by a long period of cultivation. Good cultivation takes a minimum of two to three years, frequently longer. Getting the NPO's message to the major donor prospects involves a variety of contacts and a very personal approach. Most of our large donor prospects are very busy and don't have enough time to read all that comes to them in the mail, much less their daily newspaper. So it is unreasonable to assume they will read and digest your newsletter or annual report. What everyone gets less of these days is personal mail. So send them a one-page letter on monarch-size stationery, personally addressed and signed in blue ink by the chief executive officer of your NPO. In the letter, tell just one human interest story and stop at that. Resist the temptation to add a postscript about the pending annual meeting, reunion, or special exhibit. Top donor prospects like getting personal mail with an uplifting message. They will remember the story in the short letter much longer than they will recall anything in your newsletter.

Promotion to top donor prospects is a highly personal effort requiring much time. Usually the smaller the group, the better. A luncheon with just three people is more valuable than a large luncheon for all of your major gift prospects. Smaller encounters give prospects an opportunity to ask questions and learn more. You can readily respond to each person's interests.

To reach them through advertising, pick the media they pick. A Hartford, Connecticut, NPO executive bought a page in the symphony program booklet to advertise his planned giving program and its benefits. The Salvation Army sometimes places an ad in the *Wall Street Journal* to advertise its charitable gift annuity program. Boys and Girls Clubs will occasionally place an ad in local newspaper sports pages describing the tax advantages of donating a horse or a used boat or camper.

Evaluating Advertising

Although I stated at the beginning of this chapter that firms that advertise over a long period do better than competitors, most marketing executives agree that a causal relationship between advertising and sales has never been proven definitively (Abrams, 1981a, p. B1).

Spending more will not guarantee you proportionately more enrollments or support. Advertising budgets are built on faith. We spend as much as we feel we can afford, rather than how much we confidently know it will take to do the job.

There is a good reason why we can't attribute all sales increases to the effect of advertising. We are often simultaneously offering price incentives and new programs or services. The entire staff are thus made more aware of our desire for more enrollment activity, so they produce a little better.

When we don't get the results we expect from our advertising expenditures, we conclude the advertising is weak. When enrollments or donations are good, we feel the advertising is doing its job. Although we can't fully blame or credit the advertising for our present condition, some NPO executives feel that they have little choice but to put their message out into the wider marketplace.

To make best use of the precious dollars and time we invest in all forms of advertising and promotion, concentrate on the typical customers you want to reach amid all the noise and distraction around them. Find ways to get a clear, cogent message noticed, understood, and acted on. Repeat the message. At the same time, find some rather simple ways of measuring the effectiveness of your actions. Experiment with various methods of proffering your message to the public until you feel you are getting a satisfactory response.

Chapter Nine

Media Selection

Choosing the Right Mix

What advertising medium should we use? Newspapers, magazines, flyers, catalogs, bus and subway cards, billboards, TV, radio, or the Internet? If an ad agency is making this decision for you, make the best use of your money by providing them with well-written descriptions of the targeted individuals you want to reach. Then ask agency staff, and perhaps others, to tell you how they propose to reach the greatest number of these people, with the greatest frequency. If, like most nonprofit executives, you are making the media choices yourself, then this chapter will help improve your selections by understanding the relative merits of each choice.

When evaluating a particular promotion medium use these criteria:

- *Reach*. Set a goal for how many people will receive your message.
- *Target*. Aim your message at specific customer types with similar ages, lifestyles, community, or income.
- *Frequency*. Determine the number of times a potential customer should be exposed to your message.
- *Efficiency*. Achieve the lowest promotion cost per potential customer.

Radio makes a good example of the reach and targeting concepts. Radio reaches 99 percent of teens during a week; 80 percent of teens listen to radio on an average day. They give it nearly three hours of their time. Thus, radio is an efficient method of reaching teens. By comparison, teen magazines reach 25 percent of all teens, and daily newspapers reach 60 percent. Teenagers watch a lot of television, but that medium is expensive.

Through some kind of special deal, Chuck Holmes, the Minneapolis YMCA vice president of public relations (retired), once got a free full-page YMCA ad in *Playboy* and some other national magazines. Our staff were delighted by the wide exposure. Some board members, however, expressed displeasure with their YMCA's being seen with that companion. Although I would probably encourage Chuck to do it again, I now realize that the ad (even though it was free) did little to boost the YMCA's image, because it missed the two target audiences for our YMCA: the thirty-one-year-old mothers and fifty-year-old Rotarians. *Playboy's* target is the twenty-five- to thirty-five-year-old man.

To reach your targeted audience, you must use media they use. We know, for example, that to reach the thirty-one-year-old mother we should try some daytime radio and TV, and magazines. Much of NPO paid advertising serves only to make our staff feel better. That is a worthwhile goal, but we should not be fooling ourselves that it is also reaching the intended customers. Usually it isn't. During my first $15 million capital fund campaign for the Minneapolis YMCA, staff had attractive banners hung from every light pole downtown for a week or two. The staff felt proud of the achievement, but it is doubtful many YMCA major givers took notice of the banners. None of the prospects I talked to could remember seeing the banners. They spent very little time walking the streets of downtown and looking at the lamp posts. As you learn more about media characteristics in the rest of this chapter, compare them to what you know about your target audience characteristics.

The Internet

The Internet has become the place to been seen. It is hot. By the mid 1990s, there were estimated to be about 20 million people tapping into the Internet. Not having a home page on the Internet is like not having a telephone or fax. Yet it is clearly a medium in transition and not a reliable place to put all your hopes for customer response. To get the optimum response to your listing, add some sort of service to the advertising message. The service could be in the form of entertainment (a quiz or contest), or it could be your schedule, new programs, and directions to the site.

The benefits of advertising on the Internet cannot be quantified yet. The number of hits on a site are measurable, but their meaning is unclear. At this point you may need to be satisfied with merely establishing your presence there. Having several interesting pages on the World Wide Web may boost your image among your board and staff members and among the primary audience of Web visitors—professionals and students.

Flyers

The purpose of flyers is to get a message out to many people simply and cheaply. The distribution method determines who will get and react to the message, so you can exercise a lot of control with this choice of media. You can hand flyers out at the bus stop, after concerts and athletic events, on campus, and in your own lobby. In each case, you have a good fix on who will get your message.

Many NPOs rely on 81/2-by-11-inch flyers to promote new services to the public and their membership. They are easy to make and economical. Staff in charge of each program usually design their own flyers rather than rely on specialists. You can improve staff efforts by insisting everyone attend design workshops. Your design format can be standardized and the parameters set before staff go to work on their own. A common design theme can tie together the creative work of several staff members.

Make sure that the flyers use few and simple words, state the best feature first, and make enrollment or response easy.

Direct Mail

Radio, TV, newspaper, magazine, and billboard advertising are shotgun approaches to a very wide market. Mailing your message directly to homes and places of work seems to be a more efficient way of reaching specific people. Despite increasing postal rates, more marketers, including NPOs, are stuffing mailboxes. Despite the public cries about unwanted junk mail, much of it is read.

Whom do you mail to? How frequently? What do you say each time? Do you do it all yourself, or do you hire an outside firm to handle it? These are key questions in a direct-mail program. We already know direct mail is mighty effective. The issue is how to make it pay off even better.

Very few NPOs have the staff expertise to do all their own direct-mail marketing effectively. It is a wise strategy to develop as much of that expertise as you can inside, but after a few campaigns you may get stale. There are few, if any, monetary rewards for exceptional creativity and successful risk-taking in an NPO, so I advise the occasional use of consultants and others who are paid well to be on the cutting edge.

Lists

We can mail our newsletters, announcements, promotion pieces, annual reports, donor cultivation letters, and requests for donations to people on our own lists or on lists we have purchased, rented, or swapped. A compilation of the one hundred thousand lists available is published by Standard Rate and Data Service, 5201 Old Orchard Rd., Skokie, IL 60077. Prices at local list brokers will vary but tend to cluster around $50 to $75 per thousand names and addresses. They may charge $10 extra to provide telephone numbers. Because a lot of money and time can be wasted in an effort to secure the best lists to fit your particular NPO, you may need some assistance. A direct-mail consultant who is not pushing his or her own lists may cost about $1,000 for a day's advice, but if your project is ambitious, the cost can be an excellent investment.

Measure list effectiveness by coding your brochures, return envelopes, and order forms. Sometimes the primary value of any new list is your education. By comparing the response rates of lists, you will get a sharper profile of the people who like you. Be prepared to be frustrated: you probably will not get the response you want from your first mailing. But you will get a lot smarter about whom you are reaching. So some of us use new direct-mail fundraising lists merely to uncover new supporters. Finding our supporters in the universe is more important initially than raising a lot of money.

The Franklin Institute Science Museum in Philadelphia conducted a whole series of test mailings using purchased lists containing elements common to their own membership groups. They test-mailed to members of the Philadelphia Zoo, the Philadelphia Museum of Art, the National Geographic Society, and the Smithsonian Institution and to two-income households with children under age twelve.

Keeping mailing lists up-to-date is a hard task. Figure that 20 percent of the people move each year. To keep your lists up-to-date, ask people twice a year to correct their mailing labels. Building your own list is an arduous job, but it has great payoff potential.

Few NPOs mail to their own lists often enough. Once a month is probably a good frequency to shoot for. Tell your publics about new developments, current services, and your funding needs.

Response Forms

Direct mail is response oriented, so always give the reader a way to respond: a telephone number to call or a business reply card to return by a deadline date. Because some people will pull out your response form and throw the rest of the message away, you must have your name and address printed on the form for it to be useful.

Don't ask questions on the response form that might force a prospect to put it down until he or she gets the right answers. Well-meaning camp directors, for example, will sometimes ask your child's height and weight and the names of the friends he or she would like to share a cabin with. A youngster's friends change so fast that a parent cannot confidently answer the enrollment form's question, so they set the form aside.

Make it easy to reply to you. Make the form easy enough for a child to fill out. My experience is that elementary school children love to do this when the program is for them, so allow plenty of space for them to write big. Then all you will need is the parent's signature. Piece of cake.

More Than Just the Facts

If your direct-mail piece has an envelope, include a friendly letter. Help people become comfortable with you by identifying yourself and sharing some news.

You can send a promotion piece when billing for a program people are already in. You can also insert your noncompetitive little promotion piece with the bills of a utility company or your board member's company.

Cards, Catalogs, and Coupons

Deck cards (postcard-size promotion pieces) can be used in cooperation with a large number of other advertisers. Up to one hundred cards are wrapped in plastic, allowing the recipient to respond easily by mailing the cards he or she chooses. The cost for deck card inclusion has been around $15 per thousand. You supply art work to a publisher who prints and mails the cards to its own lists.

The strength of direct-mail catalogs is that they describe everything you want to offer. The weakness is that because the catalogs promise so much, people hesitate to read them until they have time to digest all of the pertinent information. That convenient time may never come. To get your catalog read quicker, employ expert design elements and high-quality pictures. Provide a logical sequence for readers to follow. Make it seem easy for them to get the specific information they want. Use an index, large numbers, and pictures that show people just like themselves using your service. Also list items by name as well as number. You will find that most people prefer using the name.

Some shoppers cannot easily resist a bargain coupon included with the direct mail. At the Northwest YMCA we offered dollars-off coupons in our summer program brochure and got a 50 percent growth in program volume. Half of the people enrolling in four coupon-promoted programs used the coupons to save money.

Coupons effectively generate trial use and greater awareness. In 1984, some 163 billion coupons were distributed in the United States, and under 4 percent, one of every twenty-seven coupons issued, were redeemed (Murphy, 1986). By 1990, a total of 375 billion coupons were issued, roughly $1,000 worth of coupons for every citizen. Despite coupon clutter, the use of coupons is still popular and is predicted to grow.

Coupons will give you much higher readership of the advertisement, whether you get any coupons back or not. People read your ad to decide if it is worthwhile to redeem the coupon. Of course, the coupon value must be enough to help convince a customer it is worth saving and redeeming.

The average household is bombarded with two thousand coupons each year, ("Coupon Use Low," 1988) and there are marked differences between people who use them and those who ignore them. Heavy coupon users, redeeming five times as many coupons as the light users, are typically female heads of households with children and annual incomes exceeding $30,000. They are between the ages of thirty-five and fifty-four, have a high school education, and work part-time. Those less likely to clip and save are female heads of smaller households who also work full-time. If your NPO is trying to reach young, full-time working women, coupon promotions may not be the best way to do it.

Telephone

The telephone is one of the quickest ways to get a response. Using volunteers and donated office space, an NPO can contact a large number of people inexpensively. The telephone can be especially useful in securing new enrollments and renewals, making trial offers, upgrading tickets or membership, supplying information updates during times of crisis, doing market research, following up on complaints and on visitors who did not join, and securing donations.

The benefits of telephone marketing are the low cost, potential for high volume, invulnerability to bad weather, centralized control, ease of beginning and ease to accomplish, as well as the two-way communication between seller and potential buyer. You can do it on a grand scale or on a micro scale. At a typical YMCA, there usually is an hour lull in the evening once members are in their programs. I have had the reception staff call people who recently visited but hadn't joined. By following up on visitors within three days, there was a good chance the caller could persuade them to join. After three days had elapsed, however, the call was futile.

Who Does the Calling?

Telemarketing firms have special techniques, trained staff, and enough equipment to serve NPO needs. However, we can also do telemarketing ourselves when guided by an expert. The Brandywine YMCA in Coatesville, Pennsylvania, annually used board members to telephone members who had not renewed. Board members, as NPO policy setters, can simultaneously gather valuable information about membership satisfaction. Following the same format each year also allows you to compare summaries and note trends. During the eight years I was with the Northwest YMCA, four hundred volunteers, over a period of sixteen nights, called all of our several thousand program participants and past donors to ask for contributions.

Public TV and radio stations also use volunteer phone banks to respond to people calling in with their donations.

Colleges and universities hire their own students at low wage levels to seek annual gifts from alumni over the phone. If you hire people to market over the phone, you obviously want those with a pleasant voice that is easy to understand; callers should also be genuinely friendly. Customers can sense anxiety, even over the phone, and they react negatively. You can improve the quality of calls by telling your callers to smile while on the phone and to stand up when dealing with difficult calls (in order to breathe more comfortably).

It is important to practice continuous training and coaching of your telephone marketing team, whether they are volunteers or paid staff. Stay around during phone sessions to monitor the way they handle calls. When they are suffering from too many turndowns or unsolicited complaints about your NPO, or from boredom or shyness, you can act like a cheerleader. In fundraising boiler-room situations, we often gave the solicitors bells to ring and horns to blow when they were successful. Frequent breaks, some competition, and prizes encouraged a happier and faster pace. Of course, you can't fire a volunteer caller who is losing money by getting turndowns from previous donors, but if you monitor everyone's production every half hour, you can reassign the volunteer to another important task in time to prevent greater losses.

Using Toll-Free and Toll Hot Line Numbers

Investigate the value of toll-free (exchanges such as 800 and 888) and toll hot line (900) telephone numbers. Promoting a toll-free number to your prospective callers encourages them to respond. A 900 number shifts the cost of the call onto the caller, and many people are willing to assume it. The cost to the toll-free number sponsor is tied to the number of calls received. If fewer than two thousand calls are received per day, the sponsoring organization pays about 25 cents for each call below the minimum, which means that if no one calls, the organization may have to pay $500.

One of the main reasons for choosing a toll number over a toll-free number is that a toll number can do a much better job of handling mass calling. To receive five hundred simultaneous calls on a toll-free number, you would need five hundred separate lines. A 900 number can take as many as 7,200 calls simultaneously (Sharkey, 1987).

The Dial-It 900 Service was introduced in 1980 during the Carter-Reagan presidential campaign debates. By 1988, callers could use the service to register a straw vote or hear a live or recorded message and pay a fee of 50 cents for the first minute and 35 cents for each additional minute. Fundraising campaigns can have the first-minute charge raised to $2 and reap all proceeds minus the aforementioned 50-cent and 35-cent fees. So far, the most common use of the Dial-It 900 Service has been for TV audiences to register their preferences during a contest (Edel, 1988).

Figuring Cost Effectiveness

Telephone campaigns must be evaluated just like any other campaign. Here is a way to calculate the potential from cold calls, those people who presently are not members or donors (Mitchell, n.d.).

1,000	Calls
−480	No answer, busy, or disconnected
520	Potential customers reached
−310	Refusals to hear the complete presentation
210	Actual full contacts
−177	Prospects who say no
33	Customers who say yes
−2	Cancellations
31	Orders

Say you are trying to enlist people in a program that has a fee of $50. Total sales will be $1,550 ($50 × 31) per thousand dialings.

Sales equal $1.50 per dialing ($1,550 ÷ 1,000). Sales equal $2.98 per potential customer reached ($1,550 ÷ 520) but $7.38 per completed solicitation call ($1,550 ÷ 210). On the average, each of our callers might reach about fifteen prospects per hour, selling about $45 per hour. This example adds up to not quite one sale per hour per telephone solicitor. Using this example, you can now do your own calculations to fit your situation.

To appraise the value of telemarketing, look at the costs as if you had to pay for everything, including services that have been donated. Your costs include these items: list of names and telephone numbers; script design and duplication; site; equipment; telephones; long distance charges; adding machines; refreshments; prizes; wages of paid employees, plus bonuses; management study and interpretation of the report forms; general management, bookkeeping, and training; and follow-up letters.

Your estimated costs per hour per caller might include the following: caller, $10.00; WATS line, $16.00; supervisor, $1.50 ($15.00 per hour divided by 10 callers); clerical, $0.50; list cost, $1.50. Your total direct costs then would be $29.50. After you add in overhead per caller per hour (say $8.50) and workplace and training costs of perhaps $3.00 per caller per hour, $41.00 is the total cost per caller per hour ($29.50 + $8.50 + $3.00).

Let's carry the original example further to calculate the cost per hour and per sale. Assume that we are paying for ten callers and one supervisor. Each caller is expected to make twenty-eight calls per hour (a fairly standard figure).

Twenty-eight calls per hour minus thirteen no answers and busy signals equals fifteen potential customers reached. Subtracting ten refusals to hear the complete presentation leaves you with five full contacts. Of these, four prospects say no, and one customer says yes. Let's assume there is no cancellation, which means there is a total of one $50 order per hour.

By dividing the dollar amount of sales per hour ($50) by the number of calls made (28), we can conclude that we are making $1.79 with each call made. When we get a chance to tell our full story, we make $10 ($50 ÷ 5 completed messages). The cost per call is the $41 we figured earlier divided by the number of calls made per hour, 28. Our cost is thus $1.46. The cost per completed call is $41 divided by the 5 completed messages, or $8.20. If we make $1.79 in sales per attempted call and incur $1.46 in costs, our profit per attempted call is 33 cents. If we make $10.00 in sales per completed call and incur $8.20 in costs, our profit per completed call is $1.80.

Telephone Cards

Telephone cards are a new promotional vehicle currently in its fast-growth phase. The prepaid plastic cards are used in lieu of cash at pay phones and are widely sold at convenience stores. More and more NPO marketers are using telephone cards to promote their causes and, in many cases, to raise funds. Revenues from phone cards were estimated to climb from $75 million in 1994 to $1 billion in 1995 (Shermach, 1995). The ITS Readycard has a short two-day production time, so it can easily be used to gather public support for victims of natural disasters such as floods and earthquakes. NPOs that have used these cards include Ronald McDonald House, the Humane Society, the United Way, and the National Adoption Foundation.

Telephone cards were also issued to about five hundred relief workers as they assisted victims of Hurricane Opal in the Florida panhandle. In exchange for some sponsorship promotions heard at the beginning of each call, they received a half hour of free calls. Some people have warned that the prepaid calling cards end up being much more of a commercial promotion than a worthy fundraising and NPO marketing vehicle. So study the experience of others before grabbing this opportunity.

Public Service Announcements (PSAs)

Business Week magazine receives ten thousand press releases weekly. They use less than 1 percent of them. The editors like to discover and write stories themselves, preferring not to rely on the stories they are fed.

Ideally, you should match your placements with the media most likely to be noticed by your targeted audience. If the people you need to reach are most likely to listen to country music on the radio, then you shouldn't be content with a reading of the PSA on a classical music station. However, the reality is that nonprofit staff take whatever free or bargain-rate media placements they can get. They don't worry much whether the message reaches the target audience. They are just glad it got included someplace. Thus, although noticed by the NPO staff, the PSAs often go unnoticed by the people we want to reach. It is for this reason that many large NPOs supplement free PSAs with paid ads they can control.

The Advertising Council said its public service campaigns for charities and government agencies received nearly $900 million worth of free advertising space and air time in 1994, a 46 percent increase over the previous year ("Public-Service Ads," 1995). That is just a partial indicator of the value of free time and space contributed to NPOs.

Television and Radio

It is expensive to buy radio and TV time, particularly enough time to make an impact on your audience. But there are many cases where NPOs of all sorts—churches, schools, hospitals, United Way, our armed services, the Internal Revenue Service, zoos, and others— have chosen to buy time to reach their targets.

When the Metropolitan Library Service Agency of Minneapolis and St. Paul spent its first $10,000 on radio jingles, for example, the board was split on the wisdom of the strategy. They were experiencing an overall budget crunch at the time. Some board members reasoned that $10,000 would be better spent on a lot of new books. The staff won out, convincing the majority that radio advertising was necessary to build up library usage among nonusers. It was a difficult board decision.

Boys and Girls Clubs have very effectively used powerful image campaigns on television. The ads, directed to potential donors, featured celebrities who had grown up experiencing the benefits of Boys Clubs and were testifying to their value today. Now, when I ask potential major contributors who does the best job serving low-income children in the city, Boys and Girls Clubs are the most frequently mentioned, even though few respondents have actually seen these centers firsthand. The respondents are trusting the advertising.

The advantages of TV are the large and diverse audiences it can reach and the persuasive impact it can have using color, sound, real-life vignettes, graphics, and motion. Yet because it costs so much, few NPOs can afford more than a fleeting message that has little chance of standing out from the barrage of professionally produced ads. For other than the simple community bulletin board–type announcements, we should expect to spend a minimum of $3,000 to create a PSA or an ad.

Another difficultly is that in many homes, viewers are distractedly easily. The television is little more than a talking lamp. A study of 1,580 viewers in Springfield, Illinois, showed that 75 percent of those people who were not watching alone were talking with someone else in the room ("Who Watches Commercials," 1982). Twenty percent said they were doing household chores with the television on, 18 percent were eating, 17 percent reading, 6 percent talking on the phone, and 12 percent were doing something else while watching television. The study also showed that 43 percent of the audience missed one or more commercials during a half-hour television show. Mothers with school-age children are most likely to miss commercials. This serves to remind us of how hard it is for non-noteworthy advertisements on television to reach their intended audiences.

Because TV time is so expensive, an NPO should consider late-night TV time, when the cost is one-sixth that of prime time. The audience is much smaller, but it has the same demographic characteristics as the daytime audience, with the important exception that there are fewer women (Koten, 1984). At 4:00 A.M., commercials are often repeated and thus better remembered. With the lower costs, an advertisement can be stretched to two full minutes instead of thirty seconds at prime time.

Many social service agencies are trying to reach low-income and less educated people. These people watch the most TV, some fifty hours a week, compared to higher-income people who are the lightest viewers, with an average of four hours. Clearly, TV can be an effective way to reach low-income people, but the sponsoring agency would need to have a professionally prepared message that is repeated often in order for it to be remembered and acted on.

To reach an upscale audience for volunteers and donations, TV is not the way to go. They watch so little TV that the chances of their seeing your message are slim.

Our chances of getting our TV and radio PSAs used by local stations improve when we issue them regularly. Radio is the most segmented of all the electronic media, so we improve our reach and frequency when we direct our PSAs and ads to those stations most listened to by our markets.

Radio advertisements cost less than TV and can effectively reach people in a variety of situations (while they are driving, riding the bus, walking the dog, working, jogging). However, like TV, it is a cluttered medium, and the message is fleeting. A listener can't refer back to something just heard. For that reason alone, you should avoid starting any radio story with a name that means nothing to most listeners. When you must use a name, lead off with a title or description: "A South City High School art teacher, Judith Mosqueda, won . . ."

Newspapers and Magazines

Newspapers and magazines are the vehicles to use with educated and affluent markets. The same person who avoids TV is usually an avid Sunday newspaper reader, including the Sunday magazines. Sunday is his or her day to catch up on the world and find out what is happening.

Sunday newspapers are loaded with ad inserts that are read by 11 percent of the adult audience ("Marketing Briefs," 1983, p. 5), although readership varies considerably by the type of store that places the insert. On average it takes about six insert readers to get one sale, but the results are much better for large discount stores. Kmart was able to convert one in five insert readers into shoppers, whereas the figures for Sears were one in sixteen. The people who read inserts the most are those who are regular shoppers of those stores.

An NPO considering a one-time newspaper insert as a special promotion can try this calculation. A community of 100,000 people has 56 percent who are between the ages of twenty and sixty-five. Assume that 95 percent of those people get the paper with your insert enclosed—that's 52,300 people. Eleven percent of them notice and read your insert: 5,753. Only one out of every fifty of your insert readers responds because (1) you are not a discounter with the best conversion rate of five to one, and (2) you do not advertise often enough in the newspaper to develop a regular clientele of such shoppers. You would end up with 115 "sales," which you would evaluate in light of the costs of the insert program. If you could get a conversion rate of fifteen to one, slightly better than Sears, you could produce 383 sales from your inserts.

The interesting thing about newspaper ads is that readers find them more believable than those in other media. I am suspicious of industry groups that do their own research and arrive at complimentary findings, but a study by Opinion Research Corporation, commissioned by the Newspaper Advertising Bureau, found that 42 percent of the 1,001 respondents rated newspapers as having the most believable advertising, versus 26 percent for TV, 11 percent each for magazines and radio, and 5 percent for direct mail (*Advertising Age*, 1981).

The other benefits of newspaper advertising are timeliness (because of daily or weekly coverage) and durability (because readers can tear out ads and save them). NPOs have also had very good experiences getting free full-page ads in regional editions of national magazines. This is best done in cooperation with the advertising council and in collaboration with other NPOs.

Joint Promotions with Commercial Businesses

When NPOs and businesses have had customers with nearly identical demographic characteristics, some businesses have given the NPOs a discount or a feature in their advertising in exchange for the NPOs' mailing lists or purchase recommendations to their members. Sporting goods sellers have shown interest in the clientele of NPO athletic clubs and recreation agencies. Museums and concert halls have members of interest to upscale merchandisers.

American companies expected to spend $5.4 billion on sponsorships in 1996, according to IEG, the Chicago publishing firm ("Increase Foreseen for Sponsorships," 1996). Sponsorships of sports events were expected to total $3.5 billion, and those of entertainment events, $540 million. Health-related charities were expected to receive $485 million, and arts groups were estimated to receive $323 million from corporate-sponsored events. You can see there is a whole lot of money being directed toward corporate and charity event partnerships.

Half of all limited-service restaurant operators surveyed in 1995 expected to sponsor a sports team or a community event, such as a softball tournament, a local musical festival, or an entire sports league, as a way to promote their restaurants (*Restaurants USA*, 1995). Operators said they hoped their restaurant's name on team uniforms would be noticed favorably by potential customers and would stimulate more business.

Such joint promotions are certainly on the rise; however, they involve risks. Because many NPOs count on a broad base of community support, they run the risk of alienating some businesses when they align themselves with commercial competitors. The joint promotion may seem favorable to the NPO staff, but they may be trading their community goodwill too cheaply. Financially, the business may be gaining much more from the alliance than is the NPO. To improve the chances of getting a good deal, the NPO staff should involve some of their business-oriented board members in negotiations.

Discounting

As discussed earlier, lowering the price temporarily is the most common form of promotion. When considering a discounting promotion, ask yourself these questions: How much of a price discount is needed to prompt action? Will we get sufficient volume to more than offset the loss in income from transactions at the normal price? Once we offer discounts, can we ever get people to pay the full price again?

Discounting definitely works. That is why it is the number one promotion method. Yet it is questionable how deeply NPOs should get into price promotions. My experience is that people who are motivated to join a YMCA because of a bargain price do not become loyal customers. If they are stimulated to join more because of the temporarily lower prices than by a compelling desire to exercise, they are not likely to maintain the momentum of regular attendance that an effective exercise program requires.

Also, people who have paid full price during the nonpromotion period resent the discounting. When it comes time to re-enroll, they may wait in anticipation of another discount promotion.

Another worrisome feature of discount promotions is that they give the erroneous impression that the discount price is closer to our real costs and that the regular price represents an unnecessary profit for an NPO.

Guarantees

Here is a promotion method that really works: we back up our claims of good service by offering a money-back guarantee to the customer. In addition to attracting the attention of potential customers, guarantees have the positive effect of stressing high-quality, positive service delivery by our employees. At the YMCA, I promised people their money back if they were not satisfied with their child's progress in our swimming lessons. They had to let us know in writing by the fifth session. They also had to attend the parents' orientation session on the first day (during which we lowered expectations that their child was going to learn to swim right away, and instructed them about water safety at home and on vacation). Notification by the fifth lesson in a series of ten gave us enough time to switch the child to a more effective instructor. As a result of this carefully thought-out money-back boast to the community, we were able to capture the lion's share of the swim instruction market in just two years. We also did not have to give any money back, because we improved our swim lessons.

Special Events

Promotions through special events are fun and a lot of work, and take far more time than the board and staff anticipate. We are inspired to try a special event because of promises and success stories we have heard from others. We are not told enough about the unanticipated problems that are the time stealers. Thorough research of others' experiences with special events will make your planning phase much more valuable.

A genuinely entertaining, novel, or socially significant event is necessary to get good media coverage. The fact that your NPO is doing something for the first time is not enough reason for media attention.

Invite the mayor and other elected officials. This makes solving last-minute municipal problems easier. You could have unanticipated problems with the fire marshal when the parking lot overflows and people park everywhere. You may need special permits you never dreamed of.

Have an abundance of signs with your name and logo so that everyone is reminded who is sponsoring this event. Don't let a donor of soft drinks upstage you with their beautiful, professionally prepared signs. This happens too often with NPOs. We do the hard work, and for a small contribution a commercial firm gets more attention. Visit the site of the special event weeks in advance to locate the best places for signs. If the event is in your own facility, form a committee of three to discover good sign locations. Two of the three should not be on your staff or executive committee. People close to the organization know too many reasons why signs cannot be placed where they would do best.

Give staff and volunteers T-shirts and jackets to wear, imprinted with your NPO name and logo large enough to be easily read in a newspaper photograph or on TV. Colors should be bright.

Because you are using the special event to market your services, one spokesperson needs to be carefully chosen, to prevent the media from picking the wrong staff person or volunteer to quote. The spokesperson could be your chief executive, a top volunteer, or a celebrity. No matter how bright and loquacious the person is, he or she needs a full hour, or more, of coaching. Coach the spokesperson to mention your NPO name once every sixteen seconds when being interviewed. Rehearse. Quiz him or her on everything reporters might ask. Have good one- or two-sentence answers for every question. If you take too long to get your main message across, reporters may convolute it. So pick several main points. Say them simply and often.

Invite your special guests early and often. Mail, call, and hand-deliver invitations. When special guests arrive, have a quiet place for them to gather for a few minutes before you parade them through the crowd. Serve good food and beverages. Provide coat-check services so that your special guests won't have to jostle or stand in line.

Special fundraising events appeal to two groups in an NPO: board members who don't want to raise money by asking for it themselves and young adults who have little money to contribute but do have some time. The special event can give them an opportunity to socialize, express some creativity, and show support of your NPO.

Exhibits

NPOs frequently get opportunities for free exhibit space. Filling vacant store windows with NPO displays, for example, is preferable to showing signs that the local economy is suffering. NPOs also have occasional opportunities for special displays at shopping malls, trade shows, and conventions. The justification for an exhibit is in its three benefits: the cost for face-to-face contact is lower, there are opportunities for questions and answers and negotiation, and buyers usually need a shorter time to decide.

Trade shows and conventions often supply a registration list so that exhibitors can mail materials to participants prior to the event. This provides an opportunity to ask them to stop by your booth for a premium. People who stroll by the booth and notice the attractive premiums can be lured into leaving their addresses for a mailing of samples or premiums after the show. Getting follow-up leads is a major purpose of exhibiting. Often there are so many people passing by the booth that it would not be wise to consume much time making a sale on the spot.

You can create impressions and attract prospects to your exhibition booth by wearing a smile and looking more like a genuinely friendly greeter than like a salesperson and a guard. Exhibit experts say you have just four seconds to establish an impression that will remain throughout the conversation (Konopacki, 1996), so start with a greeting that eliminates any sense of sales pressure. Replace "May I help you?" with "Welcome to our booth."

During convention breaks, the exhibit floor is temporarily flooded with exhibit visitors. Staff working the booths get frustrated because they can't easily handle everyone at once. Konopacki (1996) says it is not as important how much time you spend with each visitor as much as how that time is used. According to Konopacki, 73 percent of trade show attendees report that sales demonstrations take too long; therefore, ask each person "What are the key points you would like me to cover?" You can sometimes handle multiple visitors by including them in the demonstration or conversation with the first visitor, because most exhibition hall visitors are expecting a group selling environment. If they want a private session it can be scheduled for later. Simply make eye contact with each visitor and acknowledge their presence. Research found that 60 percent of visitors who are not acknowledged within sixty seconds will walk away (Konopacki, 1996).

How can you measure the potential effectiveness of an exhibit that will cost you $1,000? You can keep track of the conversations you had with prospective buyers. If you talked with twenty-five people, the cost per contact was $40. The business trade show average is $100 per significant booth contact. You can also divide the number of personal sales calls you make that are attributable to the show to appraise its value. If you were able to get personal appointments to talk about your services with five people after the show, the average lead would have cost you $200. The industry average exceeds $250.

Marketing is an information-centered industry. Exhibiting gives you a prime opportunity to learn from the comments of the people you meet. Also important are your observations of the other exhibitors. You will find out what is new and important to them, too.

You have many wonderful ways to get your message across to the public. The discipline you must now exercise is to reaffirm your targeted audiences and look for the best return on the promotion investment. Too frequently, staff grab ideas prematurely, running with them before carefully weighing the options. With the information in this chapter you can now expect a better yield from your investments of creativity, staff and volunteer time, and money.

Chapter Ten

Packaging Programs and Services for Your Market

I can't recall anyone who has talked to me about packaging nonprofit social services. Certainly the literature about the subject is sparse. Although it may be hard at first to conceive of how one packages an ephemeral service, it is important to learn to think of our services from a packaging viewpoint.

You can bundle several different programs together into one package that sells better than the individual components. The MBF job training program in Norristown, Pennsylvania, for example, ties computer skills training for its clients with disabilities to job placement assistance and even job site coaching. These are three separate programs, usually with different staff following through to make sure their clients have the reinforcements they need to succeed. Other centers may offer their clients just one of the three services that MBF has packaged as one.

The "package" that encloses a service consists of seven major elements: brand image, price, place, service, time, volume, and frequency. After discussing how these items are perceived, I conclude this chapter with ways to discover how people want their packages wrapped.

Brand Image

Brand image affects people's desire to affiliate with your organization. Positive organizational images exert strong pulling power. Camp Fire enjoyed an excellent national reputation for years. However, in the late 1970s they decided to serve boys. Although they dropped "Girls" from their official name and showed photos of boys in their national literature, it initially remained hard for them to attract boys. Recently, when I called the national headquarters, I noticed that they called themselves "Camp Fire Boys and Girls" (boys first).

Some organizations have such powerful reputations that people seek to affiliate with them with little regard for the price. The Harvard Business School and the Stanford marching band are two examples of organizations with great draw. Conversely, community college courses in upholstery usually do not have strong affiliation powers. The courses probably sell better because they are sponsored by a college, though, than they would if sponsored by an unknown person offering to teach in their garage.

If the sponsoring organization appears to have a strong and positive image for its target market segments, then the organization should be featured prominently in the packaging. De-emphasize the sponsor when such information is not likely to be helpful. In the previous Camp Fire example, the sponsor would be touted when appealing to girls (the traditional market) and sublimated when promoting among boys during the first few years of the name change.

Price

The effective marketer will sell to people at prices acceptable to them. The packaging of fee payments ideally should be tailored for the community in which the NPO is offering its services. A large single-service facility, such as a metropolitan science museum or theater, usually has several fixed fees geared to reach a middle-income segment. The fees of neighborhood centers are more likely to reflect the incomes of people living nearby.

Coca-Cola sells more by allowing the customers many choices. Those who desire the taste of Coke can get it from a soda fountain, in a serve-yourself cafeteria line, in six-ounce cans, twelve-ounce bottles, a liter bottle, a six pack, and many other ways. Is there only one way your customers can get your services? How many different ways can a person use or sample your services? What choices are available?

Differences in buying preference can be discerned by even a casual observer of different service centers in a community. In North Minneapolis, for example, staff noticed the same bunch of fellows came regularly to the YMCA at noon to play basketball. The annual membership fee was around $100, yet they chose to pay the daily membership fee of $3 per visit. Because they attended at least three times a week, the YMCA received revenue much greater than the annual fee. The daily rate payer did not even receive the same benefits enjoyed by a person holding an annual membership. When asked why they did not pick the more economical membership rate, these fellows from the low-income inner city said they were unsure of the twelve-month future, so they weren't going to lay out that large of an investment. Staff experience showed that they would be regulars for years, not just months, but their attitude was to take one day at a time.

The basketball players may not have had the $100 to spend in one lump sum, and they may have learned that credit and loans (credit cards, bank drafts, easy payment plans) were not easy for them to manage. So they ended up not being able to take advantage of bargain long-term rates. In the same city, another YMCA unit located in a more affluent neighborhood had no trouble selling the annual rates.

Management often desires to set up one or two systems to fit all, but to derive the full market potential of a community, it can be a good idea to develop a variety of price packages.

Prices often connote the value of the service package to the buyer. High-priced services are deemed of greater quality than low-priced services, which are seen as inferior. Of course that observation is not always true, particularly with subsidized nonprofit social services. With NPOs there is often little relationship between price and quality of service. It may be good image strategy, though, to have at least one high-priced program offering. This fosters the impression that you are capable of delivering very high quality services when requested. Target the price packaging to specific segments of the market. Offer more choices to those with more money.

To those with fewer economic resources, offer simpler programs and lower fees. Price-sensitive customers can be offered no-frills products and services with fewer optional features. In difficult economic times, customers are more sensitive to the relationship between price and satisfaction in purchase decisions. They spend their discretionary dollars more cautiously.

Develop pricing packages by counter segmenting the low-price programs and hyper segmenting the high priced. Counter segmenting would meld together several small market segments, offering fewer choices to those who are most apt to use lower-priced services. Hyper segmenting would present more options to those willing to pay a premium to get them. Many YMCAs used to have a general-membership locker room with no frills but at low cost. There was another locker room called the Health Center, which cost a lot more but had the added features of sauna, whirlpool, TV, lounge, daily paper, telephone, permanent lockers, and laundry service. Hyper segmenting allows you to offer a special plan to business-people, another to families, and another to long-term members. Each has to be a viable market segment: there must be a sufficient number of people available with the ability to pay.

There are two ways to reduce the number of target markets: (1) eliminate market segments by dropping programs, and (2) fuse segments by inducing customers of differentiated services to accept more simplified choices (Resnik, Turney, and Mason, 1979, p. 101). The key ingredient for successful counter segmentation is the ability to reduce costs and pass savings to the customers with a lower fee package.

We should prominently advertise our prices when they are definite bargains. If our prices are similar to other service providers, then we should feature benefits other than price in our advertising.

Place

Place is something you can definitely promote as a benefit. The public looks at our place—our building, office, or performance area—and makes assumptions about the quality of our entire program. While experiencing a very small part of our services, people create conscious and subconscious generalizations. Let's use the example of a woman enrolling in a YWCA dance class before she decides to buy a full year's membership and the total program. She will consider investing more of her precious money and time for full membership based not only on such dance class elements as the friendliness, punctuality, and competence of the dance instructor but also on the ventilation, cleanliness, and size of the classroom, ease of parking, and feeling of personal safety.

Similarly, when an outside group uses our camp for a weekend, we should pay more attention to their subconscious sampling. Adults could be sampling our camp for a child or grandchild. Yet frequently in the off season our camps have the most attractive equipment locked up (archery, arts and crafts, canoes, volleyball). We also don't provide the rental groups with our best staff, reasoning that because the outside group has their own leadership, we can avoid the extra costs. Yet it could be the wonderful camp song leader or game leader who builds everyone's enthusiasm for the regular season.

For customers who must travel by car to our service centers, the parking lot is perhaps the most important part of our packaging. It is here that the customer starts thinking about the organization mere moments before entering the building. Consider the parking lot as part of the total building package. It should be well swept, pothole free, and well illuminated, and should provide the easiest access to the building. This means that staff and agency vehicles by strict policy should be parked in the less convenient places. Sometimes this does not happen because the staff are the first to arrive and they choose the parking places closest to the building entrance. It is also tempting for staff to reserve convenient parking places for themselves. This practice irritates customers forced to pick less attractive places. Commercial store managers do not let staff egos hinder solving this problem. They simply tell the staff that employees will park at the far corners of the parking lot, and they set the example themselves.

Parking seems such a little thing in the total marketing process, but it demands attention because the little things are what infuriate, merely irritate, or really inspire our customers. We must pay attention to the details in our packaging.

These days, remarkable numbers of people are parking themselves on the Information Highway. The services they seek are found on the Internet. Soon the Internet may completely transform our concept of marketing services. Place or location perhaps won't be as essential for the transfer of information, advice, or service.

There is general agreement that the Internet, Web, and such access services as Prodigy, America Online, and CompuServe are evolving into new forms yet to be discovered. It seems that almost everyone is jumping on board, but Don E. Schultz (1996), in a *Marketing News* column on integrated marketing, wrote: "The only people making any money on the Internet these days are the people selling stock in Web and Net technology companies, and consultants and seminar leaders who are doing all the hype. I have yet to find an advertiser, marketer, media organization, or the like who has seen anything but red ink in Internet adventures" (p. 7).

The World Wide Web was started in 1990 as a way for researchers to communicate easily over the Internet. Since then it has become an international cyberspace marketplace where companies, associations, and NPOs can advertise their services and products by setting up a Web site or home page. WebConnection helped Owings Mills establish a home page offering twenty-four-hour credit approval. Potential customers fill out an on-line application by dialing in through the Internet to the Bankers First Web site. The Northwest YMCA now has pages on the Web. A list of services are presented on screen, and viewers are encouraged to request more information.

Bob Donath (1994), in a *Marketing News* column, asks, "How will a company that cannot now adequately analyze a few hundred sales leads a year cope with thousands of inquiries pouring forth from tomorrow's media, each prospective buyer expecting an instantaneous response because everyone knows technology allows it? Database detours? Lots of ignored potential customers, probably. Technology will blossom well before we get our acts together enough to exploit it."

The Internet is clearly a very special place garnering the most attention this decade, but the warnings of Donath and Schultz should guide NPO executives who have high expectations for an immediate return on their investment.

Service

People satisfied with their service usually buy more, and they refer their friends and acquaintances to the service provider. It is much more economical to keep the customers you already have than to recruit totally new people. The way to keep them is through good customer service.

Remember the YMCA where you could buy a membership only from 10:00 A.M. to 7:00 P.M., Monday through Friday, even though the YMCA was open much longer hours and on weekends? The management reasoned that memberships were complicated and that the untrained night and weekend personnel made too many mistakes. That was nonsense! They should have simplified the system, hired more help, or done a better training job. In many NPOs, it is a wonder we get anyone to enroll. For example, NPOs may have any or all of the following policy blocks to enrollment.

- A person can enroll only themselves or their family, no neighbors.
- Enrollment must be done in person.
- The full fee is required when enrolling.
- The enrollment form asks for more information than is necessary (height, weight, names of closest friends, year in school). If I put the form aside for lack of all the answers, you failed to get my enrollment today.

- Enrollment takes twenty minutes of standing at a counter with others hovering or zooming by. Too long, too tiring, too public.

Even people who get subsidized services expect quality service. The fact that their program costs the organization more than the fees charged does not make any difference from a customer service point of view. The airlines experienced this when they significantly cut their rates to attract more passengers. Planes that had been flying half empty were now full. This meant more crowded parking lots and baggage counters and longer delays at security checkpoints. It also meant that the tired and irritated passengers encountered rushed flight attendants who were trying to be more productive. With the demands created by the increased service volume, the flight attendants often had to forsake little services such as offering pillows and magazines. Although they were getting significant air fare discounts, the passengers resented the reduction in personal attention (Flint, 1979).

Time

Among all packaging elements, timing is the easiest variable to control. We can decide when to promote, when to enroll, and how long the sessions will be. Careful attention to these variables will result in greater marketing productivity.

Programs are trending toward fewer sessions and more intensive experiences. The Marin County, California, Jewish Community Center analyzed its adult education and social programs. It found that the smaller the number of sessions offered, the greater the likelihood the course would fill up. St. Catherine's College in St. Paul, Minnesota, offered weekend college for women to complete their college educations. They could attend Friday night through Sunday afternoon on alternate weekends. The Northwest YMCA in Minneapolis was surprised by the successful parent-tot swimming lessons starting at 8:00 P.M., a time staff expected the babies to be in bed.

The market had shifted. For many working parents, this was the only practical time to enjoy a program together, late as the hour might be.

Consider seasonal cycles. There is one best time of the year to sell toys and there is one best time of the year to sign up for camp. Most toys are sold in the six weeks preceding Christmas (Birnbaum, 1980). Most campers enroll in April and May. While toy dealers are searching for ways to increase the demand for toys throughout the year (they have been focusing on promoting Easter as a toy-buying occasion), camp directors are similarly trying to lengthen their demand time. Some camp directors make the package easier to purchase by encouraging parents to sign up their children immediately after the previous season. This guarantees them the session, and perhaps even a cabin, of their choice. Others promote early enrollments at the annual Christmas reunion when emotions run high and the mosquitoes are forgotten.

The Palo Alto, California, YMCA had a special camp sign-up day each spring. The community grew to assume that was when "you've got to sign up for camp." As a bonus, free camp T-shirts were given out. The YMCA got most of their campers by packaging the enrollment timing this way.

Volume and Frequency

The College of Marin did a community demographic study in 1981, which showed that by the end of the decade there would be 50 percent fewer high school graduates in the county. That dramatic drop was important to the college because they counted on high school graduates as their primary market.

Years earlier they had extended their class offerings to attract other markets—housewives, business and professional people, people with disabilities, young children, and senior citizens—and had experienced success. Unlike the high school graduates who enrolled in the full two-year program, the nontraditional students bought in smaller quantities. They took only one or two classes at a time. Concurrently, parking and promotion burdens increased. With nontraditional students enrolled in less than a full program, the college had to make the sale more often than the customary one time for recent high school graduates. High school students bought large-volume packages whereas the nontraditional students bought smaller packages. Perhaps by awarding college degree credits that erode in value over time, the college could force larger, more concentrated package purchases from some of the nontraditional students.

If a program must be used frequently in order to be offered, it must also have lasting appeal, otherwise boredom discourages further use. Heavy users of a program are the people most likely to re-enroll. Good statistics on usage patterns will help staff monitor and avoid potential trouble spots. With an annual membership program, it is often too late to ask someone why he or she did not renew a membership. The deteriorating influences probably set in much earlier. When members get out of the habit of using their membership, it is very hard to start them going again.

The North York, Toronto, YMCA staff did an excellent job of monitoring usage patterns. In one summer study, they found the average new member used the place three times a month. That was an ominous reading. Their goal was to have members use their YMCA two to three times a week. With frequent usage, members would gain the program benefits and be likely to re-enroll a year later. The North York YMCA staff called and sent postcards to members whose attendance was low. That boosted member usage and caught negative feedback in ample time to make corrections.

Image

A service organization presents many clues to prospective customers about the nature and quality of its programs. Collectively, these clues shape the organization's image. Image, like marketing, permeates everything we do, whether we control the direction or not. Use this list of image items to more critically appraise your own NPO's corporate image.

- Stationery
    - General letterhead
    - Executive letterhead
    - Business cards
    - Envelopes
    - Statements
    - Purchase orders
    - Office memos
    - News releases
    - Special announcements
    - Large mailing envelopes with logo
    - Mailing label
    - Report forms
- Publications
    - Annual report
    - Quarterly newsletters
    - Program brochures
    - Program catalogs
    - Staff newsletters
    - Membership manuals
    - Program information fliers
- Transportation
    - Parking lot decal
    - Business car
    - Van signage
    - Bus signage

- Architecture
  Exterior design
  Interior design
  Lobby first impression
  Offices
  Service areas
- Signs
  Exterior
  Interior (permanent and temporary)
  Bulletin boards
  Directions
- Marketing assists
  Staff uniforms
  Volunteer uniforms
  Lapel name pins
  Audiovisual aids
  Portable exhibits
  Window displays
  Public service announcements
  Posters
  Pamphlet racks
  Kiosks
  Public address system
  Merchandise for sale
  Art exhibits
- Employee recognition
  Five-year service pins
  Name plate near door
  Bulletin board listing

Annual report listing

Policy manual

Safety manual

Benefits manual

House organ

Staff photos

- Dining accessories

Paper plates

Placemats

Theme music

Name tents

Menu

Ashtrays

The simplest way to discover how your organization is perceived by the public or by your members is to ask them. Telephone surveys, face-to-face interviews, and mailed questionnaires are the three tools easiest for NPO managers to use.

Ten months after opening the new Northwest YMCA building in Minneapolis, staff surveyed 2,100 of the members using a simple letter from me and a questionnaire printed on a three-by-five-inch card (see Exhibit 10.1). The purpose of the small questionnaire was to make answering look easy and thus stimulate more responses. Notice that not all the negatives on side one were on the same side of the scale. We wanted people to read each item, not make one big check mark for the whole side.

Notice that in the last question on side two, I did not ask them to list all of the bad things about the YMCA. I never want to start people making lists of everything they don't like about me or the organization. That would be dumb! When encouraged to think negative thoughts they will continue making the list for days after we have blown the whistle and called time.

Exhibit 10.1. Three-by-Five Questionnaire.

Side 1

Please rate our building-centered services by placing a mark on each scale.

Dirty building	__ I __ I __ I __ I __ I __ I	Clean building
Poor facilities	__ I __ I __ I __ I __ I __ I	Good facilities
Poor staff	__ I __ I __ I __ I __ I __ I	Good staff
Poor programs	__ I __ I __ I __ I __ I __ I	Good programs
Poor schedule	__ I __ I __ I __ I __ I __ I	Good schedule
Inexpensive	__ I __ I __ I __ I __ I __ I	Expensive
Friendly clients	__ I __ I __ I __ I __ I __ I	Unfriendly clients

Side 2

1. How often do you (or your family) participate?

Not at all	Seldom	Moderately	Regularly	Frequently
0	1/month	1/week	2/week	3/week

2. How satisfied are you with the total service?

Not at all	Neutral	So-so	Pleased	Very satisfied

3. What do you particularly like about the Y? _____

_____

_____

4. Please tell us how we can improve the YMCA for you. _____

_____

Name and address (optional)

From this study I found that most members used the YMCA frequently (a very good sign). They were positive about their experience, citing staff friendliness and helpfulness as the number one ingredient (far outstripping the brand-new multimillion-dollar facilities). The YMCA could rather easily deliver most of the improvements they wanted. They requested that we provide a cleaner locker room, fix the whirlpool, raise the temperature and pressure of the showers, and schedule the racquetball courts better. If that was all it would take to keep them happy, the YMCA could get a high rate of membership renewals. The one thing they wanted that we could not deliver on, until six years after opening, was more racquetball courts.

The Chicago YMCA built a similar but larger center on the Near North Side in 1981. Before opening, it conducted personal interviews at four shopping center locations and also had four focus-group interviews. The YMCA used the study information to help create the package it would soon be offering the public. The questionnaire was created by a private research firm, Market Facts, Inc. A similar, abbreviated model is presented in Exhibit 10.2 for the interest of NPO personnel who want to create their own study.

Seldom is the study sponsor revealed in such surveys, although a discerning respondent can guess by watching how the questions move from very general questions to quite specific opinions about an organization.

Interviewer bias can easily distort the study findings. That is why it is worth the price to hire an outside market research firm to do the study. Their trained interviewers do not quarrel or act defensively with the respondents, whereas our NPO staff and volunteers might. I remember how mad I got when showing off the new $3 million YMCA to open-house visitors and someone asked if we had indoor tennis courts, too. I thought they should be so pleased with everything we were offering them that they shouldn't dare ask for more! That attitude illustrates why you should not conduct the market interviews yourself.

If you do not have enough money to hire a professional market research firm, then consider approaching members of the local chapter of the American Marketing Association (AMA). The chapter may take on your study as a project, recommend you to a business school class in marketing research or to a large company's marketing research department, or individuals may take on the project themselves as a public service. For the downtown branch of the Minneapolis YMCA, the marketing staff at General Mills headquarters developed a questionnaire similar to Exhibit 10.1.

Exhibit 10.2. New Center Study.

1. Please check the appropriate boxes for you and your family members.

	Currently Participate		Would Use if Available	
	You	Other family member	You	Other family member
Fitness class	___	___	___	___
Basketball	___	___	___	___
Volleyball	___	___	___	___
Badminton	___	___	___	___
Ski fitness	___	___	___	___
Weight lifting	___	___	___	___
Exercise equipment	___	___	___	___
Handball	___	___	___	___
Squash	___	___	___	___
Racquetball	___	___	___	___
Swimming instruction	___	___	___	___
Swimming laps	___	___	___	___
Recreational swimming	___	___	___	___
Therapeutic swimming	___	___	___	___
Diving	___	___	___	___
Sun deck for sunbathing	___	___	___	___
Health food snacks	___	___	___	___
Sauna	___	___	___	___
Steam room	___	___	___	___
Whirlpool or hot tub	___	___	___	___
Tennis	___	___	___	___

2a. Do you belong to any health club or recreation center now?

___ Yes   ___ No (If no, skip to question 3)

2b. What is the name of this club or center?

_____

2c. How often do you use this club or center?

___ Two or more times a week

___ About once a week

   ___ Once or twice a month

   ___ Less than once a month

2d. How satisfied are you with the services you are now getting?

   ___ Very satisfied

   ___ Satisfied

   ___ Neutral

   ___ Unsatisfied

3. Please check the main program that sparked your interest and caused you to join.

   ___ Exercise classes

   ___ Individual exercise areas

   ___ Racquetball or hardball

   ___ Running or jogging

   ___ Weight lifting or body building

   ___ Tennis

   ___ Aerobic dance classes

   ___ Family recreation

   ___ Other (specify): _____

4. Considering your work hours and other commitments, what time would you most likely use a recreation/health center that offers what you want?

	Weekdays	Saturdays	Sundays
Before 6:00 A.M.	___	___	___
6:00–8:00 A.M.	___	___	___
8:00–11:00 A.M.	___	___	___
11:00–1:30 P.M.	___	___	___
1:30–3:30 P.M.	___	___	___
3:30–5:30 P.M.	___	___	___
5:30–7:30 P.M.	___	___	___
7:30–10:00 P.M.	___	___	___
After 10:00 P.M.	___	___	___

5. About how many times a week would you use this center?

   ___ Seldom or never

   ___ Once

   ___ Twice

   ___ Three times or more

Personal interview section

6a. (Point to a map of the area) Here are some sites of existing and proposed new recreation centers. From your point of view, which location would be best for you and your family? All other things being equal, which site would you prefer? _____

_____

_____

6b. Where would be your second choice? Your third choice? _____

_____

6c. Which sites would you rule out for yourself and your family? _____

_____

6d. (If the organization's preferred site is picked in 6c) Why would you rule out that site? _____

_____

_____

7. Would it matter to you if this recreation center were a private club or a YMCA?

        ____ Yes, it would matter

        ____ No, it would not matter

8a. What have you heard favorably about the YMCA? _____

_____

8b. What unfavorable comments have you heard about the YMCA? _____

_____

9. If the YMCA were to build an indoor swimming pool, four racquetball courts, locker rooms, exercise areas, and meeting rooms, how likely would you be to join, and what type of membership would you want? _____

_____

	Adult Regular Membership $150/yr	Family Membership $250/yr
Definitely would join	____	____
Probably would join	____	____
I don't know	____	____

Probably would not join ....   ___   ___

Definitely would not join ....   ___   ___

10. In paying dues, would you prefer to pay an annual fee and no added court charges, or would you prefer lower dues and a court charge each time you play?

      ___ No court charges, higher membership rate

      ___ Court charges, lower membership rate

11. Are you single or married?

      ___ Single

      ___ Married

      How many children under 21 are living with you? _____

12. Please check the box that best describes your annual household income.

      ___ Less than $25,000

      ___ $25,000–$49,999

      ___ $50,000–$74,999

      ___ $75,000–$100,000

      ___ More than $100,000

13. Please check your sex and age.

      ___ Male

      ___ Female

      ___ Under 25

      ___ 25–34

      ___ 35–44

      ___ 45–54

      ___ 55–64

      ___ 60+

14. Optional: Name_____

              Address _____

                            _____

              Telephone _____

15. Interviewer name _____

              Date _____

              Location _____

Thank you very much!

Truth in Packaging

Because this chapter has been about packaging, it is appropriate to end it with a word about truth in packaging. Post-secondary education is a good example to use because it costs thousands of dollars.

With a college education there are no warning labels, no money-back guarantees, an incomplete listing of ingredients on the package, little chance to test it, and you can't squeeze it. The price of the package is so expensive (in both dollars and opportunities lost because of the time involved), its purchase needs to be approached cautiously. A mismatch between what the student seeks and what the school offers can become a problem. Many schools have tried to use more candor in their catalogs; some will send a video to anyone showing a strong interest. To help both sides make good decisions, the schools encourage prospective students and their parents to visit the campus and talk with faculty, administrators, advisers, coaches, and college students.

Every Christmas season, the movie *Miracle on Thirty-Fourth Street* appears on television. One of its themes is the economic value of candor as practiced by the department store Santa Claus. If Macy's (his employer) didn't have it, Santa recommended that shoppers try Gimbel's (the competition). Appreciating the fresh truth, more shoppers frequented Macy's.

In a somewhat similar vein, when I showed visitors around our new YMCA, I discovered more of their specific needs and interests. We kept a supply of other NPOs' and commercial centers' brochures at the front desk. When people objected to our prices, I handed them the other organizations' information and offered them our phone to make an appointment. Rarely did anyone pursue my invitation. Most often they dismissed their objection and resumed talking about enrollment in my center.

Truth in packaging says you should not promise something you cannot deliver. On the same building tour, when people expressed an interest in our four racquetball courts, I asked how often they saw themselves playing. If they said they would want to play more than twice a week during prime time, I referred them to commercial racquetball establishments. I admitted there was little likelihood of their getting that much court time at our place. The demand for court time from all of our members was just too great. It is better to make a satisfactory referral than to sell a service that will not meet the purchaser's expectations.

Chapter Eleven

Strategies for Recruiting the Volunteers You Want Most

I have a cabin on Poplar Lake in the wilderness of northern Minnesota, where I love to fish. Because the lake is only eighteen feet from my doorstep, it is easiest for me to fish right there. My goal is simply to catch six big walleye pikes each time I go out. Sadly, I've only caught a few after untold hours of convenient fishing. The reason is that I have let convenience drastically depress my walleye pike–catching ability. There are much better lakes for walleye fishing just an hour's portage or drive away. If I seriously want to catch my limit of walleyes, I have to fish where the walleyes are always caught in greater abundance.

The same principle holds true for volunteer fishing. If you want to catch your limit of volunteers, you often have to abandon whatever is most convenient for areas that consistently produce better results. Carrying the fish analogy further, you also have to use the right bait to attract volunteers and have the right line to land them; once you have landed them, you need to know how to keep them alive and fresh. And you'll have to toss some back. It also helps to know what your walleye pike looks like and not get it confused with other fish.

This chapter identifies what typical volunteers look like. It ascribes a set of demographic characteristics to them that will help when you find yourself face to face with a potentially terrific volunteer. You will know when you have a gorgeous opportunity in front of you and also know what the odds of successful recruitment will be. You will be reminded which benefits (baits) volunteers are seeking (biting). Contract setting is next (setting the hook), during which you must pay close attention to the exchange equation—where one party gives up something of value to him or her in exchange for something of greater value from another party. Both sides feel enhanced when the deal is fair.

Volunteers serve in three distinct categories: (1) policymaking, (2) fundraising, and (3) service delivery. Each category can be considered a market segment that deserves a special market strategy.

National NPOs have developed plenty of good materials on how to attract and keep volunteers. Some of the best materials have been prepared by agencies established solely to research, train, and give recognition to volunteers. However, not many NPO professionals have paid attention to the new written materials or attended the workshops on volunteerism. They have little time for obvious information retold and repackaged. They want a fish to eat, not lessons about what fish like to eat and how big the lake is. This stance is opposite the benevolent mission dictum "Give a man a fish and he eats for a day. Teach a man how to fish and he is satisfied for life." But when you are really hungry, fish on the plate now tastes better than lessons.

NPO directors will pay more attention to the volunteer epistemology when they meet a fellow professional who honors the axioms on volunteer development, consistently uses them, and whips every other NPO professional in the sublime contest for the largest number of highly talented, highly productive volunteers. It is time for all of us to increase our skills in recruiting and keeping volunteers.

Volunteer Demographics

The dollar value of voluntary services in the United States has been estimated to be 5 percent of our gross domestic product. Millions of Americans are involved in thousands of diverse activities, such as carpools, Rotary, police patrols, and the League of Women Voters.

About half of Americans volunteer each year when the activities are broadly defined to include taking care of the neighbor's pet or plants while they are away, singing in the choir, or helping friends move. For NPO purposes, it is more helpful to know a rule of thumb. About one-third of adults volunteer on a regular, active basis—three or more hours a week (*Voluntary Action Leadership,* 1982, p. 22). Here is a more detailed breakdown showing percentages of the population that give different amounts of time.

Percentage of Population	Time Donated
16 percent	Six or more hours per week
19 percent	Three to six hours per week
25 percent	One to three hours per week
25 percent	Less than one hour per week
15 percent	None

A profile of the most likely person to volunteer in the 1980s was a white, middle-income female, college educated, married with children, and active in church. Her male counterpart was in upper- or middle-level management or a professional.

Most volunteers were in the age range of thirty to sixty, married and with children. For most NPOs, the traditional volunteer fell into one of the following categories (*Voluntary Action Leadership,* 1982, p. 25):

- *Women.* Of women volunteers, 21 percent spent twelve hours or more a month, versus 14 percent of men volunteers.

- *People who are not chief wage earners.* Twenty-three percent spent twelve hours or more per month, versus 15 percent for chief wage earners.

- *Higher-income people.* Among people earning $40,000 or more, 29 percent spent twelve hours or more per month, versus 11 percent among people earning less than $7,000 in 1980.

- *More-educated people.* Among the college educated, 34 percent spent twelve hours or more, versus 7 percent among grade school educated.

- *People living in rural areas.* Among nonurban or suburban residents, 24 percent spent twelve hours or more, versus 10 percent among urban residents.

We know which volunteer markets have the best potential. We also know that it is tougher to recruit volunteers among people in poor physical or mental health or with family members in poor health, people with extensive family responsibilities, people whose work is physically very tiring or who work long or odd hours, and people with unstable career patterns.

Right away you can probably think of exceptional volunteers who fit into some of these six categories. That is important to note because there is nothing intrinsic to age, marital status, gender, race, ethnic background, physical or mental ability or health that necessarily guarantees high or low volunteer activity. From a marketing perspective, it is worth knowing what your best prospects look like. Probably greater rewards should be given to those who are successful in recruiting large numbers from traditionally low-yielding market segments.

Seniors, teenagers, and unmarried people volunteer. Generally speaking, you have to work harder to get and keep them. It helps to know that people of distinctive ethnic or social backgrounds tend to participate mainly in volunteer groups composed of people similar to themselves.

The best volunteer markets for you are those segments similar to the volunteers you already have (and their acquaintances).

Defining the Size of Volunteer Market Segments

By ascribing particular characteristics to the volunteers you want (target marketing), you can apply the dirty demographics described in Chapter Four and some rules of thumb to determine the approximate size of the available market. Very roughly, you can estimate that 8 percent of the population is within any given five-year age range and that the gender split is fifty-fifty. Of course, in statistically small communities, retirement areas, military bases, central city business sections, college campuses, and elsewhere, the rough calculations would need to be modified. For most of us, though, there is a quick and easy method of estimating the market of volunteers to determine if we are getting our fair share. Let's look at two situations:

Situation A: A Jewish Community Center wants a mother age thirty to thirty-five to volunteer one hour per week for nine months with the drama program.

100,000 community population 50 percent female × 8 percent age qualified × 3 percent Jewish × 25 percent of the population that volunteers one to three hours per week × 3 percent interested in the arts = 2 people

Situation B: A Boys and Girls Club wants a fifty- to fifty-five-year-old male to make a significant time commitment to lead a capital funds campaign.

100,000 community population × 50 percent male × 30 percent who give extensive volunteer hours × 11 percent who do fundraising × 8 percent of people ages 50–55 = 132 people

(target market = 0.1 percent of community population)

These two examples show how to use the volunteer studies to determine target market size; they also show the absurdity of defining the target too narrowly. We double our chances of getting a volunteer when we are open to both genders. By increasing the age range we are looking for and decreasing the time commitment, we expand our market potential still further. What a case for equal opportunity!

The target market approach is valid because it enables us to focus better on the needs and interests of particular population segments. We can do a much better job satisfying the needs and interests of our key customer groups when we know them well as a group. Retail clothing merchants have certainly found this true. Whereas "one size fits all" has some universal appeal, most people prefer clothes that are tailored to fit their particular contours and lifestyle. Volunteers, like all consumers, are such a diverse lot that it is better to make specialized appeals for their time than to trust one general appeal to do the job.

Benefits of Volunteerism

When I was studying fundraising in 1980 under the mentoring of Daryl Hansen, he one day playfully surmised that some corporate executives really wanted to be generals, captains, coaches, winners, and noted high achievers. This explained the great drawing power of the Boy Scouts, Daryl said. Volunteer group leadership gives these executives an opportunity to live out some of their fantasies as soldiers, police officers, or woodsmen. Can the chair of a Fortune 500 company live out some of his or her fantasies by being on the board of the library? Maybe, but he or she may come closer as a Scout troop leader on a campout.

To be successful in recruiting more volunteer leaders, we have to study their lifestyles and appeal to their interests and fantasies. We have seen citizen crime-fighting groups such as the Guardian Angels started in twenty-five thousand communities in the United States (Morris, 1981). People's interest in both community safety and personal adventure was aroused. In exchange for risking their lives in some cases, or at least in exchange for the inconvenience of going out on regular patrols, what are these and other volunteers getting? It is helpful to know what benefits they are trading their time for.

First, we should recognize that all human beings seek the basics (Barbeito and Hoel, 1977, p. 14):

- *Survival:* the need for nourishment, shelter, warmth
- *Emotional security:* insulation from basic fears of rejection
- *Sense of self-worth:* the need to feel of value to someone

- *Love:* the need to be intimate
- *Power:* the need to control part of one's environment and avoid being controlled by someone else
- *Roots:* the need to identify with one's family, history, and some stable factors
- *Immortality:* the need to live, stay young, be remembered
- *Sex:* the need to express sexual feelings and perpetuate the race

Those are the basic elements we all seek in our actions. Seldom will anyone mention them, directly, in explaining why they have volunteered. Instead, they will mention narrower goals, but these goals will fall into the previous categories.

Here are a number of ways people commonly frame their reasons for volunteering (Schindler-Rainman and Lippitt, 1975, p. 48). Addressing these reasons in your promotion will produce better results.

- It sounds like fun.
- It will be a break in my routine, an opportunity to relieve boredom.
- They really need and want me.
- It's a chance to learn new skills.
- It's a chance to learn and help me get ahead.
- The visibility could help me on my job.
- It could help me with my personal life.
- I've received a lot of help. Now it's my turn to repay.
- It's a critical need. I've got to do my part.
- I need to do something.
- It's one of the activities we do, part of our program.
- My friend is asking me.
- I don't feel I can say no to the important person asking me.
- They wouldn't ask me if it wasn't important.

- I'll get my own desk and telephone.
- I can use the equipment and facilities for free.
- I can make some new friends.

Conversely, people may see insufficient personal benefits. They will often frame their reasons for resisting volunteer work in these ways (Schindler-Rainman and Lippitt, 1975, p. 48).

- It sounds like routine work.
- This is not where the fun is.
- I owe my time and energy to my family.
- I don't feel I have any skill that's needed.
- I'm scared of what I might get into.
- I should be paid for this.
- I think I am too old for that.
- It's not clear what kind of help and support I'd get.
- It might tie me down at times—I'd want to be free to do other things.
- It's unpopular; I'll be involved in conflict.
- My colleagues would not support my getting into that.
- My family would object.
- They are paying others for the same activity.
- It's too far from where I live.
- There is not a good place for the volunteers to have of their own.
- Their time schedule is too rigid.
- That area is dangerous.

Anticipate these objections before any recruitment session and prepare counter arguments to overcome them. This process makes a good group exercise before launching a volunteer recruitment campaign. As I mentioned before, do not make the mistake of list-ing in a recruitment brochure or newsletter all the expected objections and your solutions. Don't provide prospective volunteers with objections they had never even considered (but now that you mention it . . .).

Once you know the benefits a volunteer is seeking, you can match volunteers to specific jobs and design appropriate lures to catch your prospects. Earlier in this chapter I cited three categories of volunteers: policymaking, fundraising, and direct service. Those volunteers primarily motivated by a desire for action and personal involvement would probably be more satisfied with direct service volunteering. The association with program participants could satisfy some of the volunteer's needs for emotional associations with others.

Altruistic motivations for volunteering changed when more women started working outside of their homes. The traditional volunteer market, women homemakers, was strongly affected by the back-to-work movement of the 1970s and 1980s. According to a Sperry and Hutchinson Company report, altruism was replaced by self-fulfillment on the job and by career advancement opportunities ("Altruism Replaced," 1980). To respond, traditional women's organizations, such as the YWCA, developed more issue-oriented programming, in keeping with the interests of women's changing status in the workplace. The new type of woman volunteer was more time pressured than her predecessors. This made many organizations streamline their agendas and administrative practices. Meeting times and dates were altered to fit the tighter schedules of working women. It would have been easy for time-harassed women to give up their volunteer activities, but many found them very satisfying. Many saw active involvement, particularly on NPO boards, as helpful to both their personal and professional goals (Sautter, 1982).

Policymaking board and committee work demands volunteers who are reflective and interested in the broader community's welfare. Some people will feel more comfortable in committee work than in direct service to clients. In addition, there are some inherent benefits with strong appeal.

Being active with an NPO in which the volunteer's corporation has shown strong interest strengthens the likelihood of the volunteer being favorably noticed by the corporation. Involvement with other business leaders on an NPO board can also draw the attention of prospective employers or good reference contacts. The board meeting can be a good opportunity to demonstrate skills not used on the job. Active NPO involvement may also provide a risk-free atmosphere where a volunteer can sharpen professional skills. Members of prestigious boards are also able to watch power brokers in action and gain other opportunities not normally afforded the average person. Making new friends among the NPO board members provides an opportunity for some career mentoring or a chance to be a mentor.

Many businesspeople see volunteering with NPOs as good for business. Said the owner of a pizza chain: "Community involvement is the owner's most important part of his working day. Being an active part of the neighborhood community is much more effective than anything else as a marketing tool. Supporting things like local sports teams and community organizations is simply crucial" ("West's Pizza King," 1982).

Tim Schlitzer, head of the Pennsylvania Environmental Fund, organized volunteers from the Westinghouse Corporation in Pittsburgh in 1996 to help create a riverfront park. Schlitzer's strategy was to get plenty of corporate employees, from vice presidents to secretaries, involved in environmental projects. Schlitzer was convinced that getting employees, neighborhood residents, and other concerned citizens into projects bigger than picking up litter and planting trees increased ownership in larger environmental plans.

Attracting more volunteers for environmental projects loomed as a priority in 1996. The funding typically came from foundation grants, membership, and government grants; and all the talk in 1996 was about less government support. In an attempt to pick up more corporate support, Schlitzer changed his statewide environmental message away from confrontation and challenge. Getting all sides to recognize that environmental problems exist, the Pennsylvania Environmental Fund helped organize a wide variety of volunteers to correct problems together. One of the benefits of working with the Environmental Fund for corporations associated with pollution problems was the opportunity to improve their public image.

So far we have discussed the benefits of volunteering on the board and committee level and the program level. Fundraising, the third major segment of volunteerism, is an area where staff have seldom identified the benefits for volunteers. Some of us are almost ashamed that we have to recruit volunteers for such a distasteful task. When we are apologetic for asking them to raise money for the NPO, it is even more difficult to imagine there are legitimate benefits in it for them.

I have met very few volunteers who admit they enjoy fundraising, yet there are millions who do it each year. They get the benefits of being able to measure the impact of their actions more easily than anyone else. Fundraising can satisfy some of their needs for influence, recognition, and impact on the wider community.

When Bob Fisher was assistant to the chair of the board of Saga Corporation, he helped me compose a list of the benefits derived from volunteering in the San Francisco YMCA's annual support campaign (see Exhibit 11.1). We printed several thousand brochures and used them unapologetically when we recruited fundraisers each year. The brochures gave us greater confidence in our recruitment campaign and thus ensured greater success.

Recruiting Volunteers

An *Independent Sector* survey of volunteers ("Americans Volunteer," 1982) reveals how they learned about the volunteer opportunity and why they chose to become involved. Most people volunteered simply because they were asked (44 percent). Fewer initiated the activity on their own (25 percent). There was a greater proclivity to volunteering if they had a family member or friend who benefited from the activity (29 percent). Another large segment of the population volunteered because they were members of a group or organization that did that activity (31 percent).

Exhibit 11.1. Fundraiser Recruitment.

When You Do This	You Gain	And Your Community Gains
You support an important force for good.	You feel good making good things happen.	More fun, fitness, fellowship. Less delinquency, less stress, less heartache. Happier and healthier children, adults, families. More productive people.
You will be joining a whole campaign organization of volunteers.	This gives you an opportunity for **personal PR** and the **stimulation** and **excitement** the meeting of top folks always provides.	All levels of the community are working together. Business people, teachers, fire fighters, nurses, etc.
You work on a team with an established goal and specific time schedule.	With teams that are balanced in abilities you can enjoy **friendly** competition. Volunteers, not staff, set the goals.	Teamwork alliances create better communities.
You receive guidance and support from campaign leadership and staff. You get feedback on how well you and your team are doing.	You improve your own **leadership** skills. You end up a winner. Feedback offers excellent opportunities to succeed. Regular reports of our progress help you avoid slumps and stay on target.	Greater leadership potential at all levels.
You attend an interesting, quick-paced kick-off and victory celebration.	Fun. And a chance to build enthusiasm. Let's face it: enthusiasm really sells it. It invigorates you and provides a good stimulus for a wondrous achievement.	Fresh spirit and vitality.
You follow a definite, short-term schedule.	You make a real difference in 4 short weeks, and then rest for 48.	We get more professional staff service because they are able to limit their fundraising time.

| You raise money. | Provide greater **services** and **programs** for this community. | Counseling, child care, camping, seniors, fitness, recreation, family enrichment, delinquency prevention, tutoring. |
| You influence kids' lives. | Gain personal satisfaction and an excellent return on your invest- of time, talent, and treasure. | Many happier children who would not otherwise go to camp, receive counseling, and learn how to be even better Americans. |

You can use the data in this study to improve your success ratio in recruiting volunteers. Try these techniques:

- Actively ask people to help. Don't wait for them to ask you. (Don't wait for volunteers to volunteer).
- Ask first the families and friends of program beneficiaries. They are more likely than others to say yes when asked.
- Try getting the commitment of whole groups of people to help with your project. If an organization decides to work on your project, there is greater likelihood its members will carry out the assignment. Too often we find ourselves busily recruiting individuals in the group before we have presented the opportunity to the entire organization.

Very few volunteers reported first learning about a volunteer activity from a radio, television, or printed advertisement ("Americans Volunteer," 1982). Although it is tempting to spend a lot of time working on those media, nothing beats personal sales. Ads function best as reinforcements to these personal sales approaches, making the recruiters feel good and bolstering their confidence. Of course, some types of volunteer activity may be sensitive and potentially embarrassing. Therefore, an impersonal approach via posters or printed ads may be the only logical method of volunteer recruitment. These will be the exceptions for most NPOs, though.

Make an Offer They Can't Resist

The most commonly used seductive ploy to lure volunteers into an effort is to promise that "it won't take very much of your time." That boast is a falsehood 95 percent of the time. In reality, the volunteer experience almost always takes more time than originally imagined.

The usual ploy goes something like this: "George, we have a vacancy on our board, and I would be pleased if you would agree to join us. You know most of our current board members. You are as busy as everyone else, but we meet only once a quarter at lunch, and meetings rarely take more than two hours. You have to eat somewhere, and we hope you will accept. I won't burden you with a lot of homework. In fact, we don't send out any material prior to meetings. Your point of view as a corporate CEO, a proven generalist, would be most helpful to me" (Mace, 1976). This example was intended by its author to illustrate business practices; however, I think it is identical to what happens with NPO recruitment.

It is better to be honest about the full price of membership during the volunteer recruitment period, especially for boards and committees. Is there a fundraising campaign, and will they be expected to get and give a good sum? Are there occasional legal actions and executive staff changes to contend with? Will a new director have to call on his or her friends for something the NPO needs: new board members, donations of money and equipment, or technical assistance?

What monetary outlays do we expect of the different levels of volunteers in the organization? For some people, the dollar amounts are inconsequential, but for low-paid people they may be too taxing. Are there hidden costs such as uniforms; the annual convention; the price of luncheons, dinners, and the annual meeting; and equipment or supplies? How much time and energy is required? How much reading and preparation is necessary to be a good volunteer? How much training time is required by the organization? Where are the meetings held? Is it convenient for some but so inconvenient for others that they will have poor attendance?

No volunteer wants to let the organization down. The volunteer may want to help but is reluctant because he or she feels unable to fulfill all of the organization's expectations. This is where good marketing comes in. A sales stance would try to convince the volunteer to enlist by minimizing talk about the costs of the commitment. The marketing approach, I suggest, focuses more on the needs and interests of the volunteer. Instead of trying to fit the volunteer into an organizational mold of expectations, a marketing approach during the recruitment phase seeks to learn more about the potential volunteer. A satisfactory match between the person's interests and the organization's needs may, or may not, be made. Clearer communication should result from both parties being honest and up-front about what they desire in the relationship.

Potential volunteers should be able to state their interests candidly. The organization then needs to decide how it can respond to each opportunity. Ideally, it will tailor each volunteer contract to reflect each person's abilities and interests.

Gone are the days when many of us can demand that our volunteers fit all of our performance criteria. Now we have a situation in which much more bargaining is called for.

To make an offer prospects cannot resist, consider the following approaches:

- Emphasize moral, civic, and social obligations that can be fulfilled through participation in your NPO.
- Emphasize the benefits the community will get with help from volunteers like them, but don't overdo the "do-gooder" image.
- Make it clear how your participants and volunteers are special, different, unique. Give them a list of prominent people who are in the organization.

- Tell about some of the personal benefits they can hope to derive from volunteering with your group, but don't make promises you can't keep.

- Emphasize the sense of fellowship, the spirit of the group. Make it clear that your group is warm and accepting—nice to be with.

- Emphasize the specific contribution you hope the prospective volunteer will make to help your organization achieve its goals. Show that you respect the person's individuality and have a special place for him or her.

- Try to get support from the potential volunteer's family and friends for the new role with you.

- Impress prospective volunteers with the high quality of your recruitment effort, the place, the calibre of people they initially meet, and the printed documents used to reinforce your request.

- Give evidence of past successes so they will know they are about to join a winning team.

- Introduce them to your very best volunteers (but not the fanatics) so they can see some good role models of what you are talking about.

- Offer them guaranteed satisfaction. Find a way they can back out of the volunteer role without losing face if they find the experience unsatisfactory.

- Describe how you will help them succeed through training, orientation, and consultation.

Also essential in the marketing process are careful observation and listening. Where a sales approach seeks to persuade a person to do something the organization wants, a marketing approach reveals some opportunities and listens carefully to how the potential volunteer responds to them. It is even good during the listening period to take notes for the files, because we often forget. Your challenge is not to be so busy and absorbed in selling the volunteer opportunity that you do not hear all the prospect is saying.

Land the Transients

The traditional volunteer markets have eroded with increased job and residence instability. People are not staying put as long as they used to. We need special strategies to make use of the volunteers in transition.

NPO's need to create more short-term volunteer jobs and job descriptions. Discover for your NPO what a person can do for a short period and then leave without feeling he or she is abandoning the organization. Create smaller volunteer packages to better fit the needs of people experiencing transition in their lives.

Many NPOs have a national network of local affiliates. This feature helps when a good volunteer moves to another community. Linking former volunteers to another NPO in their new community would likely help them in adjusting to their new home.

Negotiate the Exchange Process

To make sure that the volunteer task is well understood, some organizations have developed written job descriptions that they negotiate with each volunteer.

The 1979 Camp Fire manual *Volunteer Staff: Recruiting, Selecting, Retaining* included sample job descriptions for every position as models for local councils to use (Camp Fire, 1979). The organization requested volunteer group leaders be at least eighteen years old, serve five hours per week for a year, attend orientation and training sessions, be responsible for group safety, hold periodic parents' meetings, hold regular group meetings with the children, keep records, and follow all policies of the national organization.

The Camp Fire program has moved away from volunteer recruitment using such guilt-inducing methods as saying, "If you don't become a leader your child won't have a Blue Bird Club," and misrepresenting the time required: "It doesn't take much time; only one afternoon a week for club meetings." Instead, they promise that Camp Fire volunteer jobs will provide challenging and interesting opportunities for personal growth. They offer benefits people want for themselves.

The Wichita Council of Camp Fire developed a volunteer contract to be agreed on and signed by three parties: the volunteer, her supervisor, and the council president or executive director. The contract included a job description, the responsibilities of the agency to the volunteer, a clear understanding of the specific needs of the volunteer, and the joint responsibilities of the agency and the volunteer. The council not only defined the duration of the contract but also put in writing when it would be reviewed.

Written volunteer job descriptions are probably quite palatable for well-educated, middle-income, young and middle-aged adults, the traditional volunteer market. And new volunteers will often accept a job description or contract without much negotiation. Because negotiating the exchange is critical to good marketing, it helps to have the expected roles mutually agreed on. There are always ambiguities about who should do what, so talk about them early.

Job descriptions and role expectations require that attention be paid to changing demographics. The Girl Scouts and Camp Fire are dependent on committed volunteers, and they have been highly successful for seven decades. Yet it is getting harder for them to attract volunteers for group leadership assignments. The reason is apparent: to be a good leader and gain satisfaction from the job, volunteers need to invest about five and a half hours per week, time few working women have.

When a time-harassed person volunteers to do a job, he or she wants to get it over quickly. The problem for the Girl Scout and Camp Fire organizations is that they are selling a group process, whereas many of the volunteer leaders are buying products. The group process involves helping children plan their activities and learn about group consensus and decision making. They evaluate their experiences to learn from their successes and mistakes so they can generalize and apply what they have learned to future life challenges. That learning takes a lot of work from the leader, a lot more than some volunteers want to mess with. So they seek simply to fill the schedule with activities. Do things. Make or sell products. Take trips. Do a lot of activities, but do not waste time having the children plan. It is much harder to help children learn to share loving acts than it is to drive a station wagon. The product-oriented leader demands a list of programs and places to go. She or he wants prepackaged experiences for the children.

Besides asking for five and a half hours per week, Girl Scouts and Camp Fire want a leader to serve ten months. Some of the adult volunteers respond by offering to share the leadership. It is common for an interested volunteer to recruit three others to help her provide team leadership to the group, each serving one fourth of the time requested of one person.

More and more volunteers (and staff too) are expressing preference for short-term over long-term experiences. Little League, youth soccer, and football meet this requirement well. The attractiveness to the potential youth sports volunteer is instant gratification, easy-to-understand processes, a prepackaged program, and a definite beginning and end to the task.

Potential volunteers for all NPOs may be reluctant to say yes because they feel they will be sucked into a whirlpool of successive demands until they are no longer able to please and cannot escape without making someone feel bad toward them. Allow these prospects to negotiate with you during an interview. Stephen McCurley (1994, p. 521) indicated that one of the most neglected areas of volunteer management has been the effective interviewing of volunteers and matching them with tasks and environments they will truly enjoy.

Because of the time demands, volunteers have to make their choices carefully, usually by limiting their interests. Hospital trustees, for example, should act on behalf of no more than one hospital. When properly done, the volunteer job consumes so much of their time that they cannot devote responsible thought and effort to other hospitals.

Keeping Fresh the Volunteers You've Already Got

The ball game is not over when the volunteer is recruited and presented with a job description. Even the most talented, energetic, committed volunteer needs attention, direction, and occasional confrontation.

Volunteers need constant nurture. This is a fact. Just like our own teenagers, they forget. We tell our teenage children to clean up their rooms, once, twice, a million times; similar situations exist with our volunteer annual support campaigners and many other volunteers. They need constant prodding and reinforcement to get the job done. We need to remind them what business we are in (our real mission), what our style of operation is (the values that are most important to us), who comes first, our goals, and the timetable for their activity.

Marketing is a process of not only recruiting new customers but also retaining the ones you already have. It is of value, therefore, to note why most volunteers say they continue. The top five reasons given by 843 people interviewed in one study (*Voluntary Action Leadership*, 1982, p. 29) were as follows:

1. Like helping others and doing something useful

2. Interested in the activity

3. Feel needed and enjoy the volunteer work

4. Volunteer work helps a child, relative, or friend

5. Religious concerns

Volunteers are also motivated to stay on longer when they have real opportunities to participate in problem solving. As Neil Pendleton said, "No group of non-paid workers can long be kept active without their assuming some responsibility, and thus, eventually, some voice in decision-making" (Pendleton, 1981, p. 34).

To keep volunteers' interest high we need to continually appeal to those interests and their needs. We cannot limit our marketing solely to the recruitment process. To check how well your NPO is doing in this area, answer these questions:

- In setting a contract between the volunteer and our NPO, do we allow for each individual's level of interest, ability, limited time, and other variables? Do we impose a sense of guilt or tension into the relationship because they cannot or will not buy 100 percent of the package?

- Do we publicize our volunteers' accomplishments to the public often enough? Do we save our recognitions until the event is all over and perhaps a bit too late?

- Do we encourage our fundraising volunteers to participate in the NPO's program and feel its very heartbeat?

- Do we take advantage of the unique skills our volunteers have, or do we just have them doing the tasks we want done, and in our way only?

- Do we provide them with really good training opportunities, as meaningful to them as they are beneficial to the NPO?

- Do we encourage social situations in which volunteers and staff can mix as peers? Do we allow them to have fun together?

- Do we keep our meetings interesting, avoiding too much discussion about the budget, property, liabilities, and fundraising?

- Do we have a good way of pairing experienced volunteers with newer ones? Do we encourage a mentoring process?

- Do we welcome their candid evaluations of our services, or are we constantly trying to explain things to them?

- Do we pay attention to what happens to our volunteers between sessions? Do we show that we care about their personal lives, that we are more interested in them as people than as convenient resources?

- Do we avoid any appearance of staff condescension? (Condescension is rarely intended.) Do we show real respect for the work they are doing?

Why Volunteers Quit

The primary reasons volunteers quit, according to surveys, are that (1) they become too busy to continue, (2) they have private, personal reasons, (3) they move, (4) the project or task was completed, and (5) they changed jobs or went to school. Probing the dissatisfactions felt by volunteers, some studies revealed they felt underutilized—that the staff did not release enough responsibility to them (Pendelton, 1982, p. 35). Many also complained of a lack of good communication with staff. The primary reasons volunteers quit need to be accepted graciously, but dissatisfactions should be tackled and resolved. Frequent monitoring of their satisfaction will help forestall many volunteer problems. If you express charitable, nonjudgmental acceptance when volunteers quit, you stand a better chance of maintaining their loyalty beyond their service period.

Auditing Volunteer Experiences

An organization dependent on a heavy supply of volunteers and on their goodwill should regularly audit their experiences from a marketing viewpoint. This process includes a review of the recruitment objectives, the numerical goals, the population segments attracted and the ones not reached, the orientation program, the communication vehicles, and a periodic summary of the NPO's strengths and weaknesses in the volunteer market. It is perhaps easier to see how well or poorly you are doing when you compare your NPO with another. Study the major organizations competing for volunteers to see how they do it. Find out how they recruit volunteers, which segments they are especially good at attracting, and how well they reward them.

A little market research will help determine what the volunteer benefits are in your program. Then you can assess if the benefits can be improved at negligible additional cost.

Actually talking to prospective and current volunteers is the best method of conducting market research. Remembering above all else to listen attentively to what they say, simply find some people who fit the description of your most typical volunteers and ask questions. You cannot rely on the national volunteer studies or even the information in this book to get a fine-tuning of your volunteers. You must discover the peculiarities of your own market.

Ask them the following questions: What is in it for them? What do they do now with their time? What community issues really concern them? What volunteering might they do if an organizational barrier were removed? What activities are their family and friends now involved in? What would they like to do if they had a little more time?

Recruiting Board Members

Nonprofit organizations can be very frustrating to profit-oriented businesspeople. In an excellent *Harvard Business Review* article, Cecily Cannon Selby (1978), a former national executive director of Girl Scouts USA, explained that the resilient strengths of NPOs are often perceived as their weaknesses by businesspeople. The voluntary nature of some leadership roles is perhaps the biggest source of frustration. If roles are not well understood, business executives may pull back, frustrated in their inability to help the NPO to the full extent of their potential. They may also harm the NPO. Let's say a businessperson agrees to serve on the all-important nominating committee of Camp Fire. The professional staff member can coach him or her, but cannot require the volunteer to attend briefing sessions. Only a volunteer can properly

chastise another volunteer for nonperformance. Yet that nominating committee member can have a significant and devastating
effect on the organization if the wrong leaders are nominated, the
wrong people are invited to join the board, and the remaining
board is not purged of "dead wood." This is why it is critical to pay
close attention to the recruiting process for board members and
other key volunteer positions.

Here are some suggestions for whom to recruit and how to go
about it. Be careful of selecting the easiest, most comfortable candidates. Decide what kind of volunteers your organization really
needs to make it successful, and go after them.

The Girl Scouts USA (GSUSA) national board of directors in
1993 charged the national organization and local councils to
increase and maintain the diversity of membership. Each council
nominating committee must propose a balanced slate of board candidates that reflects the racial, ethnic, and social composition of the
community. GSUSA issues guidelines that nominating committees
use in examining the slate's diversity in terms of skills, including
fundraising, finance management, community contacts and public
relations, geographic location, racial and ethnic identification, spir-
itual tradition, and gender (Weber, 1994).

During the past two decades, large NPOs concentrated on improving the management skills of their staff. They had intensive
training in strategic planning and management by objectives. As
the staffs got smarter, the volunteers had to work harder and think
sharper. Simple solutions served by the board to the staff no longer
satisfied. Policymaking volunteers who simply meant well were
replaced by volunteers with more specific desirable traits.

Good board development, it was reasoned, would result in better financial development. There was a dollar payoff value to making board development a high organizational priority.

It is arguable that certain personality traits are more conducive
to a person's achieving high levels of voluntary action (Smith and
Reddy, 1972). They include

- An open, friendly, easy approach to people
- Self-confidence and good psychic adjustment
- A willingness to take charge and lead
- A real desire to achieve
- Flexibility and adaptability
- A sense of community responsibility, morality, justice
- More energy than most people
- Good ability to communicate verbally

In addition to seeking particular abilities, connections, and personality traits, seek new people from outside the organization to keep fresh ideas flowing and to maintain a challenging atmosphere. Pick the very best or the ones who are likely to reach the top in a few years (the comers). Be aware that NPO boards are becoming more diverse in membership so that more women, those under age twenty-five, and racial minorities are represented.

For any NPO, there is a problem when the entire board gets involved in market planning or any other complex process. Pounds of paperwork are produced, but very little strategic guidance for the organization emerges. Group consensus demands that everyone's ideas are woven into the final report. This is one of the reasons no one should be recruited primarily to represent special constituencies. It kills the candor of discussion and decision making. Plans end up representing a combination of everyone's wishes rather than some hard-nosed decision making that could allay organizational grief.

When preparing to approach a potential board or committee member, assemble a recruitment team composed of people the prospect will respect. Gather preapproach information. Find out as much as you can about a prospect's interests and limitations before asking him or her to volunteer. Try to predetermine the prospect's primary buying motives. Are the motives intellectual, cause oriented, emotional, self-serving, in response to pressure? In most cases, prospects will be flattered that you wanted to learn about them before your first recruitment conversation. Also, seek advice from the "movers and shakers" in your organization before making your first move. It will help you avoid some traps and get their involvement in the process.

Recruit in person, not by telephone or mail, if you can help it. Create an informal, pleasant atmosphere in which to discuss the proposal. Expect to have several conversations to accomplish the task well. The bigger the volunteer task, the more the details need to be discussed, allowing everyone time to think about the ramifications. Major capital fund campaign leadership, for example, is seldom recruited during one lunch hour. The opportunity is presented and discussion ensues. A bargain is struck when both parties feel comfortable with the agreement. Never recruit under adverse conditions. Avoid trying to do it as the class breaks up, the luncheon club meeting adjourns, on the street corner, in a public lobby or a noisy restaurant, when the kids are around, and at other distracting places and times. Bad choice of location and time forces you to rush the presentation and reduces the opportunity for good discourse.

Predetermine your minimum time needs. Will the volunteer have to do your activity for a full year, three years, one night, one event? What is the minimum time commitment you require in order for the volunteer to be successful? Plan to reveal that there will be times when the person will be asked to devote his or her volunteer time and expertise almost exclusively to your NPO. Agreement to this paves the way for board retreats where further deliberations can take place.

In your presentation, show the big picture first. Talk about major community issues before telling what your NPO is doing to affect positively that environment. People get more excited when they feel their actions in some way will have a positive effect on major issues of the day. Present opportunities for volunteers to use their talents and resources to make an impact in the community or organization. Remember that this is a fair exchange—you need not go begging. In exchange for their time and talent, you are offering them an opportunity for personal enrichment. Talk about the community's needs, not just your NPO's needs. Instead of saying, for example, "We need an accountant on our board to improve our budgeting processes," substitute "The community has problems that we can more effectively address with your help. As a specialist, you can help our organization reach even more people in need by helping us develop a stronger and more productive internal organization." Then list the benefits the prospect can expect to receive from volunteering for a specific task.

Show your own enthusiasm for the program. Avoid much discussion about organizational problems. Stress, instead, the positive impact this new leadership team will soon have—with the prospect's help. Paint a word picture that describes the full potential of the effort.

Have an alternative offer prepared ahead of time. If the prospect says no, what else can you offer? If he or she won't chair a fundraising campaign, will the prospect consider being a division leader, or at least a campaigner? How about a personal gift, then, if the person isn't going to do any of the volunteer campaigning? This process gives the prospect more opportunity to say yes and feel good about the solicitation process. Never leave the prospect with a bad feeling about the encounter. Prospects don't like saying no, so give them something they can say yes to.

Finally, recruit privately. Don't let it be known whom you are recruiting. If that person turns you down, for whatever reason, it will be harder to get the second, third, or fourth prospect to take the job. Few are flattered when offered a job their peers have already turned down.

To return to the analogy that opened this chapter: the principles of good fishing require that we return to the water any creatures we don't intend to consume or sell. Little ones are left to grow another season, and much more often these days, the trophy-size fish are photographed and also returned to the water, left for someone else to enjoy or free to continue on with their lives.

Chapter Twelve

Your Marketing Strategy

Fifteen Steps for Putting It All Together

So where do you start? Throughout this book I have pointed out the pitfalls of various approaches and recommended others. I have mentioned a number of "first steps." Included among them were these: recognize what business (or businesses) you are in, focus your marketing efforts on a few primary market segments, and learn more about the demographics and psychographics of those key segments. I told you how to do your own market research to discover the primary buying motives of your customers, and I showed you how to audit the quality of your services.

You have already started. You didn't wait until you picked up this book. In the opening chapter, I showed how we are all marketing, all the time. It is our normal way of keeping our NPO thriving. But the value of pursuing the recommendations and adapting the examples in this book to fit your situation lies in getting much better with the effort.

Marketing is a careerlong enterprise for the effective NPO executive. We are not finished when one plan is crafted, approved, and implemented. Good management calls for one marketing plan and strategy after another. As the market changes, so must our plans. Thus I will conclude with some suggestions on how you can make good use of your initial time and effort. With limited time, it is best to pick your path carefully before stepping out.

When I have asked NPO managers which parts of the classic marketing scheme get a disproportionate amount of staff attention, they consistently identify the promotion area. "We make up for mistakes in the other fourteen areas," they often say, "by just promoting harder." The area they say suffers from too little attention is the audit phase. "We don't spend enough time measuring the results." Consequently, improvements are not implemented fast enough, and deterioration starts too soon. You can now improve on their experience by paying more attention to all fifteen steps in the classic marketing scheme; the remainder of this chapter is spent outlining these steps. Figure 12.1 depicts the total marketing effort from idea inception, through program or service development, to research and auditing.

Step 1: Choose to do something.

- "We will cut the number of youths processed by the juvenile justice system in half."
- "We will become the number one agency for volunteers."
- "With our new pool, we will capture the lion's share of the swim instruction market within two years."
- "Our theater will become financially viable and debt free."

Step 2: Evaluate your potential for success. Determine

- Market size and market trends
- Market vulnerabilities
- Financial risks
- Priority of felt need
- Compatibility with your organization, your goals, present staff, current image, mission

Step 3: Conduct market research. Determine

- Consumer attitudes toward the program category in general
- Consumer attitudes toward various organizations offering similar services

Figure 12.1. The Classic Marketing Scheme.

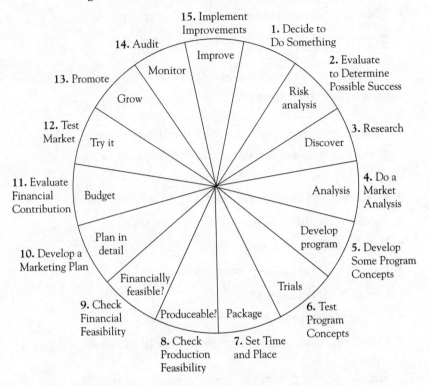

- The public image of your organization
- Customer satisfaction with current service providers
- Improvements customers and consumers want

Step 4: Do a market analysis. Consider the following market characteristics and opportunities.

- Degree of market saturation (Example: are there already too many pools, hospital beds, theater seats, camp slots, or day-care openings?)
- Relative market shares of the top five service providers
- Present consumer satisfaction
- Present consumer loyalty
- Significant market segments
- Competitor retaliation
- Amount of felt need
- Demographics: census, geography, household income, and so on

Step 5: Develop some program concepts to meet the expected demand. Notice that we do not develop the program—an answer to perceived problems—until step 5. Too often we come back from a conference inspired with a program idea, the solution, and try to lay it on the organization and our community without enough attention to the first four steps.

Step 6: Test the program concepts.

- Find out if anyone is likely to buy.
- Determine where the strongest consumer demand likely will be.
- Test various program variations.
- Determine your competitive advantages in price, quality, and convenience.

Step 7: Package the program.

- Determine timing, place, and amenities.
- When will it be offered?
- How long will the sessions last?
- How many sessions will be offered the first year?
- Where will it be done, and what location factors will affect your success?

Step 8: Check the production feasibility. Even if we are successful in introducing this program, can we continue to produce it? Will it receive enough nurture? Will it have room to grow? Features to consider include the following:

- Facility capacity
- Highest volume that can be served
- Leadership requirements and size of our leadership pool
- Time slots available
- Subsidies available

Step 9: Check the financial feasibility. Not until step 9 are finances seriously considered. The easiest way to kill a good idea is to prematurely attach finances to it. Because resources are perpetually tight, it is best to ignore negative fiscal features until new ideas fully develop.

Step 10: Develop a marketing plan. Do detailed market planning after completing the first nine steps. Prepare written statements about strategies required to create demand for the program. Market plans differ from organization to organization. There is no fixed format. The plan must be written, and must cover anything important to your decision makers. Usually this includes elements from the following list.

- Marketing

  Facts

  Opportunities

  Problems

  A means of capitalizing on opportunities

  Program definition

  Competitive performance

  Delineated segments of potential customers and consumers

  Benefits of the program to consumers and others

- Advertising

  Promotion techniques

  Tying consumer benefits to features advertised

  Ways to realize short-term and long-term volume objectives

- Proof

  Documented evidence the program will produce the espoused benefits

  Endorsement letters from satisfied users

  Endorsement letters from others (hospital president, police chief, United Way executive)

  Documented consumer research

- Pricing

  Fees charged by similar service providers

  Consumer attitudes toward price variations

  Break-even analysis

  Production costs

  Value to the consumer

  Minimum acceptable revenue

  Pricing objective: make money, recover costs, gain publicity, start with a new market, increase overall service volume, provide a high-quality service to a limited clientele

- Production targets
    Enrollment goals
    Attendance expected
    Mail and telephone responses

Step 11: Evaluate the financial contribution. Aim for a specific return on the investment.

- Forecast three-year volume
- Study experience of others in the field
- Calculate length of payoff period
- Determine annual subsidy requirements
    Staff time
    United Way
    Contributions
    Other supports
- Evaluate the financial risk
    Is it worth it?
    What are the alternatives?
- Schedule three distinct phases
    Introduction: high cost, low return
    Fast growth
    Leveling off of demand

Step 12: Test the market. Pick the most likely response area, then analyze the reactions of consumers, other service providers, and potential funders. Test their receptivity to these variables:

- Program
- Packaging: number of sessions, length of sessions, time offered, and attractiveness of setting

- Price
- Advertising and promotion

Step 13: Promote and grow.

- Modify strategies to fit improvements suggested in the test marketing step.
- Pick areas to expand.
- Schedule activities.
- Assign personnel.
- Prescribe performance standards.

Step 14: Audit developments. Gather information about

- Service
- Quantity
- Quality
- Points of customer contact
- Staff performance
- Levels of satisfaction
- Punctuality of schedule

Step 15: Implement improvements. By step 15 you have gone full circle with the marketing process. Then you have to start over again, because marketing is a continual process: it is every purposeful thing you do to get and keep customers and consumers of your services. But each time around you can get better and better. This is not to say that practice makes perfect, though. The internal and external market forces are very dynamic. Unfortunately, practices that worked well for you in the past may wear out or become outmoded.

Christopher Lovelock (1991, p. 6) wrote, "Customer loyalty to established service businesses is proving quite fickle in the face of price cutting, product differentiation, and provision of more convenient delivery systems." He went on to say that not only is competition intensifying but the rules of the competitive game are changing just as quickly. "The ability to run a good operation, while as important as always, is no longer sufficient" (p. 6).

There is more information available to us particularly because of computerization and telecommunications. Keeping up with the technological changes may enable you to survive and prosper a few more years. For example, in 1995 The Achievement Center (TAC) in Worthington, Minnesota, a vocational training and placement program for people with disabilities, bought a CD-ROM listing surveying and engineering companies all over the United States. This enabled the center to bulk mail a simple flyer promoting wooden survey stakes made by its clients with disabilities. The mailing got good results. The center bought another CD-ROM to mail flyers promoting a new product suggested by a nurse on its board of directors. She asked if TAC clients and staff could manufacture infant and adult wooden measuring boards for use in medical clinics. After developing the new product, the staff learned it was beyond the capability of their clients, so they contracted with a local cabinetmaker to manufacture the units; they used the CD-ROM for addresses of clinics that might be interested. The units cost them $140 but sold for $300. This small sheltered workshop using mid 1990s technology sold two hundred boards to Puerto Rico alone.

Be a Hero

"Up, up, and away," said Superman as he leaped tall buildings in a single bound (circa 1940s) and later, in a 1980s movie, circled the globe to turn back time. Few of us can be superheroes, but most of us can be special heroes in the eyes of our peers and our organization. By following marketing principles and adapting the techniques described in this book, you should now be better able to focus your limited and precious resources. Your personal investment should improve your own and your organization's service quality and return on the investment.

References

Abrams, B. "Industry Veteran Challenges Conventional Wisdom on Ads." *Wall Street Journal*, Apr. 9, 1981a.

Abrams, B. "Umbrella Tactics Can Help Sell Products and Cut Costs." *Wall Street Journal*, July 16, 1981b.

Abrams, B. "Data General Turns to TV Ads to Reach Company Executives." *Wall Street Journal*, Oct. 8, 1981c.

"Ads Glorifying Career 'Superwomen' Can Alienate Full-Time Homemakers," *Marketing News*, May 1, 1981, p. 1.

Advertising Age, Nov. 23, 1981.

"The Affluent Market." *Yankelovich Monitor 1982 Special Report*, Sept. 1982, p. 15.

Allen, F. "Most Bosses Shun Symbols of Status, Help Take Care of Household Tasks." *Wall Street Journal*, Nov. 1981.

"Altruism Replaced as Prime Motivation for Volunteerism." *National Business Woman*, June 1980, p. 15.

"Americans Volunteer." *Independent Sector*, Apr. 1, 1982.

"Appealing to Four Groups of Women." *Advertising Age*, Oct. 1981.

Barbeito, C., and Hoel, R. "Recruitment: A Supermarket of Volunteers." *Voluntary Action Leadership*, Summer 1977, p. 14.

Bartos, R. "What Every Marketer Should Know About Women." *Harvard Business Review*, May-June 1978, pp. 73–85.

Bartos, R. "Marketers—All Women Aren't Sisters Under the Skin; Need Research to Hit Moving Targets." *Marketing News*, May 1, 1981, p. 11.

Bartos, R. "What Women Like, and Don't Like, in Ads." *Advertising Age*, Mar. 8, 1982, p. M-3.

Baugher, R. "The Motivation to Exercise: Why People Do It." *Journal of Physical Education*, Nov.-Dec. 1978, p. 42.

Bergen, H. "Panning for Gold." *Contributions*, Jan.-Feb. 1996, pp. 6–8.

Birnbaum, J. H., "Toymen Seek Ways to Make Christmas a Year-Long Event." *Wall Street Journal*, Feb. 21, 1980.

Boulding, K. *Economics as a Science*. New York: McGraw-Hill, 1970.

Bryson, J. B. *Strategic Planning for Public and Nonprofit Organizations: A Guide for Strengthening and Sustaining Organizational Achievement*. San Francisco: Jossey-Bass, 1995.

Camp Fire. *Volunteer Staff: Recruiting, Selecting, Retaining*. Kansas City, Mo.: Camp Fire Girls, 1979.

"Communication with Children." *Journal of Advertising Research*, June 1965, p. 2.

"Coupon Use Low Among Young, Working Women." *Marketing News*, Jan. 1988, p. 24.

Donath, B. "Roadkill in the Backroom." *Marketing News*, Apr. 25, 1994, p. 13.

Drucker, P. F. *The Five Most Important Questions You Will Ever Ask About Your Nonprofit Organization*. San Francisco: Jossey-Bass, 1993.

Dupont, T. "Research Suggests Nine Rules for Advertising to the Elderly." *Marketing News*, Apr. 16, 1982, p. 1.

Edel, R. "900 Numbers Add Up for Telemarketers." *Advertising Age*, Jan. 18, 1988, p. S-7.

Flint, J. "Air Travelers Resent Cut-Rate Courtesy." New York Times Service, cited in *Minneapolis Tribune*, Jan. 21, 1979.

Gigles, N. "Why Y&R Took Bull out of the Herd." *Advertising Age*, Nov. 9, 1981, p. 82.

Goldman, A. "Market Segmentation Analysis Tells What to Say to Whom." *Marketing News*, Jan. 22, 1982, p. 10.

Hardy, J. *Managing for Impact in Nonprofit Organizations*. Erwin, Tenn.: Essex Press, 1984.

Herman, R. D., and Associates. *The Jossey-Bass Handbook of Nonprofit Leadership and Management*. San Francisco: Jossey-Bass, 1994.

Housewright, E. "Do Church Ads Work or Compromise Gospel?" *Marketing News*, Mar. 13, 1995, p. 22.

"Increase Foreseen for Sponsorships." *Chronicle of Philanthropy*, Feb. 22, 1996, p. 13.

Ingrassia, P. "Adding Friendship to Worship." *Wall Street Journal*, Oct. 27, 1977.

Johnston, D. "PSAs Are Powerful Promotional Tools, but Experts Warn of Potential Pitfalls." *Non-Profit Times*, June 1988, p. 15.

Klein, H. "More Workers Are Refusing Promotions." *Wall Street Journal*, May 18, 1982, p. 32.

Konopacki, A. "Tricks of the Trade Show." *Marketing News*, Jan. 29, 1996, p. 7.

Koten, J. "Big Advertisers Are Waking to Benefits of Late-Night TV." *Wall Street Journal*, Feb. 9, 1984, p. 27.

Leaming, G. "Discussing Price Isn't Done in Polite Focus Groups." *Marketing News*, May 27, 1991, p. 16.

Leavitt, T. "Marketing Myopia." *Harvard Business Review*, July-Aug. 1960, pp. 45–46.

Leavitt, T. *Marketing for Business Growth*. New York: McGraw-Hill, 1969.

Lentini, C. "Balancing Act in Women's Magazines." *Advertising Age*, Oct. 19, 1981, p. S-62.

Lovelock, C. H. *Services Marketing*. (2nd ed.) Upper Saddle River, N.J.: Prentice Hall, 1991.

Lovelock, C. H., and Weinberg, C. B. *Public and Nonprofit Marketing*. (2nd ed.) Redwood City, Calif.: Scientific Press, 1989, p. 11.

Lynch, M. "Slimming Down, Many Firms Are Selling Off Acquisitions to Clarify Their Images, Lift Their Stocks." *Wall Street Journal*, Dec. 4, 1980, p. 48.

Mace, M. "Attracting New Directors." *Harvard Business Review*, Sept.-Oct. 1976, p. 48.

Makens, J. C. *The Marketing Plan Workbook*. Upper Saddle River, N.J.: Prentice Hall, 1985.

"Marketing Briefs." *Marketing News*, Dec. 23, 1983, p. 5.

McCurley, S. "Recruiting and Retaining Volunteers." In R. D. Herman and Associates, *The Jossey-Bass Handbook of Nonprofit Leadership and Management*. San Francisco: Jossey-Bass, 1994.

McKenzie, R., and Tullock, G. *The New World of Economics: Explorations into the Human Experience*. (3rd ed.) Burr Ridge, Ill.: Irwin, 1981.

Mitchell, G. "How to Market by Telephone." Chicago: Extension Institute, American Management Associations, n.d.

Morris, B. "Thousands of Patrols Are Formed in Suburbs to Supplement Police." *Wall Street Journal*, Sept. 2, 1981, p. 1.

Murphy, L. "Redemption Isn't Always Salvation in Couponing." *S&MM*, Jan. 13, 1986, pp. 45–47.

Nickles, E. "The Newest Mass Market: Women Go-Getters." *Advertising Age*, Nov. 9, 1981, p. 56.

Nissen, B. "When Disaster Strikes, Workers for Red Cross Are Never Far Behind." *Wall Street Journal*, June 14, 1979, pp. 1, 33.

Novelli, W. "Toothpaste, Political Candidates, and Health: Examples of Marketing Approaches." *Community Focus*, Oct. 1980, p. 4.

"Older Consumers Affected by Major Life Events." *Marketing News*, Jan. 15, 1996, p. 6.

Ostrow, J. "What Level Frequency?" *Advertising Age*, Nov. 9, 1981, p. S-4.

Peckham, J. "The Wheel of Marketing Change." *Harvard Business Review*, July-Aug. 1976.

Pendleton, N. *Fund Raising, A Guide for Non-profit Organizations*. New Milford, Conn.: Prentice-Hall, 1981.

Percy, L., and Rossiter, J. "Ten Ways to More Effective Ads via Visual Imagery, Psycholinguistics." *Marketing News*, Feb. 19, 1982, p. 10.

Potter, H. "IRI Ad Study Confirms Some Conventional Wisdom." *Marketing News*, Jan. 6, 1992, p. 22.

"Public-Service Ads Enjoy Big Growth." *Chronicle of Philanthropy*, Aug. 10, 1995, p. 41.

Rabin, A. "Top Execs Have Low Opinion of Marketing Research, Marketers' Role in Strategic Planning." *Marketing News*, Oct. 16, 1981, p. 1.

Resnik, A. J., Turney, P.B.B., and Mason, J. B. "Marketers Turn to Counter-Segmentation." *Harvard Business Review*, Sept.-Oct. 1979, pp. 100–106.

Restaurants USA, Dec. 1995, p. 21.

Ricklefs, R. "A Cultural Institution Succeeds by Marketing Its Wares Aggressively." *Wall Street Journal*, Jan. 23, 1979, pp. 1, 33.

Roessing, W. "Commerce on Campus." *Sky*, Nov. 1981, pp. 46–52.

Rosen, M. *Marketing News*, Feb. 19, 1982, p. 16.

Rotwein, N. *Get Off on the Corner of California and Presidio*. San Francisco: Jewish Community Center, June 24, 1981.

Rubright, R., and MacDonald, D. *Marketing Health and Human Services*. Rockville, Md.: Aspen Systems, 1981.

Salamon, J. "Instead of a Toaster, How About a Few Tips on Handling a Mugger?" *Wall Street Journal*, Nov. 19, 1980, p. 25.

Salamon, J. "Marketers Start to Help Banks Recognize Gains from Selling," *Wall Street Journal*, Sept. 3, 1981, p. 25.

Sautter, C. "How to Succeed in Your Spare Time." *Savvy*, May 1982, p. 72.

Schindler-Rainman, E., and Lippitt, R. *The Volunteer Community*. Fairfax, Va.: NTL Learning Resources, 1975.

Schlossberg, H. "Latest Image Study Finds Mixed Results for Researchers." *Marketing News*, Sept. 14, 1992, p. 9.

Schultz, D. E. "Why Marketers Like the Sales Promotion Gambit." *Advertising Age*, Nov. 7, 1983, p. M-52.

Schultz, D. E. "Losing Attitude." *Marketing Research*, Fall 1995.

Schultz, D. E. "Integration and the Internet." *Marketing News*, Jan. 15, 1996, p. 7.

Schumacher, E. *Small Is Beautiful: Economics as if People Mattered*. San Francisco: Harper San Francisco, 1973.

Selby, C. "Better Performance from Nonprofits." *Harvard Business Review*, Sept.-Oct. 1978, p. 92.

Sharkey, B. "Dialing for Dollars and Data." *Adweek*, Nov. 16, 1987, p. 6.

Sharn, L. "Orthodox Synagogue Turns to Unorthodox Recruiting." *USA Today*, Feb. 8, 1996.

Shermach, K. "Phone Cards Ring Up Profits." *Marketing News*, Nov. 20, 1995, p. 1.

Simon, M. "Survey Probes Strengths, Weaknesses of Promotions." *Marketing News*, June 8, 1984, p. 3.

Sloan, P. "Retailers Ready for Change." *Advertising Age*, Jan. 27, 1987.

Smith, D., and Reddy, R. "Any Volunteers?" *Adult Leadership*, Jan. 1972.

Smith, K. "Most Research Firms Use Mall Intercepts." *Marketing News*, Sept. 11, 1989, p. 16.

Stiansen, S. "Ogilvy Study: Advertising Works." *Marketing Week*, Dec. 14, 1987, p. 2.

Strang, R. "Sales Promotion: Fast Growth, Faulty Management." *Harvard Business Review*, July-Aug. 1976, p. 121.

Torrens, P. "What Is Hospital Marketing? And How Did It Get a Bad Name?" *Hospital Forum*, July-Aug. 1980, p. 6.

Voluntary Action Leadership, Winter 1982, pp. 22–31.

Weber, J. C. "Something for the Girls." *Advancing Philanthropy*, Winter 1994, pp. 25–27.

"West's Pizza King." *San Francisco Business Journal*, Feb. 15, 1982, p. 15.

"Who Watches Commercials." *Wall Street Journal*, May 20, 1982, p. 33.

Wilson, A., and Atkin, B. "Exorcising the Ghosts in Marketing." *Harvard Business Review*, Sept.-Oct. 1976, pp. 117–126.

Winter, R. "Survey Indicates Bosses Savor Jobs, Fear Inflation's Effect on Income." *Wall Street Journal*, May 12, 1981.

Yankelovich, D. "New Criteria for Market Segmentation." *Harvard Business Review*, Mar.-Apr. 1964, p. 84.

Yao, M. "Big Pitch for God: More Churches Try Advertising in Media." *Wall Street Journal*, Dec. 31, 1979.

Index